I met two people who had an extraordinary influence on my life: Pierre Wack and Nelson Mandela. The first taught me how to see into the future by correctly perceiving the present; the second how to change the future by having the correct moral compass. To both my heartfelt thanks.
—Clem Sunter, Chair of the Anglo American Chairman's Fund, U.K.

In this book, Thomas Chermack had the talent to highlight the complexity of the character of Pierre Wack. Faced with many unique challenges, my husband was able to transform them into a deep inner fulfillment. Being able to "see," he was able to free himself of many contingencies and to emerge as one of the brightest figures of his generation. This book allows one to discover the role played by Pierre Wack in Shell and shows how it is essential for any economist to have clear and structured thinking.

—Eve Wack

Pierre Wack was a truly remarkable man, who searched for others like him to gain insight into the future. Thomas Chermack has written the outstanding story of the life of this remarkable man . . . a true opportunity to get inside the mind of the greatest all-time seer in the world of business.
—Peter Schwartz, Senior Vice President for Strategic Planning of Salesforce.com, US, former Head of Scenario Planning at Royal Dutch Shell, U.K.

Pierre Wack was a visionary ahead of his time. His work on scenarios laid the foundation for looking at the future in new and actionable ways. Any business leader, or MBA student who aspires to be one, has much to learn from his remarkable story.
—Michael E. Porter, Harvard Business School, US

Thomas Chermack has written a compelling biography of an exceptional man. Pierre Wack applied a timeless and enduring discipline to "see" the present, understand its possibilities and identify ways forward. He was the pioneer of scenario planning.
—Ged Davis, Executive Chair, Scenarios, World Energy Council and former Head of Scenario Planning at Shell

# Foundations of Scenario Planning

Pierre Wack was head of scenario planning at Royal Dutch / Shell Oil in London for just over ten years. He died in 1997. He was a pioneer of what we know today as scenario planning—an alternative and complement to strategic planning.

Scenarios explore a variety of possible futures for examining decisions in organizational planning. Pierre was a unique man with interests in Indian and Japanese cultures and traditions. He travelled extensively and led a unique life that involved long periods of visiting gurus in India and extended sabbaticals in Japan. His experiences with Eastern thought no doubt shaped his ability to evolve the scenario method at Shell, and as a result he was able to lead a team that foresaw the oil crises of the 1970's and 80's.

This new volume will cover the basic context of his life timeline and attach it to the development of his thinking about scenario planning over the course of his career. After his death, Wack's materials, papers and documents were collected by Napier Collyns and have recently been made available at the University of Oxford where the Pierre Wack Memorial Library has been established. These documents contain a variety of clues and stories that reveal more about who Pierre Wack was, how he thought and will provide details about scenario planning that have never been seen or published. They also reveal a curious man and include a timeline by his wife, Eve, which details their relationship over the course of 40 years.

Written for management and business historians and researchers, this book will uncover unseen contributions by a scenario planning pioneer shaped by significant events in his personal life that helped him to see the world differently.

**Thomas J. Chermack** is Associate Professor of Organizational Learning, Performance and Change and Founder and Director of the Scenario Planning Institute at Colorado State University, US.

# Routledge International Studies in Business History

Series editors: Jeffrey Fear and Christina Lubinski

For a full list of titles in this series, please visit www.routledge.com

# Foundations of Scenario Planning

## The Story of Pierre Wack

Thomas J. Chermack

Routledge
Taylor & Francis Group
New York  London

First published 2017 by Routledge

711 Third Avenue, New York, NY 10017
2 Park Square, Milton Park, Abingdon, Oxfordshire OX14 4RN

*Routledge is an imprint of the Taylor & Francis Group, an informa business*

First issued in paperback 2018

*Library of Congress Cataloging-in-Publication Data*
A catalog record for this book has been requested.

ISBN: 978-1-138-19019-1 (hbk)
ISBN: 978-0-367-02656-1 (pbk)

Typeset in Sabon
by Apex CoVantage, LLC

This book is dedicated to the future students of scenario planning. I hope this "origin story" compels your curiosity to remember the past so we may create a better future.

Thomas J. Chermack,
Fort Collins, Colorado, 2016

# Contents

**PART IV**
## Reflections and Legacy

# Charts and Figures

## Charts

## Figures

# Foreword, Part 1

Pierre Wack changed my life! I had been slowly climbing the ladder at Royal Dutch Shell and was in my forties when my boss at the time Karel Swart who was the Managing Director responsible for Planning called me to The Hague and told me he wanted me to go to London and work with "a crazy Frenchman". "Where is he?" I asked. "He is in Japan on a sabbatical," he said "But he will soon be in London and we want you to work with him." I soon met Pierre Wack for an interview and the only thing he asked was "What can't you do?". "I can't write a book" I said. The irony was that I was to work with Pierre and Ted Newland on and off for the next thirty years or so, first in Shell and later in Global Business Network and none of us ever wrote a book. But by now there have been numerous books written about the scenario practice we first developed in those days.

This is the first book written that is truly dedicated to Pierre and I hope it will enable me to share with you how he changed my life. It didn't have much to do with business or the bottom line. There was just simply a presence about him that was immediately something you felt. You couldn't be around him and look for certainty. The only thing certain about being with Pierre was that on his desk he would have a little holder for a small stick with a glow at the end. He always had this marvelous incense burning which would pervade the whole room. It was difficult not to feel a sense of magic when you were with Ted or Pierre or not to believe what they were saying however unlikely.

A few years after our Shell days I was visiting Pierre at his chateau La Johannie in Curemonte in the Dordogne in central France. We were sitting in his beautiful garden when he produced a few pieces of paper and said "I'd like you to read this." He gave me the pages, which were in French, and it was about the gurus he had met over the years. It started with Gurdjieff and a few others, and covered several failed attempts at finding a match until it finally described how he met this special guru, whom he eventually shared with a number of other French people interested in Asian mysticism. One of these, Daniel Roumanoff, decided to write a book about the guru and collected stories of their experiences with this special guru and asked Pierre to contribute his own story to the collection. I sat there in the sun, with Pierre's favorite sunflowers in full bloom and was captivated by the words of my friend who did not like to write. While I was reading Pierre said to me, "Look I really learned to see with the guru and having learned to see, I was able when I joined the Shell Group in London to see the world in a way no one else had done". He went on further, "Although the guru knew nothing about oil prices or the Royal Dutch Shell Group, he really helped me see the things they needed to see." When I got to the end he leant over and snatched the four pages right out of my hands. "That's not for you, Napier". So for several years I was wondering if I would ever see them again.

The last time I saw Pierre was in 1997 when he was with his wife in a nursing home owned by his father-in-law near Chartres. I arrived early so I spent a couple of hours in Chartres Cathedral with an amazing man who knew every inch of this most beautiful building. I was in a special mood when I reached Pierre and after giving him some papers to read I asked him in front of his wife Eve whether I could preserve what I could of his personal papers. He seemed excited by this prospect and a few weeks after he died I went with my wife and our friend Don Michael to stay with Eve at Curemonte. After two or three days we had sorted Pierre's papers into three categories: the personal, professional and esoteric. Eve kept the personal and esoteric papers but had translated into English the four pages I longed to read and which I have shared with many people since. We packed up the professional books and papers and shipped them to The Hague where we kept them in the GBN office opposite the Queen's Palace. Cynthia Selin helped me sort them out and when she went to Copenhagen to work on her doctorate she wrote the first deep account of Pierre's work: Professional Dreamers.

After a few years GBN had to give up its library space and our close friend Kees van der Heijden suggested we give the collection to Templeton College. Kees was then working there and it had been the location of the first business school at Oxford University. In due course Templeton merged with Green College to form Green Templeton College in the centre of Oxford. In May 2014 the Pierre Wack Memorial Library was officially opened at Oxford University under a partnership arrangement between Green Templeton College and the Said Business School with professional help from the Sainsbury Wing of Oxford's Bodleian Library. This book is heavily based on materials which the library maintains and have not been published elsewhere, and it is supplemented by interviews with former colleagues of Pierre. Increasingly the library is being used for research on the development of scenarios and Pierre Wack's contributions.

There is no question that Pierre Wack was a charismatic figure who changed the way many companies have tended to deal with the future. It is true that not every scenario exercise will result in profound insight, but commitment to the process over time cannot but change the future of any company. In today's world, scenarios are more relevant than ever, and the lessons we might take from considering the life of scenario's most enigmatic figure will not be easy. But if we pay attention, accept the nature of today's reality and dedicate our efforts to really thinking about the future, we cannot but help come away with a different way of seeing the world. I should like to thank Tom Chermack, whom I first met with Cynthia Selin in Arizona at a conference on the plausibility of scenarios, for the amazing effort he has made to track down the story of Pierre Wack and to help us all better understand his achievement. Pierre always believed that an understanding of history was essential for studying the future. In the same spirit as the dedication of this book it is my great hope that Pierre's story will provide a foundation and inspiration for the next generation of scenario planners.

I can think of no better way to introduce Pierre or this book than by providing those four pages that enthralled me so long ago. I hope they are as much an inspiration to you as they have been to me.

Napier Collyns
London, 2016

# Foreword, Part 2

## Pierre Wack's "Four Pages"

Original text

Pierre Wack, born in 1922, met Svamiji for the first time in the spring of 1961. He was the first Frenchman who ever visited the Channa ashram.

"Before meeting Svamiji," Pierre tells us, "I had already been in the presence of many spiritual masters. In Paris, I had known Gurdjieff; I had been to Zen monasteries in the Far East, practiced meditation in Burma and in Thailand, and I have visited several other masters in India.

When I met Gurdjieff in February 1943, I was twenty years old and I was exceptionally well received. You could say that Gurdjieff cured my tuberculosis because he 'fed' me both spiritually and over some extraordinary dinners, in the middle of the war, at a time when everything was scarce. What's there to say about him? I thought of him as a formidable, yet dangerous power, whereas Svamiji always seemed to be good without any dark sides. I do feel very grateful towards Gurdjieff, because he welcomed me and because he was the first to make me see that higher states of consciousness could exist. He gave me my first tasting and this, in a way, roused my appetite. But even though it wasn't a culture 'fit' as often is the case in the East, I did feel after several years that the road he took was not mine.

In Japan, I met So-en Roshi of the Ryutaku-ji monastery, as well as the Roshi of Nanzen-ji. Although I was very impressed by these two masters, one of whom spoke perfect English, I understood that to make real progress, I would have to stay in Japan for at least a couple of years, and this held me back. When I presented Svamiji with one of the Roshi of Nanzen-ji's books, *A flower does not talk*, his reaction after reading it was: "Yes, that man has found the truth."

In Burma, in a temple that was located in the suburbs of Rangoon, I practiced the Satipathana, and I visited Buddhist monasteries in the north of Thailand.

## Meeting with Svamiji

When I visited India for the first time at the end of 1960, I had a couple of addresses in my pocket. Svami Prajnanpad is at the bottom of my list—I had an image of him like Vedanta's 'theologist.' Once I got to Calcutta, my first visit is to a yogi in Puri who is said to be 125 years old. He is a massive man with atrophied legs from constantly sitting in the lotus position. Wristwatch in hand, I measure that his respiratory cycle lasts for two minutes. "Start by disciplining your food," he tells me, but I am not yet ready to appreciate the relevancy of this advice and leave the next day. Next, I meet a Sikh master, then, in Bombay, Rajneesh, and finally Ma Ananda Mayee. Each time, my decision emerges rapidly—This is not the road for me—and I move on.

Then I meet a Sufi master in Kanpur, Bhai Sahib, with whom I stay for three weeks. I visit him every morning and every afternoon. Communication with the master, albeit in total silence, is exceptionally good, and I become familiar with extraordinary states of consciousness. Still, I can't stay with him for longer than that. Before leaving France, I have imposed a couple of strict rules on myself that I have sworn to obey:

- to distrust anything that looks like a demand for money
- to leave for several days after a stay of three weeks at the most, no matter what happens, to avoid being brainwashed;
- to observe carefully the entourage and the goings-on amongst the disciples.

Bhai Sahib demands total obedience from his disciples. When, after three weeks, I announce to him that I will leave for a couple of days, the master is furious. He bursts out in violent maledictions and calls me names. I leave him anyway, but I can't suppress the idea that he has cast an evil spell over my future.

It is because of this bad experience, however, that I meet Svamiji. When I go back from Kanpur to Calcutta by train, with the intention of going back to Thailand, I notice that my train makes a stop-over at Khana Junction, the station that is nearest to Svamiji's ashram. I arrive there at five o'clock in the morning, leave all my luggage at the station—feeling certain that I will leave again soon—and walk over the rice-fields for two and a half hours before arriving at the ashram. Svami Prajnanpad is there alone, which is exceptional. The ashram is a marvelous enclave. I stay there for three weeks, then for another two. I have a sitting in the morning and one in the afternoon. It is the strongest experience I have ever had. For the first time in my life, I feel fulfilled.

What's there to say about Svamiji that hasn't already been said? I would like to put forward more specifically the personal and operational side of his teachings, for this made him truly unique amongst the masters that I have known. He himself certainly found it very important: he forced himself never to speak to more than one disciple at once, not even to a little group. I can only give you a sample of Svamiji's teachings. I could tell you about how he made me grasp and realize "acceptance," but this is very much linked to some personal experiences of mine, and I have no desire to expose my private life. I will therefore choose "seeing" which, for me, is linked to something objective that I can describe much more easily.

## The Art of Seeing

It is one thing to say "One must see, simply see things the way they are, and not give oneself over to games of the mind . . ." It is not common to see what is there. Naturally, we "look" with our minds—with our interpretations, inferences, preconceptions, comparisons, expectations and through all our previous experience. To "see" is a function of a pure consciousness. It is an enchantment with what is that goes beyond "liking" or "disliking," and enchantment precisely because it is like that ("that-ness," Svamiji said)—and this has a taste of existential certainty: when I see, I am and I am with what I see . . . In Sanskrit, Rishi, the sage, is a seer—Paripasyanti, he who sees all around him. India has always celebrated the fact of seeing things directly as they are—not believing, imagining, speculating, but seeing. Still it is quite a different matter to be able to transmit this wisdom into personal and operational terms. This, in my opinion, has been the true greatness of Svamiji.

Perhaps a metaphor will clarify what I want to say. It's like trying to split with an axe, an old tough tree trunk, knotty and with lots of curious difficulties. Svamiji was without equal when it came to discovering the right angle of attach, coming up with an adequate axe and inspiring his disciple with the will to use it, because in this case the disciple was both the trunk and the one who was to use the axe. In this manner, I must have had at least fifty sittings over the course of thirteen years, dense and intense, personal and operational, only to "see things as they are," to learn the art and the discipline of seeing. These sittings transformed my life, and firstly, my professional life. This is how it happened.

When I came back to my job at Shell, where I was occupied with economic studies, I was asked to make market forecasts. I talked to Svamiji about it when I went to see him the following winter. After he'd asked me precisely what my work consisted of, he said: "That is your yoga. It will be the test that will allow you to verify whether you see things as they are. See, establish interrelations, see through and be one with it."

By nature, I was not very predisposed to see. I would have been much more inclined to give myself over to interpretation and to mental constructions. Still, I launched myself into this activity with an enormous zeal, that I wouldn't have had if I wouldn't have been literally set afire by the taste, the sensation of "seeing."

At the time, forecasting was essentially an econometric activity, that consisted of looking for "development laws" in the past course of a phenomenon and applying them to the future. This way, it was possible to make forecasts from behind one's desk about elements with which one didn't have any contact whatsoever. This way of doing it was almost the rule. Svamiji's obligation for me to "see things" was revolutionary.

Instead of econometric calculations from global statistics, "seeing" demands, firstly, the identification of the forces at work and the chain(s) of cause and effect behind the development of a market, and secondly, information about the chain that is much finer than global statistics, a ladder where significant differences appear. "Seeing" certainly was a much more demanding and strenuous discipline than regular forecasting, but the managing directors who had to make use of forecasts quickly saw the difference and my field of activity expanded first to the entire Shell France and then, on an international level, to the ensemble of the Royal Dutch Shell group in London.

This was an exceptional opportunity: more than ever, the predictions would form a merciless test. I arrived in London a couple of years before the period of great turbulence that would shake the oil business: prices would rise enormously, the growth of consumption would be broken, concessions in the producing countries would be nationalized . . . and most of all, nobody in the industry was expecting any of this. I have described elsewhere some of the stages of this struggle to see things as they are, as opposed to the assumptions that one has of things. Every time I experienced difficulties, or had doubts about how to proceed, I went to ask Svamiji for advice. I would feel like a piece of wood floating on a river that gets stuck in the reed; Svamiji always found the way to release me.

Here's how Michel Albert, former head of the French Plan, described the result of this approach: "I witnessed how, several years in advance, the economists at Shell were probably the only ones in the world who were able to foresee the oil crisis and convince their superiors to build their strategies from these views of the future." Svamiji had made it very clear to me that it wasn't only important to see, but also to make others see. Without this, scenarios, which went so much against the ruling expectations of the day, would be nothing but "water on a stone," that would dissipate without leaving a single trace.

Obviously, Svamiji didn't know much about oil, and he knew practically nothing about a company as big and as complex as Shell International. But because his teachings concern the optional functioning of a person in his entirety, and because of his ability to be present and focus entirely on the person who was with him, his advices could very well be applied to professional life. His spirituality was very much *alive*, and extended far beyond the partial aspect that I have described here."

Pierre Wack

# Preface

## How This Book Came to Be

I never met Pierre Wack. It would be easy to argue that I have no business writing a book about him. As is the case for many, I first came across the name Pierre Wack when I became interested in scenario planning. The more I learned about him, the more fascinated I was. When I met Napier Collyns in the 2000s, we began a friendship that led to several unexpected projects and furthered my curiosity. In 2014, I had the good fortune to be invited to the Oxford Futures Forum, by organizers Rafael Ramirez, Cynthia Selin, Lucy Kimbell, and Yasser Bhatti. While there, I visited the Pierre Wack Memorial Library at Egrove Park in Oxford. Once I realized the volume of unseen material available, it was clear that a book about Wack could, and should, be written. In particular, the detailed accounts that his wife Eve wrote in the weeks after he died established some important details and raised many additional questions. I remember being in tears after reading her manuscript *PierrEve*. After the Forum in Oxford, my luck continued with an invitation to visit Napier Collyns' home in Putney, just outside London. There he shared with me more papers, scenario books from Shell, and we watched a few videos of Wack he had on a VHS tape. I had heard of Wack's legendary presentations, but it was the first time I saw him speak, heard his voice and was able to witness his magic—even if only on a television screen. That was the beginning of this project. I knew I simply had to try to write his story.

Over the next two years, I conducted more than 40 interviews with Pierre's friends, colleagues and adversaries to tell this story. Those closest to him, particularly his wife Eve, were clear that Pierre was no saint and he was quite capable of showing his bad side. I have no desire to hide those parts of his story. He was a human being like any of us, yet for many, he had a mystic way about him.

There has been some controversy over what happened during his era at Shell. Recent publications hint at the debates about what credit is deserved and by whom. Some of Wack's adversaries declined to be interviewed, so

I have done my best to tell the story with the widest possible range of views available. I have tried to submit a fair perspective and be transparent about the sources for what I have written.

While I checked the sources many times, it was sometimes difficult to balance accounts with conflicting details. A letter may have held an event in 1975, when an interview with a different source held the same event in 1976. Much of this could be the simple fading of memory over the years, which I am sure was a challenge for my interviewees. Every effort was made to ensure the highest possible degree of accuracy, yet I am sure some readers will have different recollections. Nonetheless, any factual inaccuracies are my responsibility which I fully accept.

Some portions of this book, (like the excerpts from Wack's conversations with his guru, or the longer sections pulled from actual scenario books) will be of more or less interest to different readers. I encourage readers to simply move on if a section is deemed less relevant as it is the story that matters most.

This is a book about the unique life of a remarkable man whose passion for his work was so intense, he often said he would have paid to do it. He bent the universe to his will at times and at others worked intensely to try to accept the things with which he was confronted. He opened a new way to think about the future and a new approach to wondering about the dynamics of industries, nations and the world.

This is also a book about really thinking. In a time when leaders of companies claim they are completely overwhelmed and when every business book begins with a statement about how the world is changing faster and becoming more uncertain, Wack stands out as a person who refused to consider short cuts. He knew that deep commitment to thinking and reflection are requirements for any who wish to arrive at novel conclusions or see into the future in ways that lead to genuine insights. He was aided by a relentless curiosity and a serious dedication to logic and rigorous analysis. When it comes right down to it, I simply believe that in order to understand scenario planning, we must first begin by understanding Pierre Wack. In the spirit of that conviction, this is his story.

Thomas J. Chermack

## A Note about Sources

Interviews were conducted between 2014–16, (and transcripts of interviews provided by other sources were obtained during the same time period) with the following participants:

Cheryl Aldons, Eve Baudoin, Napier Collyns, Jimmy Davidson, Ged Davis, Joop De Vries, Michael Jefferson, Guy Jillings, Cho Kong, Ted Newland, Peter Schwartz, Bruce Scott, Clem Sunter, Ray Thomasson, Kees van der Heijden, Eve Wack, Jean-Pierre Wack, Pierre Wack (provided by Art Kleiner), Fiona Youlton.

Documents and Letters were contributed by Eve Wack from:

Peter Beck, Napier Collyns, Jimmy Davidson, Michael Jefferson, Ted Newland, Allan Newey, Michael O'Connor, Bruce Scott, Luc Smets, Clem Sunter, Kieth R. Williams, Ian Wilson.

Sources relevant to the content are listed at the end of each chapter. Sources are not identified in-text to improve readability.

# Acknowledgements

I am deeply grateful to Napier Collyns, Eve Wack, and Jean-Pierre Wack for their support, suggestions, and contributions. Their time and energy were critical in launching and sustaining this project. Further, their efforts in preserving Wack's materials in Oxford have made this project possible and kept his story relevant. I want to thank Christopher Jones, the Information Support Officer at the Pierre Wack Memorial Library, University of Oxford. His assistance with the various Pierre Wack Archives is sincerely appreciated. David Varley and Brianna Ascher at Routledge were extremely helpful in assisting with the completion of this book and their suggestions along the way were invaluable. I could not have completed this project without Laura Coons and her assistance with interviews, reviewing the many drafts, and providing careful editorial advice, or Emily Frost who redrew many diagrams from old, difficult to read copies. I would like to sincerely thank everyone who agreed to be interviewed over the last two years and share their memories. It was a privilege for me to speak with each of you and I will remember these conversations for the rest of my life. In particular, Ged Davis' insights and thorough review are greatly appreciated. I am grateful to Colorado State University for supporting me in pursuing my path of disciplined inquiry. And finally, I am most indebted to my mentor Dr. Richard A. Swanson for always believing in me more than I believe in myself.

# Introduction

Silently a flower blooms,
In silence it falls away;
Yet here now, at this moment, at this place,
    the whole of the flower, whole of
    the world is blooming.
This is the talk of the flower, the truth
    of the blossom;
The glory of eternal life is fully shining here.

This poem is the introductory verse from a small book titled *A Flower Does Not Talk*, by Zenkei Shibayama. Pierre Wack lived in Kyoto, Japan with him for a time studying Zen in the 1960s and he found the book to be particularly enlightening.

Wack was famous for using his words sparingly and with intention, for getting directly to that which was most essential within his message. In that same spirit, this introduction is brief. To begin, it is helpful to consider a quote from Andre Gide: "One does not discover new lands without consenting to lose sight of the shore for a very long time." This was not a line Wack himself is known to have used, but it suits him. For some who knew him, Wack was the constant explorer—willing to lose sight of home shores in favor of adventure, discovery and the quest for greater insight. For others, he was one who could range far and wide in his thinking all while keeping his feet anchored firmly on the shore. This duality is one of the remarkable parts of Wack's unique make-up and is a theme that framed much of his life.

For now, you are invited to leave the shore for just a little while, in order to visit the new lands discovered by this man half century ago—lands that reshaped how the future could be told.

## Introduction Sources (in order of use)

Shibayama, Z. (2012). *A flower does not talk: Zen essays*. North Clarendon, VT: Tuttle Publishing.

Gide, A., & Appelbaum, S. (2003). *The immoralist*. North Chelmsford, MA: Courier Corporation.

# Part I

# Who Was Pierre Wack?

Pierre Wack has been called the most influential management guru you have probably never heard of. For those to whom he is unfamiliar, welcome to the story of a most remarkable man. The contributions made by Wack and his scenario teams at Shell in the 1970's have created a discipline and shaped strategic thinking throughout the world. The roots of his unique approach to planning are mysterious and one goal of this book is to clarify the background and context for what happened in the development of scenarios at Shell.

Part one of this book covers the early history of Pierre Wack's life, including his childhood, his education and other important events that shaped who he became. Part one consists of chapters 1 and 2, and they fill in the foundations of his life based on accounts of those who knew him best. These chapters bring together information from the available documents, interviews with many who knew him, and the very important contributions of his surviving wife Eve, for whom he described elements of his life history that are not documented anywhere else. These chapters lay out the forces that influenced Wack most. From fleeing mandatory enrollment into the German SS Army in World War II, to the height of mystic culture in Paris, to the Zen gardens of Japan, these chapters highlight the spiritual foreshadowing to scenario planning. They describe a man who made a habit of being free, of seeking to see things as they are and working to accept the facts of his life.

Chapter 1 provides a frame for the early years that shaped Wack's life. It is a high-level summary of the major forces that motivated him to become a "seer." The stories and people briefly described in chapter 1 are elaborated on in later parts of the book. While this chapter does not provide a high degree of detail, it does provide the scaffolding required to understand and situate later chapters. It is an organizer, and a general timeline of Wack's early life. Though it will raise more questions than it answers, it is intended to provide an essential foundation for understanding Wack.

Chapter 2 delves deeply into Wack's spiritual history and contemplative pursuits. It is a tour through Wack's esoteric influences as a child, leading him to study with Gurdjieff, Japanese Roshi (senior spiritual teachers), and a guru for more than 10 years in India; further, it explains the initiation of his lifelong pursuit of "remarkable people." This chapter includes stories and anecdotes from his travels and worldly interactions as told by Wack himself. The stories shed light on Wack's experiences in the unusual situations that helped him develop the senses which would later yield great insights for a variety of people, in a variety of circumstances, in a variety of companies. These stories present, in essence, the spiritual foundation of scenario planning.

Part one of this book summarizes the dynamics that settled down around Wack and allowed him to guide his and others' thinking about the future in a way that had never been done before. For some, Wack was deeply influential, while for others he was off-putting. Yet there is no denying that his life has left us a truly extraordinary legacy, a mystical story and a discipline called scenario planning.

## Part 1 Sources (in order of use)

Ertel, C., & Solomon, L.K. (2014). *Moments of impact: How to design strategic conversations that accelerate change.* New York: Simon and Schuster.

Solomon, L.K., & Ertel, C. (2014). Lessons from the godfather of strategic conversation. Excerpt from Ertel, C., & Solomon, L.K. (2014). *Moments of impact: How to design strategic conversations that accelerate change.* New York: Simon and Schuster. Published online: http://sparksheet.com/lessons-from-the-godfather-of-strategic-conversation/ Accessed July 28, 2016.

Selin, C. (2007). Professional dreamers: The past in the future of scenario planning. In B. Sharpe & K. van der Heijden (Eds.), *Scenarios for success: Turning insights into action*, pp. 27–52. Sussex, England: John Wiley & Sons.

# 1 Pierre Wack's Personal Motivation to "See"

*Pierre's foot slipped on a rocky slope and he instinctively reached for the boulder next to him to steady his step. Gaining his grip, he watched as a rockslide developed and washed down over the cliffs below. It was getting dark, but not too dark to see. He dusted off his hands and remembered his father's ability to talk to animals—he hoped he would not find himself in a situation that required such powers. He thought of his brother, Raymond, with whom he used to collect strawberries and eat them all, igniting his brother's rage. He worried about his brother serving under the French flag in Africa, and for his parents, whom he instructed to inform the authorities that he had died in the bombings. It was not clear where this path would lead him, but surely, not to war. He remembered cycling to Czechoslovakia when he was 15 years old and wished, only for a moment, for a flat gravel road and a bicycle. He made a fire in a cove of boulders and in a shiver, decided to wait out the long, cold night. The terrain was too difficult to navigate in the darkness. He would begin again toward Switzerland in the morning.*

Pierre Andre Wack (pronounced as the French "Vaque") was born on April 11, 1922 in Colmar, located in the Alsace region of France. Alsace is a borderland between France and Germany—a place of two cultures. Alsatians generally do not regard themselves as French, and in fact, they refer to France as "*L'exterior*," the exterior. Wack thought the French were far too emotional—they allowed feelings to interfere with structured and rational thought. His father Jean-Jacques Wack was a minister in a local Mennonite community and owned a dry cleaning business. Wack's grandmother lived upstairs. His mother Elisabeth attended to him, his older brother Raymond, and the home. Not many details of Wack's childhood are known, but we do know he loved cycling and had a relatively stable and loving childhood.

At 16, he refused to be baptized and enter what he called "the clan," a decision that his father accepted and respected. Wack won a scholarship and then graduated from Bartholdi Lycée High School in 1940. He immediately enrolled in Heidelberg University to study Economics. Shortly after he began his education at Heidelberg, he transferred to the University of

Frankfurt to study Economics, Politics, and Statistics. Wack quickly became fluent in German and during this time, usually spoke the language.

The start of World War II, and his desire to flee, meant that his studies would be delayed. Wack secretly decided to leave Germany for France when the German army began to enroll Alsatians. So strong was his opposition to the war that he told his parents to inform the authorities that he had been killed in the bombings. Somehow, he even arranged for his parents to receive his official death papers to protect them from being arrested. His route took him south, and with the help of a smuggler he was able to cross the border into Switzerland where he was captured and imprisoned. It was only with the aid of his uncle George who came to negotiate his release that he was able to gain freedom out of Switzerland and head to Lyon, France. Once he arrived in Lyon, he enrolled as a student with the Faculty of Law in the free zone.

In October of 1941, Wack moved in with a family where the rent was affordable. His wife Eve remembered: "Every weekend he would go to Bonneval, in the Alps, where he camped." There Wack encountered a hostage situation; he was able to negotiate the release of three Germans. In exchange, the parents of the hostages offered Wack a hut in the mountains "where he lived like a hermit, at the end of a path, several kilometers from Bonneval" for about two years, hiding from the destruction of the war. It is clear that World War II had a profound effect on Wack, and he was ultimately changed by the war. This was a similarity Wack would share with his counterpart, Ted Newland, many years later.

In 1943, Wack moved to Paris and enrolled in L'Ecole libre des Sciences Politiques, which changed names in 1945 to L'Institut des Sciences Politiques: "We had in France university like any other country but we have Grandes Ecoles and Grandes Ecoles is way above university. There is a competition to enter. And a competition to exit and the competition is very important. I came number one off the Institut des Sciences Politiques. At this time I wanted to become a civil servant . . . I could choose whatever I wanted." History is not always forthcoming – there is no record of Wack's enrollment there, and L'Ecole libre des Sciences Politiques did not actually have a program in Political Science in 1944. In February of the same year, he met one of his first remarkable people—a man who would become his teacher—G.I. Gurdjieff. This meeting altered the course of his life forever by opening his eyes to alternative ways of seeing and knowing.

Upon leaving L'Ecole libre des Sciences Politiques in 1944, Wack took a position briefly at the Commissariat Regional de la Republique in Strasbourg. This position would have been impossible without a degree in Political Science, though Wack's official education is simply not clear: "My first job, I was at the time 23 years old, was Chief de Cabinet. And Alsace Lorraine were part of Germany so there was German money, German wages, everything was German. And to bring it back into the French economy it was like what West Germany had to do with East Germany. We did it much better. But I had an enormous job because of this." His wife Eve recalled Wack's descriptions of this time: "He was happy to have subordinates much older than him, but not with the restrictions of the administration." His happiness did not last long as Wack grew tired of the minutiae. Official records indicate that Wack was largely unemployed for the majority of 1945 after he left the Commissariat Regional de la Republique, though his passport shows several entries and exits from Switzerland and Italy throughout 1946. From December 1947 to July 1948, he had several more visas for Switzerland and in July 1948, his final Italian visa was issued.

Toward the end of 1946, Wack went to Paris and met with friends Herve Henzi, Andre Taillade and Claude Jaudel. Jaudel was a childhood friend, and Wack had worked with Henzi at the Commissariat Régional de la Republique in Strasbourg. The group had in mind to recruit other "literati" and publish a monthly fashion magazine. Wack became the Director General and in 1947 the first issue of *L'Occident* was published. This effort was a stark contrast to those who knew him later as a scenario planning guru. His wife Eve recalled that when he first told her the stories about *L'Occident*, she could not at all see him in that role. In fact, she broke out in laughter in remembering Wack's story of an obsession with a particular pair of very fashionable, yellow shoes. Unfortunately, the effort at *L'Occident* did not last long. The Swiss investors decided to stop financing the magazine when Wack's father died (he had been contributing a portion of the funding,) and in February / March 1948 the fourth and final edition was printed. From 1949–50, Wack worked as an independent economics consultant for various companies in Paris until a Michelin company executive led an effort to "liberalize the French economy" and recruited Wack to oversee the economics aspects of the project.

Accounts by people who knew Wack indicate he was actually quite fascinated with the efficiency of the German economy before the War, which led him to enroll at the University of Frankfurt. Trained as an economist, Wack is said to have admired the swiftness with which Germany's position in Europe was improving both economically and socially. Growing up in Alsace, which was essentially a mixture of the French and German cultures, Wack appreciated aspects of the German way of life. Wack felt betrayed once Hitler's evils came to light and the horrors of his rule were evident.

Though he did not personally experience battle, Wack was deeply, personally affected by the events of the war and he made the choice to avoid being trapped, relentlessly pursuing his freedom instead. This initiated the overriding theme of Wack's life. Above all, he sought freedom. According to Eve, he frequently spoke of his early experiences and he was "always looking for something—to be free—he did not like to feel trapped at all, by anyone or anything."

The events and history that have been described here were important aspects of Wack's life that no doubt made him who he was—no different from anyone else, yet impossibly unique. However, the nature of Wack's experiences and the things that shaped him tended to push him toward ways of understanding and knowing that are not typical. He sought alternative consciousness, mystical interpretations of the world and intuitive understanding. These kinds of pursuits are not common for executives in global corporations.

By all accounts, Pierre Wack was a rare, remarkable and magnetic person. Because of the events of his life, he was personally motivated to see the world in different ways—and here "different" truly has the sense of the unconventional, using alternative perspectives and varied techniques. The events of Wack's life gave him his own mental model and personal experiences that, in a certain place, with certain people, framed what remain the most famous cases of scenario planning success to date. The insights generated by the scenario team at Shell under his leadership have become legendary, and this book is a tour of the legend's most mystical character.

To understand scenario planning, it is essential to understand its roots. Scenario planning needs us to wonder about the things we do not know rather than try to analyze only what we do know. Wack was an advocate of relentless curiosity, and he was a man *genuinely interested* in the world. He promoted the utility of intuition and the magical flashes of insight that emanate from stilling the mind in Zen meditation, yet he simultaneously prioritized facts and the ability to perceive them accurately. On this topic, Wack was fond of quoting Paul Valery, the twentieth-century French philosopher. He said, "Un fait mal observe est plus pernicieux qu'un mauvais raiseonnement." A poorly observed fact is more treacherous than a faulty train of reasoning.

Let us now do our best to observe the facts of Pierre Wack as accurately as we can.

## Chapter 1 Sources (in order of use)

Wack, E. (n.d.). *Quelques dates et événements de la vie d'un "homme remarquable"*: *Pierre Wack* [draft; 12 pages with note by Eve Wack]. Document retrieved from the Pierre Wack Memorial Library, University of Oxford.

Wack, E. (1998). *Pierreve: 1977–1997*. Curemonte, France, Unpublished manuscript.

Excerpt from personal communications with Eve Wack. Author held interviews and discussions in 2014–16.

Kleiner, Art, James C. Davidson telephone interview: Spring 1993. (n.d.). 21 pp. The annotated transcript of a telephone interview between Art Kleiner and James Davidson regarding the development of Shell's Group Planning Department. Retrieved from the Art Kleiner Archive, University of Oxford.

Kleiner, A. Pierre A. Wack interview in Curemonte. (n.d.). 53 pp. The annotated transcript of an interview between Art Kleiner and Pierre Wack regarding the development of Shell's scenario planning. Retrieved from the Art Kleiner Archive, University of Oxford.

Valéry, P. (1967). *Eupalinos: And, L'âme Et la Danse*. Oxford: Oxford University Press.

# 2   Travels to the East
## Japan and India

*The stone steps at Nanzen-ji Temple in Kyoto have been worn smooth from the centuries of visitors. Pierre ascended slowly, studying the spectacular and massive central gate at the temple entrance. He recalled the teachings of his gardening mentor—to really see things as they are—a leaf blown across his feet, the wonderful patina on the old beam supporting the Mon gate he was about to pass through and the crimson red of the maple leaves over his head, no two of which were the same. He was to meet Roshi Zenkei Shibayama, for whom he had a very important question . . .*

Some form of mindfulness practice exists in every culture around the world. For some, these practices take the shape of organized religion. For others, they are less formal and may take the form of carpentry, sailing, yoga and unlimited other possible variations. What all of these practices have in common is an emphasis on reflection and introspection—what some people might call "magic"—the things we cannot yet explain that allow us to wonder about life. More than most cultures, the Japanese have elevated seemingly mundane activities to paths of enlightenment. Gardening, tea ceremony, martial arts, calligraphy and flower arranging are among the most well-known. However, the quintessential Japanese practice is Zen meditation. While meditation had existed as a practice for centuries before finding its way to Japan, the Japanese interpretation and development in several of its schools remains among the most mystic of traditions.

There is far more research, of far better quality than most people realize that rigorously demonstrates the benefits of meditation and spiritual practice. A vast collection of close and careful study related to Zen Buddhism houses surprising outcomes for the naysayer. Of the many important contributions, Austin's two manifestos titled *Zen and the Brain*, and *Reflections on Zen and the Brain* stand out, particularly because they so comprehensively report on and summarize the considerable body of research related to cognitive function under meditative states. These volumes detail the remarkable conclusions of many authors, some of which Wack was known to have studied with great interest.

## Hara

Wack's path to the East truly began in his childhood. While little specific evidence remains, the stories he told others are important clues to the roots of his curiosity. Wack's father is said to have believed he could talk to animals, and he was known to have a great love of nature. Wack's fondness for animals and nature were passions they shared.

There is little surviving information from Wack's school years that seems relevant to his spiritual practice, and there are no stories of academic mentors or particularly influential figures over this period of his life. However, in 1949 Wack met Karlfried Dürckheim who planted a seed:

> I got [the idea of Japan] from a German, very remarkable man, who has made an excellent book on Japan. He was an attaché in the German embassy and he was always sitting on his floor and painting, making calligraphy and he made a very interesting book which is in English. It's well worth reading—It's called Hara. Hara means the center on which Japanese concentrate when they do painting, they paint from hara, when they do judo, aikido, archery.

Hara generally refers to the abdominal area and has a long history in eastern medical and spiritual practices. It is one's foundation and creates stability. The Japanese focus on this area as a source of strength and energy in their everyday posture, as well as during the performance of martial arts and other meditation practices. As Dürckheim wrote, "When we find the physical center of the body, we also find the psychological center of the soul. According to Zen masters, by correcting posture and breathing to balance this center, one can cultivate inner tranquility." Wack's interest in such ideas clearly reaches back to the early parts of his life, but a major source of inspiration came in 1943 when Wack met Gurdjieff.

## Gurdjieff

George Ivanovich Gurdjieff (also referred to as Georges Ivanovich Gurdjieff, or G.I. Gurdjieff) was an eccentric music composer, writer, and mystic teacher. Although he had many occupations throughout his life, he is known to have been a businessman selling carpets, at some points, on and off. He had amassed a degree of wealth over his activities and eventually settled in Paris in 1936. There, he focused on his teachings in the later part of his life throughout World War II. Originally, Gurdjieff drew from the traditional teachings of monks, fakirs and yogis as he had travelled extensively throughout the Middle East and India. Accounts suggest that his later teachings were based on his personal travels, jokes, and other interactions he documented in his book, *Beelzebub's Tales*. Gurdjieff was a controversial figure to be sure.

In Paris, Wack met this charismatic man in February of 1943. Wack was suffering from tuberculosis at the time due to malnutrition given the scarcity of food during WWII. He recounted the story of their meeting:

> I was in Lyon because it was still unoccupied and Lyon was a strange capital of strange things. All kinds of secret societies and things like this. A friend and I were already interested—we were looking around and then Lyon became occupied and I went to Paris. This friend told me, "Look I saw a very interesting chap and I have an appointment at this address at 4:00 Friday." At 4:00 Friday I rang the bell. I didn't know where I was. I opened the door, I only saw the back of some feet. I sat down, 14 people were sitting. I heard a voice of a woman speaking, Madame Jeanne de Salzmann, and I was abruptly put in a quite advanced course with Mr. Gurdjieff. I had probably the wrong day . . . I think 4 or 5 months afterwards I was presented to Mr. Gurdjieff with a quite famous man in France who had worked in India . . . And we were both presented to Gurdjieff at the same time. Happily, Gurdjieff started with him first, and really agonized him. Afterwards we came back through the metro. He hardly could walk it was so shattering.

Wack further clarified the circumstances under which he met his first great master: "When I met Gurdjieff in February 1943, I was twenty years old and I was exceptionally well received. You could say that Gurdjieff cured my tuberculosis because he 'fed' me both spiritually and over some extraordinary dinners, in the middle of the war, at a time when everything was scarce." The affinity for alternative explanations was mutual and was mutually beneficial. Wack stayed with Gurdjieff in his Paris apartment even when other disciples were celebrating the end of the war out in the Paris streets in 1945.

By his own account, Wack stated that Gurdjieff "was the first to make me see that higher states of consciousness could exist. He gave me my first tasting and this in a way, roused my appetite." Wack was grateful to Gurdjieff, though he eventually saw a dark side and later on reflected: "the road he took was not mine."

Some accounts of Gurdjieff question the legitimacy of his later practices and have suggested a degree of self-promotion and arrogance. This may be the dark side to which Wack was referring. The time Wack spent with Gurdjieff ignited a lifelong interest that would take him down many paths, though it is not clear if he ever found the understanding he sought. Yet those paths undoubtedly and profoundly influenced the ways in which Wack saw the world and therefore, eventually, the evolution of scenario planning at Shell.

## Sufism

Some have written that Wack studied Sufism—generally the mystic Islamic belief in which the practitioner experiences the Truth through a direct personal experience of God. However, there is no evidence or anecdote that Wack had much interest in God at all. His refusal to be baptized, and opinion at just 16 years old that religion represented a "clan," illustrates this disinterest. The exposure Wack had to Sufism principles would have been through Gurdjieff's teachings, though Gurdjieff was known to blend various philosophies into his own systems rather than to follow or promote any specific religious tradition. Gurdjieff is nonetheless regarded by some as a Sufi master, and while he spent time in the Middle East, and indeed studied with Sufi practitioners, his teachings do not reflect a strict adherence to Sufi principles. Gurdjieff was also famously vague and unforthcoming about the sources of his teachings.

Wack's interests were far more focused on learning and insight about the world. Wack was interested in the human mind. He believed it was a remarkably sophisticated instrument not well understood. So it is important to draw a distinction that Wack's energies were spent on understanding how people engage with what they believe is reality, how they influence it, how they understand it, how they come to accept it and how they can reframe it. As his life unfolded, he was increasingly concerned with the philosophy of acceptance, most likely related to personal experiences, and it became a foundation of his thinking. It was this, far more than any set of prescribed religious beliefs or practices that he was seeking. And Zen Buddhism was a natural fit for his pursuit.

## Japan

Wack visited Japan for the first time in 1953 and felt instant connection. He knew immediately it would be a place he would return to again and again. By this time, Wack had become a good listener, deeply influenced by his experiences with Gurdjieff and he wanted to continue developing his pursuit of insight. He had come to know there were ways of understanding beyond the five senses.

Wack had obviously developed an interest in worldly ideas and all they had to offer—and had initiated his cultivation of remarkable people. His travels to other countries were built around meeting someone he heard was interesting. He recalled how his first visit to Japan came together:

> I was living in Paris in a house where I was the only one who was not paying the rent. It was a duplex house and my neighbor was Fujita, a very well-known Japanese painter. And I told him I wanted to go to Japan and he gave me two pieces of advice, he said, "Don't go to Tokyo, when you arrive go immediately to Kyoto," and he gave me the address and a recommendation of the best Japanese traditional restaurant, not restaurant, hotel, Japanese inn [*ryokan*]. At the time it was not very expensive, I didn't remember at all that it was a big weight on my budget. Now it's you know . . . but nevertheless they accepted me and

I stayed three weeks. And then I got a recommendation for a Japanese designer and I stayed with him again one month.

## Garden Design—Seeing Things "As They Are"

His trip had two purposes—one, to gain some understanding of the Japanese economy and how it was growing so fast (related to his work for La Libre Entreprise to jumpstart the French economy), and two, to further his own spiritual practice by learning about Zen. Japan was in the middle of the Showa period (1926–89) and the time later became known as the "Japanese Miracle" because Japan's economy grew three times faster than any other nation. Wack thought he might learn how the Japanese were fueling and managing their growth so efficiently. He had also made a connection to a Japanese garden designer and was to apprentice with him for a few weeks.

Before Buddhism had arrived in Japan, the historical religious practice was Shintoism—the worship of nature. Mountains, rocks, trees, waterfalls—all could be considered sacred. Kyoto and other old cities in Japan feature many sacred aspects of nature in a variety of shrines. The deep connection to nature is obvious to anyone who visits during the spring for the cherry blossoms, the autumn for the magnificent maple leaves, or quite honestly any other time of year.

Garden design, then is a perfect mixture of Shintoism and Buddhism. Gardeners are esteemed members of society, highly paid and respected:

> In Japan, my first trip was with a garden designer and you know a garden designer is one of the highest grand artists in Japan. At least as much as a painter or sculptor. He was a very remarkable man— Kokobe-san. You did not need to be Japanese to experience what the game of garden design was. Usually when we look at the landscape it's mechanical. The mind works, talking to itself. You compare it with this green, or so on. But sometimes it happens—you see a branch, a rock or a leaf—very intensely. And when you see, you see its uniqueness. Designing gardens—you don't use anything exotic. You just use normal things. This is called the art of garden design. So I spent some weeks with him and at the end, my last day, he took me to a corner where there was only vegetable brush and he told me, "Look at this. Look at it really. This is real. It is. And it is much more important than to be beautiful. Never forget, what is, is." It was my first feeling of really seeing.

The idea of seeing things "as they are" would become a central theme throughout the rest of Wack's spiritual journey and would have profound influences on his later work in planning. On the same trip, he also made arrangements to visit with several economists in Japanese companies.

## Nippon Steel

Wack made connections to perhaps the most famous Japanese corporation—
Nippon Steel. He was comparing their planning practices to what he was
doing in Paris and his mission was to take insights away about how they
were so astutely perceiving their markets:

> It really is Nippon Steel that helped me a lot when I was working on the
> French National Plan. And Steel being a major user of energy of course
> I looked at all the big projects of Steel and I was very aware of what
> they do and how they looked and how they justified their investment
> and so on. And it was completely consistent with these interpretations
> of the market. Completely.

## Throwing Stones at Bamboo

Because of his profound gardening experiences with "seeing," Wack
returned to Kyoto the following year to get a different view of Japanese
spiritual practices and to visit more companies. This time, however, he made
arrangements to visit So-En Roshi (Roshi is an honorific title for senior
teachers in Zen Buddhism):

> It was in a monastery, with one of the few Roshi who spoke English,—
> the monastery of Hakkuin, the remarkable Zen painter and monk. The
> Roshi was a painter himself. I asked him a question which was impor-
> tant for me. And he pondered for a few seconds and then he told me,
> "If you take a stone and throw it against a bamboo, and really hear the
> sound, you will have your answer." Needless to say, after this, I threw
> some stones at bamboos. And it's not easy. You must really feel com-
> pletely one with the bamboo to hit it, and if you hit it on the side, there
> is no sound; you must hit it in the middle. And then there is a sound.
> And to hear it deeply; it will change your state of mind.

Wack would retell this story many times throughout his career to communicate some of the key purposes of scenario planning—changing your state
of mind, hearing a sound deeply, striking the mental models of managers
like the stone against the bamboo—these are all powerful images he used to
get ideas across.

## Family in Paris

In 1954, Wack was able to afford an apartment on the Rue Campagne Premiere in Paris. He met fashion model June Pruce and a short time later she
was pregnant. In 1959 their daughter Nathalie was born and he married

June a year later. Wack helped June gain a work-permit in France, and she had a very successful career as a fashion model, "working for such houses as Gres, Lanvin and Revillon." After her modelling career, she eventually transitioned to salon and make-up artist work for television and film under the Carita sisters, Rosy and Maria. Wack did not take to married life at the time, and he never actually lived with June.

Wack was working for a law association called *"La Libre Entreprise,"* created by a Michelin executive named Monsieur Morisot. The purpose of the association was to free the French economy via three key strategies:

1  Analyze and publish data about the French economy (called *"Voici les Faits"* [Here are the Facts]),
2  Force French companies to clarify their operating statements to support the employee / management relationship, and
3  On Wack's recommendation, create a publication focused on more global economic trends and visions aligned with global practices.

## Zenkei Shibayama

In 1959, Wack returned to Japan to visit the Roshi at Nanzen-ji temple—a man named Zenkei Shibayama. Wack heard he was interesting and he spoke English which was rare in those days. Surely, the Roshi would be a great addition to his growing network of remarkable people. On arrival, the monks didn't open the door right away—Wack was left in front of the old wooden door of the temple for a night in the freezing cold. Still, he persisted and the next day, the Roshi invited him in.

Shibayama was a celebrated monk in Japan, Nanzen-ji being one of Kyoto's oldest and most famous temples. A few years later, in 1966, Shibayama would publish a collection of Zen essays titled *A Flower Does Not Talk.* Uniquely, the original text included a set of Ikebana (flower arrangements) photographs composed by one of the most famous masters, Jowa Hirohata to accompany the Roshi's thoughts. It is likely that Wack's love of Ikebana began in the years he studied with Shibayama and it is also likely the Roshi was working on his poems and essays at the time Wack was visiting him. A particular passage that is said to resemble Wack is as follows:

> Why fret away your life?
> See the willow tree by the river;
> There it is, watching the water flow by.

Many years later, Eve said that Wack spent a lot of time on their terrace. She made a garden that could be viewed from the terrace, "And he would sit for hours and hours, just watching, meditating, just watching a tree, and . . . just looking . . . I think he had the capacity of when looking at a tree to become a tree."

Wack stayed for three weeks in the monastery, meditating, cleaning the temple and living as one of the monks. After this experience, Wack was able to see that if he wanted to make any serious progress in his spiritual understanding according to the Japanese tradition, he would need to remain under the tutelage of a Roshi for several years. This was not feasible given his position in economics and planning, and he settled for taking his vacation there as often as he could. Throughout the rest of the 1950s, Wack continued to visit Japan and it became one of his favorite places.

While Wack was fascinated with Japan, he explored other remarkable people in their places around the world. He had another important insight on a trip to Bangkok in late 1959. While Wack did not describe the experience in detail, he did reflect on its importance for him:

> The real experience came later in Bangkok with a very remarkable man. Usually we see with our minds—with influences, with expectations, with all our past experience. To see—and I mean, not in the narrow sense, but to perceive totally, to see through. To see is a function of true consciousness. It is a wonder of what is, because it is so. He describes it, Heidegger: "It is a shock when you really perceive." The word "wise man" in Sanskrit is Rishi. Rishi means "a seer." Bodhisattva—the "one who sees all around." This by the way is the best definition of a scenario leader I know. The greatness of seeing is that it puts all emphasis on things as they are, as an access to truth. Not believing, in operating things—just seeing things as they are. He asked me what types of things I did, and I explained I was involved in some future study. He told me all about the chance—take it as a test, if you see things as they are. I was really, from this time I used future study as a test if I could see things. And it was a very powerful notion. He told me for instance, if your seeing is complete and perfect, at the right state of observation, there is immediate understanding. And I identified it several times. It's true. So this was one of the things that helped me a lot. To see is the best antidote against a crisis of perception. You heard me many times using the word "see," "perceive," and so on. It is not by chance. It is the way.

## Chantal Livry-Level

In 1960, Wack met Chantal Livry-Level in Paris. Chantal was 25 years old when they met. Wack was 38. They began travelling together. He took her to Japan, the French countryside, and Morocco. Chantal became interested in Ikebana—the Japanese art of flower arranging, which fit perfectly with Wack's established connection to Japan and his own previous experience with Shibayama Zenkei in Kyoto. They kept a tent permanently pitched in a farmer's field in Brittany, France about four hours outside of Paris. Their love grew quickly and intensely. Professionally, Wack was making contributions to the French plan.

## Svamiji Prajnanpad

The most profound influence and mentorship in Wack's life came from Svamiji Prajnanpad, the story of whom is captured in the Foreword to this book. The reason Wack wrote those pages helps with the context. Wack received Svamiji's name from Daniel Roumanoff who he contacted through Arnaud Desjardins. Roumanoff provided a list of remarkable teachers and put Swamiji Prajnanpad at the end of it. Wack visited India for the first time in at the end of 1960 seeking a teacher. It was a year before he joined Shell Francaise, (and almost a decade after his first trip to Japan). The role of spirituality was firmly established for Wack, and he had absorbed tremendous insights from Gurdjieff and his years of tutelage in Japan and other places in Asia. He was about to open a new chapter in India and had made a list of many remarkable yogis he wanted to visit:

> Once I got to Calcutta, my first visit is to a yogi in Puri who is said to be 125 years old. He is a massive man with atrophied legs from constantly sitting in the lotus position. Wristwatch in hand, I measure that his respiratory cycle lasts for two minutes. "Start by disciplining your food," he tells me, but I am not yet ready to appreciate the relevancy of this advice and leave the next day. Next, I meet a Sikh master, then, in Bombay, Rajneesh, and finally Ma Ananda Mayee. Each time, my decision emerges rapidly—This is not the road for me—and I move on.
>
> Then I meet a Sufi master in Kanpur, Bhai Sahib, with whom I stay for three weeks. I visit him every morning and every afternoon. Communication with the master, albeit in total silence, is exceptionally good, and I become familiar with extraordinary states of consciousness. Still, I can't stay with him for longer than that. Before leaving France, I have imposed a couple of strict rules on myself that I have sworn to obey:
>
> * to distrust anything that looks like a demand for money
> * to leave for several days after a stay of three weeks at the most, no matter what happens, to avoid being brainwashed;
> * to observe carefully the entourage and the goings-on amongst the disciples.
>
> Bhai Sahib demands total obedience from his disciples. When, after three weeks, I announce to him that I will leave for a couple of days, the master is furious. He bursts out in violent maledictions and calls me names. I leave him anyway, but I can't suppress the idea that he has cast an evil spell over my future.

Those who knew Wack say he always looked for the positive aspects of a difficult situation, and in his view it was because of his failed attempts, that a useful solution presented itself:

When I go back from Kanpur to Calcutta by train, with the intention of going back to Thailand, I notice that my train makes a stop-over at Khana Junction, the station that is nearest to Svamiji's ashram. I arrive there at five o'clock in the morning, leave all my luggage at the station—feeling certain that I will leave again soon—and walk over the rice-fields for two and a half hours before arriving at the ashram. Svami Prajnanpad is there alone, which is exceptional. The ashram is a marvellous enclave. I stay there for three weeks, then for another two. I have a sitting in the morning and one in the afternoon. It is the strongest experience I have ever had. For the first time in my life, I feel fulfilled.

Svami Prajnanpad was born Yogeshwar Chattopadhyay on February 8, 1891 near Kolkata [Calcutta]. He entered a Channa ashram around 1924 and attended Calcutta University, though he increasingly tended toward spiritualism. A Brahman coming from a very poor family, he was writing poetry but graduated in Physics, according to the wishes of his elder brother as his parents died when he was very young. He taught English literature and Indian philosophy in several colleges. In 1922 he met Niralamba Swami, who became his guru. He discovered the first books of Freud in Bénarès in 1923 which inspired him to complete the Upanishads [a collection of ancient Indian texts of a religious and philosophical nature]. In 1930 he gave up teaching entirely and became a disciple of Niralamba Swami, considered by many to be one of the great Indian yogis—also an Indian nationalist and freedom fighter. Niralamba Swami asked Prajnanpad to take over his ashram as he approached his death in 1930.

Starting in 1959, Svami Prajnanpad cultivated a following of French disciples that included Daniel Roumanoff, Pierre Wack, Frédéric Leboyer, Roland de Quatrebarbes, Arnaud Desjardins, Denise Desjardins, Olivier Cambessedes, Anémone Cambessedes, and Colette Roumanoff. Wack was an early disciple and his connection with Svamiji created a path for others. Svamiji was known for his teaching methods that involved working with only one student at a time. He did not give sermons, speeches, or religious talks, and many regarded him as a skilled psychoanalyst. Wack would continue to visit Svami Prajnanpad each year until the master's death in September 1974. Wack's own brief description (some of which is excerpted here) is provided in full in the Foreword of this book.

Wack regarded Svamiji as a most skilled advisor, helping him work on his own perceptions and acceptance. He was clear that Svamiji helped him extend the idea that began in Japan—to "see"—to "see things as they are and not give oneself over to the games of the mind." Wack described "seeing" as it related to his work at Shell:

> Instead of economic calculations from global statistics, "seeing" demands, firstly, the identification of the forces at work and the chain(s) of cause and effect behind the development of a market, and secondly,

information about a chain is much finer than global statistics, a ladder where significant differences appear. "Seeing" certainly was a much more demanding and strenuous discipline than regular forecasting, but the managing directors who had to make use of forecasts quickly saw the difference and my field of activity expanded first to the entire Shell France and then on an international level to the ensemble of the Royal Dutch Shell group in London.

Wack did not believe he was predisposed to think this way, and he said that he was naturally attracted to give himself over to those games of the mind. But his persistence in finding a guru who would question him, and his development of a network of remarkable people throughout the world, gave him the ability to come to the insights that were so effective later at Shell.

## Shell Francaise

In April, 1961, Wack had to decide between offers from two of his favorite consulting clients—Shell and Michelin. Wack learned that Michelin forced employees to take their holidays in August, when the whole company would shut down. August in Japan and India, Wack's favorite spots, are not pleasant due to the heat, humidity and insects. Shell allowed more freedom in when their people could take leave, so the choice was easy. Wack accepted the role of Chief Economist at Shell Francaise and immediately went to work. His assistant, Huguette Joligeon recalled a story about Wack that would characterize his uniqueness throughout his career. One day in 1968 she entered his office to ask something about a file. Wack was in a yoga posture on the floor and answered: "Je suis loin de toutes ces contingences" (I am far from all these incidental things.) Huguette left the room feeling guilty to have disturbed her boss. She said she will never forget!

## The God of Wind

In 1962, Wack and Chantal bought an afghan dog and named him Indra, after the Hindu God of wind: "Indra became the most beautiful and the most intelligent of all dogs. He loved luxury hotels, big restaurants, where, adult, feeling admired, he walked proudly between the tables. But his arrogance became humility when his master took him to his office at Shell Francaise, where under the desk, he waited until the day would end." Indra would play an important role in his life a few years later.

Tragically, Chantal died suddenly in Paris in 1964. She was 29 years old: "They had returned together from a weekend. He had taken her home. Then he'd called her: the telephone did not answer. He'd gone back to see what had happened . . . It had been impossible to find a doctor that holiday fast enough." She had fallen and hit her head on a door. Wack immediately sought his guru in India to help him deal with the loss: "I could tell you about how he made me grasp and realize 'acceptance,' but this is very much linked to some personal experiences of mine, and I have no desire to expose my private life." Wack saved many of her possessions, including a Japanese funeral sculpture that remains at Wack's home in Curemonte, France. His later wife Eve remarked: "I imagined the tragic side of this event, but he talked about it without emotion. He told me only facts—but in the manner he told me this story from the beginning, when we'd met, without apparent reason, I felt that Chantal may have been the only love of his life."

### Recordings with Svamiji

Wack continued visiting Svamiji in Channa each year, usually in January. In 1964 and 1974, Wack's sessions with Svamiji were recorded. After Swamiji's death Daniel Roumanoff collected all the recordings and letters from the disciples who were willing to give them. He spent several years on the transcription of a considerable volume of material. Then "Svami Prajnanpad un Maître Contemporain" was published by La Table Ronde, then by Albin Michel with a résume called "ABC d'une Sagesse." The nine recordings of 1964 and the thirteen of 1974 were published in French in 2002 by l'Originel under the title of "l'Eternel Présent". The recording with Pierre Wack on 9 January 1974 is available online (http://www.svami-prajnanpad. org/extraits.html).

Conversations with Svamiji were in English as he did not speak French and the recordings were translated into French for Roumanoff's publication. Shortly before Roumanoff's death in December, 2015, English transcriptions of Wack's talks with Svamiji were made available for this project by Daniel's wife, Collette. What follows are the passages that concern important themes in his life, planning and those judged to hold a particular relevance in understanding Wack.

### Sittings in 1964

The recorded sittings in 1964 consist of nine conversations between Wack and Svamiji, which occurred on January 6, 7, 8, 9, 10, 13, 14 and 15. The conversations were each focused on a different topic usually chosen by Wack (with titles provided by Daniel Roumanoff). The listing of these conversations is as follows:

1   Sense of Separation and Uniqueness: Is There Contradiction? (6.01.64)
2   Imagination and Memory (7.01.64)
3   Emotions and Samadhi (8.01.64)
4   Habits Life After Death Buddhism and Hinduism (9.01.64)
5   Throwing Back and Growing Out (10.01.64)
6   Maya: Is Rivermaking Zigzag? (11.01.64)
7   Opinion of others: Speaking to an Audience (13.1.64)

8    Expression, Ananda, Sânti (14.01.1964)
9    Why Usually Knowing Is Not Being? How to Make Awareness Last? (15.01.64)

This section provides excerpts from each topical session that gives insights about Wack, what he may have struggled with and how he thought about both practical and spiritual aspects of life. There has been no attempt at interpreting these passages, rather they are simply provided so that the reader can observe Wack's efforts at learning to "see" and make connections to his later work in scenarios.

## Sense of Separation and Uniqueness: Is There Contradiction?

S. By acceptance, mentally and emotionally, you become freed. And all your energies are at your disposal at that moment. You can utilize anyway you like. And if you don't accept, a major part of your energy is bound there. So what can you do?

P. And it comes quite clear what you told me day before yesterday on positive action. Because positive action follows immediately our acceptance.

S. So without aim, without idea of result, no action is possible. So now when you accept, then . . .

P. . . . you are free for action.

S. You are free for action. You just see the circumstances, see your resources and act.

P. Yes. You don't act on reaction, you act positive.

S. This is positive action. And this positive action brings results. If you see your resources, if you are at one with the circumstances, then . . . ? The two combined cannot but bring the result. So the result will take care of itself. You take care of yourself. That is the law.

## Imagination and Memory

P. I know that in my life imagination is very important. On the good side and on the bad side. Sometimes I have ideas and, in my work, I use creative imagination without any doubt. And at other times, imagination is just dreaming and projecting things and not seeing things as they are. So what is the place of imagination?

S. «What is the place of imagination?» Yes, you know, fundamentally, everything is neutral, so imagination also is neutral. It depends on the subject or the position of the observer or the nature of the subject to appear as good or bad. But imagination is neutral.

   What is the nature of imagination? Imagination is nothing but a sort of wish-fulfilment. What you imagine? That which you don't find here but wish . . . What do you imagine? «I imagine: Oh! If I like that . . . if something will be like that and so on and so forth . . . « That which is not here.

P. And also seeing eventualities in the future?

S. Quite all right. But eventualities in the future . . . on the basis of the present. You cannot imagine anything what you don't know. What you don't feel, you can't . . . You may mix one aspect of you here with another and so on and so forth and you can figure . . . That's a different point. But it all depends upon your own present position. So imagination is nothing but an elongation, so to say, of your present experience.

So generally, which sort of people imagine more . . . are given more to imagination and which not?

P. The one who are not satisfied from the present.

S. There you are! One who is not in harmony, so to say, with reality or with the circumstances in which he is placed, gives himself up to imagination.

So . . . but there is imagination . . . until one can imagine, one cannot go forward. That is also a point. Finer the imagination, more the way to progress. But that imagination should be based on reality, otherwise it will be something airy. It will lead to nothing but airy. Life will be airy, haphazard, nothing more than . . . It will not be tangible and cogent and real.

So whatever is in every imagination you are to see: «What is this?» One is to see only. To be man or to attain enlightenment or anything else, one is to see.

Because you know, the whole conception, so to say, of enlightenment, of wisdom or anything else . . . Here they say: one who is wise, perfectly wise is called a seer. *Paripaśyanti*: they see all around. *Pari* means all around. *Paśyanti*: they see . . This is from the Upanishads: «Those who are balanced and calm and cool (*dhîrâh;.*), they see all around (*paripaśyanti*) that whatever manifests is nothing but a form of *ânanda* and blessedness (*amr;. ta*).

For man it is only to see. What does actually this so-called man do? He thinks and not sees. So if thinking is not at one with . . . or not in harmony with seeing, life is a tragedy. So it is said: «Just see . . . just see."

## Emotions and Samadhi

So, emotion is the outcome of your thinking that you see a thing as it is. But, really, you don't see the object but you think that you see the object.

P. I see it coloured, I see it . . .

S. . . coloured by your own colour. That is you see the thing as it is not or you see a thing otherwise than as it is, So, you get emotion. So, emotion is the result of a wrong seeing.

P. I remember quite well that when I have an emotion and I try to see it practically, it's a sign that I see a thing as it is not. But, Svâmiji, how can I live without emotions? How can I act, how can I . . . ?

S. Who says you are to . . . ? You are acting with emotions. Don't jump to conclusions. Just accept yourself first. «How can I live without emotions?» that is not the question. The question is: «The emotions are here, how may I be free from the emotions?» And if you will be free from the emotion, you will live without emotion. Your task is to see the nature of emotion and to be free from it.

P. But not to suppress them. Yes, yes, yes . . . Oh! I see . . .

P. Now, I see quite well, even so well that sometimes I try to feel no emotions, to have not the change. So, I feel it quite well and I feel also that it is an impoverishment and this is not the right way.

S. So, in order to do that, you must have awareness first. You must be aware of each and every one of your actions, so that you can very easily say: «Oh! Now, there is emotions there is this . . . there is this . . . Now, let me see that. Why does the emotion arise? And I know that emotion arises only when I don't see a thing as it is, or I see a thing as it is not. So, what is this here? What is the fact here which I don't see or which I see otherwise? Let me see . . . ».

P. The emotion can be a very good lesson, a very good experience.

S. It teaches you. It leads you to truth, from untruth which you take to be truth now. So, emotions are an asset. The more emotions one feels, more awakened is he. A dull man doesn't feel any emotion. His ego, so to say, is not awakened. He is dull, he is asleep. Those who are very emotional should be taken as more alive, more awakened and they also do more work.

So, emotion is an asset. So, you are to do what then? You are to utilize this power or strength or energy behind the emotion to your benefit. Now it is frittering away your energy and so on. You are to see that first, see the nature of emotion first.

S. You know that. So, how to be free then?

P. To live it . . .

S. To live it . . . to see . . . to go . . . Have the courage to see through. «Quite all right, here, when I get emotions, I know that I am not seeing things as it is. I am seeing something else. And that is a fact to me now. Quite all right». Take it . . . test it . . test it whether it is a fact or not. And you will be free. Go and test and: «Oh! No, no, no! It is not . . . it is not . . . it is not, otherwise.».

P. It's not always easy to test it!

S. It is very difficult to test it, because you are carried away by your emotions. In order to test you shall be master of your emotions. Emotions will never carry you away, but you shall allow the emotion to have its play. That's the difference. When you are carried away by emotions, you can't see what is taking place. But when you say: «Yes, I feel emotion, yes, I feel.». Feel it! Don't deny! Yes, there it is. Feel it through. And then ( . . . ) «What is it? It is the product of wrong seeing. What is wrong seeing here? What is the nature of it? Let me see».

## Habits, Life after Death, Buddhism and Hinduism

*S.* The natural relaxation that everyone, or every animal or every being is having is sleep. Without sleep you can't work. What is sleep then? Natural relaxation. You become free from all struggle, all activity, everything. So similarly also consciously, there is manner that you can relax for some time daily and in that case if you have got that habit to relax, then you will always be relaxed during your work too.

*P.* Do it regularly also this voluntary . . .

*S.* Yes, regularly, for half an hour, for an hour, thus, complete relaxation.

*P.* But always at the same time?

*S.* Always at the same time. Yes, because you were functioning, you are over external works and so on and so forth. So, if you do it regular, that will be of benefit. And, even in that case, during work also, you are engaged in your work fully, but sometimes you feel: «Oh! Am I relaxed or not?» Relax and work. So, this relaxation is to be cultivated consciously and that will be actually converted into habit, as you call it. It will be your own and you will always be relaxed in a way. You will be accustomed to relaxation.

And in order to do that, sometimes during the day, take some time and relax completely. If you have got an easy chair, quite all right. In your office you have an easy chair. Relax completely: physically and mentally. Don't think, don't plan, nothing of the kind at that moment. Complete relaxation. If you do that, then you will at once be refreshed.

So, you can arrange your life in such a way that work and rest may be adjusted properly. The more work you do, the more rest you need. So, rest also depends upon the nature of the work. A physical work: some rest. A mental work: another kind of rest. And mental and physical work: another kind of rest. So, you can very easily accommodate, that is, you must have rhythm so to say.

## Throwing Back and Growing Out

*P.* I can feel it and see it through emotions and sometimes with dealing with people and so on. But how can I realize duality by just ordinary . . . ? I walk in the morning in the field, I feel my movements, I see palm trees, I see other trees, my emotion is not involved. I don't see things through my emotions because there is no reason to have likes or dislikes. How then to realize? How to see things as they are and how to realize duality?

*S.* Yes, this duality. When you see, you see, when you walk, you see a palm tree, you see and see everything, you don't see duality. No. Why? Duality: when there will be two. Duality meaning two. So, there should be presence of two. When you see a palm tree, that's all. Oh! Feel it . . . feel it! You have got no emotional or intellectual reaction within. So, your emotional reaction shows that you are different from that, from which you get the reaction. The emotional reaction shows that there is something there. Otherwise? Nothing. Nothing, because you are not bound. It is there. As soon as you say it is there, that shows you and it are different. It is there only. That's all. Palm-tree is there. Finished. That shows at once you become the palm-tree at that moment. Is there any difference? Or rather, when you say it is palm-tree, different from a mango-tree, so intellectually different you see there. As soon as you say it is a palm tree, that shows that you differentiated from a mango-tree, so you are in duality then.

## Maya: Is Rivermaking Zigzag?

P. But now there is a point which is important for me. I quite agree that there is no future for the individual psychology. It is as there would be a never-changing present, coming and . . . But what I do? Part of my work for Shell is to forecast the future. And for instance, the energy requirement in 1970 are completely different from the ones now. And this is something I don't project. This is something which has to do with the number of people going to marry and this is nothing you have to figure out because the people, who are going to marry and have children need dwellings and need fuel to heat their dwellings. They are already born. So, with the life expectation, with the . . . it is completely statistics and nothing else.

S. Quite all right, yes, yes.

P. So, I can say, in 1970 there will be so and so many dwellings more and so and so fuel more and so you see . . . And this is a change. It has nothing to do with the present. So future exists objectively.

S. Yes. Is it? Now see through. You forecast on what basis? On the basis of the past?

P. Not only, not only.

S. But? Come on. On the basis of what? What is your data? You build your future, so to say, you build your data, build your result or picture of 1970 quite all right. What is your data on which you build?

P. My data . . .

S. . . . as a scientist.

P. . . . are not only the symptoms which I project . . .

S. Not only the symptoms. But what is that?

P. My data are the causes of energy consumption.

S. Quite all right.

P. And they are the number of cars, the number of dwellings for people and so on . . .

S. Quite all right. So you stand on what? You stand on? Reality data. It doesn't depend on your liking or disliking.

P. Oh! No! Not at all . . .

S. So that creation is a reality. But that is what you do. You create now and here. You don't go to 1970. But here you see: «This is so . . . this is so. . . . this is so. If I calculate and doing so and so . . . so 1970 will be this." Where is 1970 now? Here.

But there may be another man who says: «Oh! I am so miserable. Oh! Oh! Now if I go on saving thirty francs and so forth and then something like that will happen and after that in 1970 I shall have a house and so on and so forth and so on . . . ». What is he doing?

P. Oh! He is dreaming!

S. What is he doing? Doing anything?

P. No. He is projecting . . .

S. As for example, you know, a potter. Very nice, in Aesop's Fables . . . you know Aesop's very instructive anecdotes?

As for example, a potter was there. He made some earthen pots and he has a shop. He has put all these earthen pots and he was selling all those things. During noon, he rested and lay down and he was thinking: «Well, I am going on with this work, quite all right . . . in this way I shall go on and after that I shall have profit . . . that much of profit. And then I shall get a bigger shop and I shall do like that. And I shall have so much money and so on and so forth. And I shall give my wife so much ornaments and so on and so forth. And if she comes, she is very spendthrift. She doesn't control herself. But then if she comes and says: «Well, give so much money to me," oh! I shall never give it! I shall kick her!» At once he kicks. What does he kick? All those earthen pots!

P. Yes, very good story!

S. So see it through. So you are only to be a scientist, be an economist, yes, yes, be a scientist through and through. In economical problems you never bring in your likes and dislikes. You have got data on which you stand, on which you work. So you are with truth.

## Opinion of Others: Speaking to an Audience

P. I have rather often to make speeches or conferences. Now sometimes, it's very easy. Other times, the same subject . . . I know it quite well, but I don't know why, the audience is different. I am quite paralyzed. I know quite well that I know the subject, I could . . . And I know quite well that I couldn't care less of the opinion of others, but there is . . . how to go to the root when one feels like . . . ?

S. First of all, to feel . . . to be oneself. So the idea is «everything is different». So what you are, you are. When you feel that «I am what I am», that's all. So, you needn't care about others. At once it will come.

But then, about audiences. The nature of the audience makes difference. It may be. If the audience is of older people, that will make some effect and if the audience are of your age or something like that, that will make another effect.

As for example, you go to lecture. What do you do? You are to be at one with the subject. That's all. You are to be one with the subject. As soon as you feel that there are the audience, you are half with the subject, half with the audience. So you cannot do full justice. And when you are one with it, you go and you see your own ideas and joys are reflected in their eyes. You do not see so many people. You will not see so many faces and so many eyes. You will see yourself reflected there. You are one. But if you see them, you are divided there. You cannot lecture. So for lecturing you are to do what? Only to be at one with your theme. And again, go talk to yourself, not to others.

P. Talk to yourself?

S. Yes. When you lecture, whom do you lecture to? To others? No you cannot lecture. You lecture to yourself. The thing is you just feel and express yourself as fully as you can. Have a delight of expressing yourself. And that delight will be contagious. It cannot but be contagious. As soon as you feel the audience, you are divided. You are not with the subject.

## Expression, Ananda, Sânti

P. So, there are two ways in awareness: One Svâmiji told me last time to see how my ego expresses at the moment, in thinking, in emotion . . . and another way is how am I in this situation? Who am I now?

S. Here ego is in action and there ego in itself. When you are away from all actions, so to say, you see that. And again in action too, try to see that: «How do I feel? How do I do?» Yes, do it.

P. And the first way also is probably good when you try to see how you expressed yourself, one hour or two hours ago.

S. Yes, comparatively, you can very easily see. Yes. That's all. Now then?

P. It's a very agreeable feeling because you get out of dreaming to come into . . . it is like an awakening.

S. Yes. Because you are true always. Here you are always true to yourself. So you are always free. You are now in this situation, you are true. Now you need to go to another situation: you are in that situation. So you are as elastic . . . as adaptable as anything. No rigidity anywhere. So you become free.

## Why Usually Knowing Is Not Being? How to Make Awareness Last?

P. Yes, I see. So when I am back in Paris, far away from Svâmiji, what can Svâmiji give me as a rule to watch?

S. Oh! That is given: awareness.

P. Yes, yes. And awareness cannot fade away?

S. Cannot fade away. You are to try to be aware. If it fades away sometimes, no doubt now, at once you will see: "Oh! Where I was?" You may feel like that: "I was absent." So, sometimes you will see the very anomaly and the work of *mâyâ* is so ludicrous and so interesting! You say «I, I, I.». as if you are a single entity, but you are not. That is to be watched. You are to be aware of that first.

P.  This I catch quite well: how my ego expresses . . .

S.  Yes, and in that case only to be . . . Formula was given: always try to be where you are. That is, always challenge or ask yourself: "Who am I now?" And that's all. And be that.

Throughout the 1960s Wack continued working on economics and planning at Shell Francaise. He generally enjoyed his position there, living in Paris and continuing to explore his spiritual growth whenever he could. He also worked on the French Plan, rebuilding the economic stability of France along with people like Pierre Mendes France. In early 1961, Wack and several others were already agitated and dissatisfied with the straight line forecasting based on regression models. There was no attention to short and long-term planning cycles and the core concepts of uncertainty, circularity and "longue echeance" were already in Wack's mind. Wack met Leslie Dighton, a young addition to the Shell team who was being sent to Algeria to help with planning and economics. During the summer of 1961, Wack and Dighton shared an office in Shell Francais. Dighton had come to his own realization that the continued use of regression lines in Shell's planning were fraught with potential error, and when considering the volatility of the situation in Algeria, he thought there must be another way. Wack was already headed down that path and fanned the flames of Dighton's curiosity. There was not yet the thought of developing scenarios but the idea of considering different versions of the future was well underway. Wack suggested to Dighton that it was essential to study the history of Algeria before officially transferring there, and so he did. Dighton experimented with some early versions of what might be called scenarios, and his superior indicated they were not based enough on hard data to make decisions. Dighton went on to his post in Algeria, which was surely a nightmare, but he was eventually able to convince the top leadership in Shell that there was a real problem in Algeria and it needed serious attention, or the withdrawal of the two expats stationed there.

To this day, Dighton recalls Wack as a very warm person, someone "who was not part of the hierarchy, working usually all on his own with very few people around him." Wack taught Dighton about context—the context of decisions—if he wanted to make a difference. "I saw Pierre as a fountain of thought, there was no crazy intention, but for me, Pierre was a catalyst. He really did not want to sit and talk about gas prices, oil supply and demand, no—he wanted to talk about different ways of thinking." According to Dighton, "The upgrading of forward thinking to the CEO level from planners was key to empowering the whole system change which nourished scenarios."

Wack and June were divorced in 1965. In the late 1960s he was asked to lead what would be his first scenario assignment for Shell Francaise, drawing from what he learned with Herman Kahn, the details of which are provided in the next chapter. It is clear that during this time, Wack was experimenting with applying "seeing" to his planning work at Shell Francaise and for his home country. He was actively seeking different views on various economies around the world and how he might be able to learn from them.

## Sabbatical in Japan, 1971

Wack had gained a positive reputation for his work throughout the 1960s in France with his extensive work in Shell Fracaise and on the French Plan. In the late 1960s the wheels were turning at the larger Shell in London to overhaul the planning system. A detailed version of this story is told in the next chapter. Wack was chosen to head up the team, but he had something he needed to do first.

When Wack accepted the offer to move to London and work on a new planning system, he had been studying Zen Buddhism for almost 20 years, and had been meeting with Svamiji Prajnanpad in Channa for 10. He decided to negotiate the ability to spend a year in Japan which afforded him the opportunity simultaneously to develop his spiritual practices as well as his study of planning. India could not offer a comparable chance to study planning in a developed economy that would reveal insights relevant to his new task at Shell in London. Of course, Newland had flagged Japan as a country likely to be a global force over the next decade which gave Wack confirmation on his path. These facts gave Wack what he needed to make the case for his sabbatical to Andre Benard and Karl Swart. What is less well known is what he was doing there and the impact it would have on his own thinking and, therefore, Shell. In early 1971, Wack made his arrangements:

> I knew I wanted to go inside Japanese companies and it would not be easy . . . So I went to the Keidanren . . . Then I got the Vice President of the Keidanren who acted like my Godfather. We picked out the companies which were interesting to look at, which had something to do with planning. And we decided—sometimes it was a planner who was interesting, sometimes it was a vice president, sometimes it was a chairman. Each time, my godfather would introduce me. Happily, I knew from my experiences in Japan how to approach them. I gave them a list of 30 or 32 questions and I told them I would come back in two months' time. Because if you ask them directly, you have you know, no answer at all. When I came back two months later I got, really, very substantial answers. Very, very fascinating.

Unfortunately, there is no available record of the questions Wack asked, or the detailed responses he received. Yet Wack was very clear that everything he learned about strategic vision, he learned in Japan, and most likely, from those interviews. He distilled some of the major insights:

> When you speak to a Japanese company about planning, they will usually tell you, "We do not share your enthusiasm in the West for planning." They will add with a smile of satisfaction, "We have just a clear vision of what company we want to be." Now if you live with them, and I have spent some time with Sony, Honda, Mitsubishi, and so on, I found they see a strategic vision and planning like any animal in a habitat must rely on some strengths—on its claw, on its beak, on its capacity to hide. A strategic vision is a combination of strengths on which you want to rely in the future. It is a formula for success, not for the present, but distinctly directed toward the future. Sony, for instance, at the time when I was with them, had decided to be an innovative company but limited itself to only consumer electronic groups. For this they wanted to be excellent—ichiban—in three technologies at the same time—color, solid state, and magnetic tape recording. They said, other companies may be as good, even better than Sony in one of those three technologies, but none will be as good as we are in the three of them. They had some other elements of strengths. They had a very different financial approach from a normal Japanese company: Usually Japanese companies had at the time a tremendous amount of debt. You want to decide on the strengths you want to have in order to survive in the habitat you have decided to live in. None of these strengths are given, each is achievable with effort, and there must be a congruence with all of them. They must fit together. It's an ideal counterpart of scenarios. You do not often change your strategic vision. I see that Sony in 22 years now, since I had my sabbatical, has changed 2 ½ times. They are in the process of changing it again now.

Wack's metaphor of the company as an animal using its claw or beak is a perfect example of what was so engaging about him. And it was a preview of his later interest in competitive positioning. Companies could behave like animals to take advantage of their assets. They could run and hide—take care of their corner of their habitat. Or dominate and attack—again based on their assets and strengths. And every company is likely to employ all of these techniques at some point. In these ways, Wack had the ability to connect things he experienced and learned throughout his life with his professional world. In this case his love of nature influenced the way he described and explained strategic vision and competition. His use of metaphors and the ability to succinctly explain complex ideas became one of the most important factors in getting scenarios accepted in Shell.

After his sabbatical in Japan, he arrived in London ready to take on a role that had not yet been defined, but that would define him and Shell for years to come. Wack was very grateful for his time in Japan—expressing that it provided an absolute foundation for his later success, and it gave him a way to start conversations in London where he was unknown:

> I came back to London with a nice story to hear and while nobody knew about me, I organized presentations on Japan, so suddenly I became known. And if I would have not had the risk to say it, I think people would not have come. I was a nobody. So it's really the Japan thing, it's such a happy circumstance. And in fact I came to London largely in order to think . . . having given me this sabbatical in Japan. But if I would not ever have had it I don't think I would have been successful afterwards.

## Sittings in 1974 (February—Eight Months Before Svamiji's Death)

Another set of sittings with Svamiji were recorded in 1974—precisely a full decade after the first set and after three years of working inside Group Planning on scenarios. The conversations took place on January 10, 11, 12, 13, 14, 15, 17, 18, 19, 20, 21, 22, and 23 and included the following contents:

1  Thinking and Seeing (10. 01.74)
2  To Be Is to Express (11.01.74)
3  Truth Is: Application of the Teaching to Private Life (12.01.74)
4  To Know Is to Be (13.01.74)
5  Awareness (14.01.74)
6  About Prayer 15.01.74
7  What My Being Is? 17.01.74
8  All Actions Are Negative (18.01.74)
9  Justice of the Situation. Positive And Negative Action (19.01.74)
10  Aim of Life (20.01.74)
11  Mind is Desire (21.01.74)
12  Necessity and Dignity (22.01.74)
13  Aim of Life
13/2 Dharma (23.01 74)

## Thinking and Seeing

P.  I would like to understand better "seeing" opposed to "thinking." Seeing suggests an immediate understanding, something like intuition. Is it only this?
S.  Yes.
P.  It is immediate?
S.  Yes. Seeing is, so to say, complete, perfect, immediate understanding . . . and if understanding is not immediate, that shows there is thinking. Meaning? There is the play of the emotion or there is the play of the

past, which covers, which intervenes between you and the object.

P.  So there can be a mixing of seeing and thinking?

S.  That may be. But two things cannot occur at the same place . . . either seeing or thinking. When you think, there is no seeing . . .

You are to start from thinking, because thinking was originally there. It is still there. It is the cause of the past. Everything is there. So when there is thinking, there is disturbance here: positive or negative, either elation, joy or depression, dejection, conflict . . . It is tested here at once.

## To Be Is to Express

As the days have changed in this age . . . Svâmiji saw from his early childhood to these at least sixty years: Oh! What a tremendous change has taken place! People have become so materially minded! And it is going fast, fast! So higher mental, and moral or social instinct is going down and down.

To do for others was so natural fifty years ago, sixty years ago. Not now. Pleasure . . . amusement . . . : "Oh! We must have, we must have, we must have!" All people collect with their . . . now, amusement, individual . . . Each individual goes away without any connection.

So, in this age, if you go and talk of higher things, there may be people as yesterday, some people there may be, but not much. Some will come with intellectual curiosity, no doubt. Because this is the age of intellectualism, not intellectuality.

P.  What is the difference?

S.  Intellectuality means proper, right functioning of intellect.

Intellectualism is a luxury of the intellect . . .

P.  And proper, right functioning of the intellect . . . is seeing?

S.  Oh! Yes! Seeing! Ah! Right. And wrong, luxury of the intellect is thinking. Oh! Yes, yes, yes!

P.  Svâmiji thinks that this evolution . . . things going worse will continue? Is it not possible . . . ? I am impressed by many signs in advanced industrialized society of a change.

S.  Oh! Yes, no doubt.

P.  If one has only, let's say, his own life as time horizon, one might get pessimist. But if one sees things, with a longer horizon, because society can last longer, I find that presently it is a transition period in which we got plenty of bad things and already one sees, in the young generation, completely new signs of something different. I know many people who do not work anymore for material things, because they have . . . So they are free from it and they work for any interest . . .

## Truth Is: Application of the Teaching to Private Life

When I came in London, first, English people were not so happy that a Frenchman was doing planning and I had no such a priori good reception. And I evolved and I came out with quite a revolutionary at this time story which is just happening now. That the price of energy will increase very much. People at the beginning did not want to believe me. Well, everything which has happened now that producer country is going to restrict production, they do not need, they are going to have so much money, they just do not need. At the beginning, people told me: "This is much too logical. This will never happen. This is much too logical, it is impossible that the price of oil will rise so high, this is just impossible." And when they saw things becoming . . .

Then also, in another way, what Svâmiji told me became very effective. About speaking. You remember, I told Svâmiji that I sometimes felt embarrassed speaking before people with very high ranking and Svâmiji told: "Just be the speaker when you speak." Now I have to speak before Governments, before men . . . and I do not feel embarrassed at all, I just have a message and I put it across and . . .

So on the professional life, I really can test Svamiji's teaching and it is very good and I am sometimes surprised that I am paid for doing what I do, because it is a very useful job. I should pay for doing it. It is very good.

But in my private life it is not so. I still am completely . . . I am not having a real life . . . When I make every day an examination of what happened in the day, I have half a dozen roles . . . main actors in which I can always see myself being in and . . .

It is kind of phantom life, it is not real life. It is a phantom . . . and I say it is phantom number one who was there present. Then here is number three, I know him quite well. Is it because I am emotionally involved in my private life and I am not emotionally involved in my professional life?

S. Exactly, exactly. But you cannot detach yourself from your private life. You are involved with that private life, whereas in the other field, professional life, you are not involved in that. That is the point. That is the mind's play here, not there. Simple test.

P. Yes.

S. And truth can be tested in any field, whatsoever. Otherwise, it is not truth. Truth is. Where? Everywhere. When? Always. Definition of truth is this . . . what is truth? Truth is what is. Means? It cannot be applied "was and will be." "Is," only definite "is." "Is" meaning? Where? Wherever. When? Whenever. There is no distinction and comparison and differentiation here. Private life, professional life, mechanical life, economical . . . any, any, any, any. It is.
Apply that "it is." What is there? That's all. Simple test. Truth means "is." Nothing else.

## To Know Is to Be

P. Svâmiji said yesterday that understanding is always hundred per cent . . . is not partial understanding, is complete understanding.

S. Yes, yes, these adjectives and adverbs: partial, complete . . . all these things are illusory and unreal and untruth. Because truth is: yes or no. There is nothing in between. So in between is dependent and relative and so it is untruth. "I did it completely," as if there is some doing which is not complete! What is that doing?

Understanding is understanding. Because the test of understanding is to be. To know is to be. What you know, you are that. The test of knowing is in being. So in being there is no . . . ?

P. . . . no shades.

S. No shades, no shades, no shades . . .

P. The test of knowing is being?

S. Yes. Being meaning? Intellectually, in feeling and in action. It must go intellectually and percolate to feeling. And that must come out in action. Then you know. Otherwise not . . . otherwise partial. Meaning? Not-knowing is there . . . Knowing is coming . . . Not-knowing is mixed.

## Awareness

P. I practiced yesterday afternoon, this morning. For instance, this morning for over one hour, nearly always, completely aware. With seeing tree, observing the many, many extraordinary variety, each singularity, noticing many things I have never seen. With village people, also feeling really oneness, feeling . . . for more than one hour, nearly without interruption, without mixing of the mind. How can this deepen . . . ? I also felt very strongly that this is the real way to do it. When mind plays, it is like an usurper . . .

S. Yes, an usurper.

P. How to deepen it?

S. Only to feel it. Feel what? "Mind is nothing but an usurper. It comes and usurps me. Shall I allow it to do it? Is it not below my dignity that I am nothing, mind comes and . . . ?" If this feeling is deepened, then it will go. You allow your mind to play. That's all . . . If you don't allow . . . ? No!

## About Prayer

P. Is prayer not a way to get communion, to get the feeling of oneness. I just observe, in Indian Scriptures, there are many occasions mentioned about prayer. Svâmi Ramdas got his enlightenment by prayer. Is prayer just a play of the mind or is it just a way . . . ?

S. What is the meaning of prayer? See that. What is the meaning of prayer? Whether it is the play of mind or not will be proved or tested by a clear idea of what is prayer. You see, prayer meaning . . . first of all fundamentally, there are two . . .

P. Yes . . .

S. You pray to another and this another is not a definite thing. It is a creation of the mind.

P. But if another is the real Self?

S. . . . real Self, then? Where is the prayer? And if a small boy did not pray to get adolescence? Do you see that?

P. Yes, yes, yes . . . he has no need.

S. . . . even if he sees adolescence, he sees adolescence objectively, is not a play of the mind, he sees objectively. But still if he prays "let me have it . . . let me have it" will he get it? No! Rather prayer dupes, because it keeps two intact, which is an illusion play of the mind. So, you see, prayer is an illusion of the mind.

P. Is it always so?

S. It is always so.

P. Sometimes, prayer . . .

S. Prayer . . . the very meaning prayer! You pray to somebody to get something . . .

P. Yes, in this sense. But sometimes by mystics, prayer is a way of achieving oneness.

S. What is the meaning on prayer then? What do they do? Find out. You have got the rule, so to say, then apply. If there is two and the play between two, it is the play of the mind.

## What My Being Is?

P. I would like Svâmiji to help me to see clearly what my being is. It is easy to see my personality: I was born in a family, I had in the past, in my early childhood, some experience, a certain type of school, a certain type of experience I have some friends, I have some position, I can see my personality.

S. Yes.

P. What is my being? It is much more difficult.

S. Much more difficult? Yes. How?

P. The only thing I feel is a taste which is completely different from anything else . . .

S. That's alright.

P. . . . which is "I am," which is completely different.

S. It is alright. If you feel like that, that is significant. As you described, so it was nothing but a general panorama of experiences, and identifications.

P. Yes.

S. So behind all those things is there anything particularly significant, distinct from all those? Or rather that takes all those things and goes forward? Do you follow?

P. Yes.

## All Actions Are Negative

P. Svâmiji, I tried to see what were my fundamental wants. And to be honest, material ones are nearly fulfilled. No problem on this . . . I see no urge . . . also no fear . . . no professional fear. Two years ago, when I came to London, people were not happy that a foreigner came, it was difficult . . . then slight fear of . . .

S. . . . instability?

P. Yes . . . Now no fear . . . also no risk of failure, I feel confident, so very quiet on this side too.

S. No fear of insecurity?

P. No . . . no . . .

S. That's alright.

P. Only small material urge, but I could do without . . is I got a new flat in London . . . to arrange it. It is the first time that I will have one of my own. I lived in furnished flats which is not agreeable. This is a small . . . but it is only material want.


## Justice of the Situation. Positive and Negative Action

Positive action is; "Yes, I have done . . . I have done as best as I could, so that I feel I am doing. I have done . . . I have done . . . I have done, I left nothing for me to do." Positive action.

So life is an anomaly and contradiction. So, from this contradiction, you are to grow out.

P. In negative action, one never makes any use of the action, one learns nothing . . . , no experience . . .

S. Negative action is nothing. Negative action depends upon the mind only.

Positive action depends upon the fact only. It is based on the justice of the fact . . . justice of the situation. "I am nothing. I only see and calculate and "this is so, this is so, this is the connection, this is the connection, Oh! Yes this I shall do."

And what is negative action? "Oh! I like to do it . . . go on, go on." What are you doing? You deny the situation, the fact and you are goaded by your own emotion? No. This is negative action. And by this negative action you get only negative result. That is failure, division, discontent, anxiety and everything . . .

And by positive action, you come to stability, respect, confidence, and that saves you from this little *confidences?* Seeing facts. You go on seeing facts, facts, facts, Oh! Then fact. Clear?

P. Very clear, very important.


## Aim of Life

Be free from this desire! To be free from this desire or to be free from the illusion of the mind is the negative aspect of human life. And positive aspect to return to . . .

P. . . . his original Nature.

S. . . . his original Nature. To be free from . . . that is the aim of human life. In short take this scheme . . . you can elaborate if you like.

P. What an illustration of to see! What Svâmiji exposed is the best illustration of to see.

S. To see, yes, yes. And this whole thing comes out of seeing. So you see what is it. What is it? So Svâmiji says: "What is the aim of life? And what is the aim of human life?" To understand human life, first of all, take general life and find out the aim of it and see how can you apply here. Or the same thing: to come back to his original Nature.

P. How does it happen that man and only man has this sense of infinite inside. How does it happen?

S. It happens because, the man . . . he becomes, in tune with Nature, by observing, by seeing, by finding the laws and so on and so forth. And by being and trying to be all powerful in Nature.

And still you see: "However much I do, I am not satisfied! No, no, no, I am not in peace! And about power, about energy of life, this is the best age to illustrate that. Rockets and etc. . . . Where is sun? Where is moon? (Before) you only imagined. Now you go there. And from here you control. Ough! There is a leak in this ship. From here they say: "Oh! There is a leak, see, see, see.""

## Mind Is Desire

Some old people get a kind of philosophy . . . some French retired men . . . retired people put on the front of their small house: "Ca me suffit" which means "it is enough for me." So they deliberately cut desire. This also is . . .

S. They cannot cut desire . . .

P. They cannot?

S. Cannot. They think they cut desire, they only stupefy themselves by repression. Energy can never be trifled with. You cannot play with energy. Either it must exhaust itself or you must be above it. But to be above it, you must be free from it. And for being free from it, it cannot but exhaust itself. No, no . . .

P. Clear. I wanted just to . . . clear.

S. Two quotations, so to say. One from your Yogavâsis;.t;. ha, very nice:

*icchâ mâtram;. viduś—cittam;. tac-chânti moks;.a ucyate*
*Etâvan-tv-eva Śâstrân;.i tapânsi niyamâ yama*

It says: mind, mind, mind, it is nothing but *icchâ* desire. Only desire, that is mind. You say conscious, unconscious, unconscious, but anything you say, it is only *icchâ* And *tac-chânti* and pacification of this *icchâ* is called *moksa*: liberation. And this much, is all *Śâstra* scriptures, all tapasyas, all penances, all things are nothing but *icchâ* and to be free from *icchâ*. Finished. If you want to know what is mind, it is *only* desire.

## Necessity and Dignity

P.  I see the direction very clearly and it's up to me to find why I am going to devote all my attention to this. The significance of a day is, what material it brings for seeing clearly why?

Yesterday, for instance, I have several occasions, just one . . . After Svâmiji's sitting on desire, Svâmiji used it to illustrate that desire can never be satisfied. Svâmiji used an example dealing with another person and making the point that he is different, he cannot be . . . Then, I wanted to ask Svâmiji well, what with an object? Because there the question of difference doesn't play.

While looking in my little note book, it so happened that I had notes on my last trip, just the day after when I left here, I stopped in Rome where I had some business and afterwards, I just had some hours to spend and I wanted to buy a pair of shoes. Italy is famous for shoes and I remember I read my notes . . . four hours completely lost, completely . . . I was just looking around for shoes. I am not interested in shoes. I can wear different types. But this, I realize that an object, when it focuses the attention, it . . . I am looking after the object, I am running after myself. I got the taste very clear and I got material . . .

Around this, I would like to ask Svâmiji, he uses several times a key word, I understand the general meaning, "feeling of necessity." I understand the meaning. I would like to know what is the inner experience behind the word? Svâmiji always has inner content behind the word . . .

S.  Feeling of necessity, the inner content is that . . . What is the meaning of necessity? I am feeling . . . ?

P.  I must do it.

S.  Necessity meaning?

P.  Something which is necessary.

S.  That is? Necessary meaning? Without which . . . Take the negative way.

P.  Without which I cannot do . . .

S.  Ah! This point: "I cannot do . . . I can't find relief . . . I can't find satisfaction . . . and so and so on and so forth." This is the inner necessity. And to feel it . . . one must be aware of this necessity, and feeling for it, then one can see what to do. First of all, he sees: "I want this. Why? Why? Oh! Without which I don't feel at ease, don't feel satisfied and don't feel anything, anything. But main point is, that I will not be satisfied. So what is there? First of all, what is there that I feel without which I cannot satisfy?" What is there?" See what is there, see the nature of it and why you want it. You can easily see. So your connection with it, you will be able to see.

## Dharma

P.  Oh! Yes, yes. What is *dharma*?

S.  *Dharma*? Oh! Very nice question. Very useful and very particular word this is. *Dharma: Dharma ity ahu* . . . Exact definition of *dharma*: that which holds is *dharma*. That which holds. *Dhr;.*: holding. That which holds is *dharma*. What is the meaning of it? That which holds means that which makes any existence possible.

That characteristic which is responsible for a particular existence is his *dharma*.

As for example water. What is its *dharma*? To flow. That which flows is liquid, is water. What is the *dharma* of fire? To burn.

There may be a big picture of fire. It is not fire. Because if you put your hand, it doesn't burn. You make a . . . so to say, earth or marble lion. Put it just near your door. It exactly . . . Quite all right. In darkness you will say: "Oh! Oh! This is a lion!" But this is not a lion, because it doesn't kill. So it is an image of a lion, semblance of that, but it is not that. Because his *dharma* is not there. That shows that *dharma* is that characteristic which makes any existence possible. That's all.

So what is the *dharma* of man? You can ask . . .

P. Yes.

S. What is the characteristic that distinguishes man as man distinguished from animal or anything? What is that which makes the existence of man possible, that is the *dharma*.

As for example you see: a man that said foolish things, you will say: "You are an ass!" What is that? He can say: "Yes. I see. I am this, I am not an ass. Why do you say I am ass?" What is the meaning? Though it appears to be man, actually his behavior is like an ass.

P. His *dharma* is the one of an ass.

S. *Dharma* is that.

P. I see, I see, I see.

## Summary

The passages from Wack's sittings are important because they reflect the things he was most curious about in both his professional and personal lives. In some cases he directly references his work at Shell and how he was able to connect the concepts of "acceptance" and "seeing" to scenario work.

Wack also made a brief comment about Svamiji himself, of course with the use of a metaphor. He used them frequently, though understood they were no substitute for genuine, rigorous inquiry. Those who knew him best, said that the metaphor of the axe and the tree trunk was his most profound:

Perhaps a metaphor will clarify what I want to say. It's like trying to split with an axe, an old tough tree trunk, knotty and with lots of curious difficulties. Svamiji was without equal when it came to discovering the right angle of attack, coming up with an adequate axe and inspiring his disciple with the will to use it, because in this case the disciple was both the trunk and the one who was to use the axe. In this manner, I must have had at least fifty sittings over the course of thirteen years, dense and intense, personal and operational, only to "see things as they are," to learn the art and the discipline of seeing. These sittings transformed my life, and firstly, my professional life.

Wack continued to visit his guru in Channa, India each year and returned to Japan many times for holidays, Shell presentations and personal visits or conferences. The stories and examples in this chapter have attempted to capture Wack's long history of meditative practice and frame what is known about Wack's major spiritual "foundations." It is critical to reiterate that Wack had been studying Buddhism and visiting Svamiji for almost 20 years when he moved to London to join Group Planning. This rich history and related experiences provided a context for understanding how he blended his curiosities and struggles in life with his intellectually focused and deeply analytical work as a planner for one of the world's largest corporations.

## Chapter 2 Sources (in order of use)

Sharpe, B., & Van der Heijden, K. (Eds.) (2008). Interview with Napier Collyns. In *Scenarios for success: Turning insights in to action*, pp. i-ix. New York: John Wiley & Sons.

Austin, J. H. (1999). *Zen and the brain: Toward an understanding of meditation and consciousness*. Cambridge, MA: MIT Press.

Austin, J. H. (2010). *Zen-brain reflections*. Cambridge, MA: MIT Press.

Austin, J. H. (2013). Zen and the brain: Mutually illuminating topics. *Frontiers in Psychology*, 4, 784.

Pagnoni, G., & Cekic, M. (2007). Age effects on gray matter volume and attentional performance in Zen meditation. *Neurobiology of Aging*, 28(10), 1623–1627.

Austin, J. H. (1990). Zen and the brain: The construction and dissolution of the self. *The Eastern Buddhist*, 24, 69–97.

Ritskes, R., Ritskes-Hoitinga, M., & Stødkilde-Jørgensen, H. (2003). MRI scanning during Zen meditation: The picture of enlightenment. *Constructivism in the Human Sciences*, 8(1), 85–89.

Grant, J. A., Courtemanche, J., Duerden, E. G., Duncan, G. H., & Rainville, P. (2010). Cortical thickness and pain sensitivity in Zen meditators. *Emotion*, 10(1), 43.

Dürckheim, K. (1977). *Hara: The vital centre of man*. New York: Inner Traditions Publishing.

Dürckheim, K. (1973). *Hara*. New York: Inner Traditions Publishing.

Dürckheim, K. (1971). *The way of transformation: Daily life as spiritual exercise*. Melbourne: Allen & Unwin.

Kleiner, A. Pierre A. Wack interview in Curemonte. (n.d.). 53 pp. The annotated transcript of an interview between Art Kleiner and Pierre Wack regarding the development of Shell's scenario planning. Retrieved from the Art Kleiner Archive, University of Oxford.

Gurdjieff, G. I. (1960). *Meetings with remarkable men*. New York: Penguin Group.

Gurdjieff, G. I. (1964). *Beelzebub's tales to his grandson: All and everything*. New York: Penguin Group.

Gurdjieff, G. I. (1976). *Views from the real world: Early talks in Moscow, Essentuki, Tiflis, Berlin, London, Paris, New York and Chicago.*

Gurdjieff, G. I. (1950). *Beelzebub's tales to his grandson* (Vol. 1). Alexandria, Egypt: Library of Alexandria.

Wack, P. (1993). Original text, as dictated to Eve by Pierre (English Translation of Chapter XII Les Disciples of Svâmiji Prajnânpad). In D. Roumanoff (Ed.), *Svâmi Prajnânpad: Biographie*, pp. 1–4. Paris: La Table Rhonde.

Collyns, N., & Tibbs, H. (1998). In memory of Pierre Wack. *Netview, 9*(1), 4–10.

Transcript of tapes 1, 2 and 3 from GBN Scenario Planning Seminar 19 April 1993 [transcription by Peggi Oakley, 2 copies]. Document retrieved from the Pierre Wack Memorial Library, University of Oxford.

Transcript of tapes 4 and 5 from GBN Scenario Planning Seminar 19 April 1993 [transcription by Peggi Oakley, 2 copies]. Document retrieved from the Pierre Wack Memorial Library, University of Oxford.

Transcript of 'Wack @ Curemonte' from Tape 1/Side A to Tape 5/Side A [94 pages, 2 copies]. Document retrieved from the Pierre Wack Memorial Library, University of Oxford.

Wack, P. (1994). *Speech & interviews* [37 pages, 2 copies]. Document retrieved from the Pierre Wack Memorial Library, University of Oxford.

Photocopied pages from Srinivasan. (1987). *Talks with Swami Prajnanapada*, pp. 114–137. Document retrieved from the Pierre Wack Memorial Library, University of Oxford.

Roumanoff, D. (1986). *Svami prajnanpad un maitre de vedanta contemporain* (Doctoral dissertation, Paris 4).

Prajnanapada, S., Srinivasan, R., & Desjardins, A. (1984). *Entretiens avec Swami Prajnanpad*. Paris: L'Originel.

Prajnanapada, S., & Desjardins, A. (2003). *Les formules de Swami Prajnanpad*. Paris: Table ronde.

Prajnanpad, S. (1984). *Lettres à ses disciples, vol. 3: La Vérité du bonheur*. Paris.

Roumanoff, D. (2009). *Svami Prajnanpad, un maître contemporain: Le quotidien illuminé* (Vol. 2). Paris: Albin Michel.

Maraini, F. (1959). *Meeting with Japan*. London: Hutchinson.

Patel, A. (2016). Gaining insight: Re-thinking at the edge. *Technological Forecasting and Social Change, 107*, 141–153.

Suzuki, D. T., & Jaffe, R. M. (2010). *Zen and Japanese culture*. Princeton, NJ: Princeton University Press.

Suzuki, D. T. (2002). *Mysticism: Christian and Buddhist*. New York: Courier Corporation.

Poodry, C. A., Hall, L., & Suzuki, D. T. (1973). Developmental properties of shibirets 1: A pleiotropic mutation affecting larval and adult locomotion and development. *Developmental Biology, 32*(2), 373–386.

Wack, E. (n.d.). *Quelques dates et événements de la vie d'un "homme remarquable": Pierre Wack* [draft; 12 pages with note by Eve Wack]. Document retrieved from the Pierre Wack Memorial Library, University of Oxford.

Wack, E. (1998). *Pierreve: 1977–1997*. Curemonte, France, Unpublished manuscript.

Pruce, J. (2000, January 11). [Letter to Napier Collyns]. Copy in the Pierre Wack Memorial Library, University of Oxford.

Shibayama, Z. (2012). *A flower does not talk: Zen essays*. North Clarendon, VT: Tuttle Publishing.

Excerpt from personal communications with Eve Wack. Author held interviews and discussions in 2014–16.

Roumanoff, D. (1993). *Svâmi Prajnânpad: Biographie* (in French). Paris: La Table Rhonde, pp. 262–266.

Wilkinson, A., & Kupers, R. (2013). Living in the futures. *Harvard Business Review*, *91*(5), 118–127.

Wilkinson, A., & Kupers, R. (2014). *The essence of scenarios: Learning from the Shell experiences*. Amsterdam: Amsterdam University Press.

Transcripts of Recordings with Svamiji 1: Contributed by Collette Roumanoff.

Transcripts of Recordings with Svamiji 2: Contributed by Collette Roumanoff.

Excerpt from personal communications with Leslie Dighton. Author held interviews and discussions in 2014–16.

Kleiner, Art, James C. Davidson telephone interview: Spring 1993. (n.d.). 21 pp. The annotated transcript of a telephone interview between Art Kleiner and James Davidson regarding the development of Shell's Group Planning Department. Retrieved from the Art Kleiner Archive, University of Oxford.

Excerpt from personal communications with Ted Newland. Author held interviews and discussions in 2014–16.

Presentation by Pierre Wack to the manufacturing function in Shell, transcribed by Kees van der Heijden, Shell Int'l Petroleum Co., Amsterdam, Holland, 1982, Unpublished manuscript.

Williams, R. J. (2016). World futures. *Critical Inquiry*, 42, 473–512.

Davis, G. (2010). Preface. In Ramírez, R., Selsky, J. W., & Van der Heijden, K. (Eds.). (2010). *Business planning for turbulent times: New methods for applying scenarios*. New York: Taylor & Francis.

# Part II
# The Shell Years

The 1950s and 1960s oil industry could be characterized as relatively stable. Planners relied on forecasts of demand, supply, and price to anticipate each year's investments. All in all, it was a relatively simple operation. All that started to change in the mid to late 1960s when forecasts started failing more frequently but the failures did not provoke a response from most executives as anything more than a "blip" on the radar screen. There were some, however, with a wider, more dynamic view that things were about to change in dramatic ways, never to settle down again.

Part two of this book covers Pierre Wack's "Shell Years." These are roughly 1960–82, and these years are detailed in chapters 3, 4, 5and 6. This is the story of how scenarios came to be used and developed at Royal Dutch / Shell. As the godfather of scenario planning, Wack led the teams that revolutionized planning under uncertainty.

Chapter 3 describes the major players in the formation of Group Planning—Shell's new planning system. It is a summary of the people involved in dislodging an old planning approach called "Unified Planning Machinery" (UPM). Backgrounds are given on the characters who could see the world was about to change, and the difficult task of convincing their superiors is described.

Chapter 4 continues the story with details on the early trials at developing scenarios and how they began to see success. To be sure, it was a roller coaster ride of gaining support, only later to lose it, and then earning it back again. Wack's insights from the early scenario trials are described as well as the pitfalls along the way.

Chapter 5 covers the era just as scenarios gained credibility and the practice garnered support from Shell's executives. Indeed, there was a flurry of scenario activity. Chapter 5 also provides an account of how Wack discovered the importance of mental models that fundamentally altered his approach to scenarios. The evolution of the scenario team is also described as well as the famous "in the green" sessions—the off-site meetings for scenario development.

Chapter 6 documents Wack's later contributions to Shell leading up to his retirement in 1982. This chapter documents more scenario work and his search for a successor. Wack's cultivation of "remarkable people" is described as his travels took him across the globe. Chapter 6 covers his reflective thinking as he approached retirement and his realization that scenarios were one part of a more complex strategy system. Finally, as Wack's reputation became legendary, a variety of other opportunities began to emerge that would shape the next phases of his life.

## Part 2 Sources (in order of use)

Schwartz, P. (1996). *The art of the long view*. New York: Currency-Doubleday.

Wilkinson, A., & Kupers, R. (2013). Living in the futures. *Harvard Business Review*, *91*(5), 118–127.

Wilkinson, A., & Kupers, R. (2014). *The essence of scenarios: Learning from the Shell experiences*. Amsterdam: Amsterdam University Press.

Ertel, C., & Solomon, L.K. (2014). *Moments of impact: How to design strategic conversations that accelerate change* (Vol. 36, No. 7). New York: Simon and Schuster.

# 3  Bringing the Scenario Team Together
## Two Pieces of Jade

Jade has a history in China of several thousand years. Jade has been an important part of religion and civilization in Asia; it has been used as a decoration, a magic icon, a charm for rites of worship and burial, and a status symbol. While other materials like gold, silver and bronze have also gained prominence in Asia, none of these materials has exceeded the position that jade has acquired—it is associated with merit, morality, grace and dignity.

*Pierre boarded the Pan Am Boeing 747 in the same quiet manner he usually did, situating himself in the cabin with a seat and a separate bed. He had a lot of work to do to prepare for his meetings in Tokyo, but he knew he needed to sleep. The Vice President of the Keidanren provided access to some of Japan's top-performing companies, and he needed to look over the bios of the CEOs he would be meeting. He also had the familiar feeling of excitement, knowing that at the end of this flight he would be back in Japan—a place he loved deeply. The rush of the engines lifting the plane into flight always brought a smile and within what seemed like seconds, they reached cruising altitude.*

*The pilot exited the cockpit and left the door open—he worked his way through the central lounge, stopping for a chat with several of the passengers. Most passengers were enjoying their cigarettes and cocktails by this time, and the cabin was filled with thick smoke—but it did not disturb Pierre. Svamiji had taught him a breathing technique to relieve him of his need for cigarettes. As the seven course meal was about to begin, Pierre noticed the small flight bag under his bed and wondered why anyone thought he would want such a thing. Another gift for Fiona . . .*

In 1964, after a Standard Oil of New Jersey Executive visited the Shell offices in London, two Managing Directors at Shell were convinced the company needed its own group dedicated to studying the future. The conversation had been focused on countries with a high potential for future growth. The visitor from Standard mentioned their success in identifying South Korea's potential for explosive growth and development. They were so proud of their success that they decided to set up a team dedicated to the study of various emerging economies. At the time, Shell's planning practices were known as UPM (Unified Planning Machinery). Thus began the search within Shell for creative people who could imagine an entirely different system for thinking about the future. However, not everyone agreed and it would take time to bring this vision to life.

## Jimmy Davidson

It wasn't until July of 1967 that the Committee of Managing Directors (CMD) created a new Group Planning Division and recruited Jimmy Davidson to take the helm. Davidson had previously been Head of the Exploration and Production Economics Division, and before that, he had worked with the Shell Group's companies in Colombia and Ecuador. Speaking of his introduction to the new division, Davidson remarked: "I had always been interested in the whole question of uncertainty and risk but I hadn't known anything about scenarios until I went to planning and Ted Newland starting talking to me about scenarios." He recalled early (literal) missteps as he described: "And I put my foot wrong, right from the beginning because in January of 1968, when I'd just taken over this outfit, I lacked the merit and perhaps diplomacy—surely the lack of diplomacy to voice the need to change the system. Now this bombshell from somebody who had just taken on this organization, provoked a furious outburst from McFadzean." McFadzean was the Managing Director responsible for planning, and he instructed, "on no account was any change to be made to the system into which so much effort had been put." The political negotiations inside the CMD could be characterized as classic change management problems—stances were taken for historical reasons and few people liked to see their work undone.

At the time, the chairman of the CMD was Jan Brouwer "who was an absolutely outstanding intellect." He was very supportive of a different approach to planning along with David Barran, then the Vice Chairman of the CMD. The regressions lines they based their forecasts on were too simplistic and failed to take several factors into account. With the support of Brouwer and Barran, Group Planning quietly pursued its task of long-term thinking and deep questioning of forecasts. Davidson remembered: "so I went to Jan Brouwer, who was then chairman, and told him that in view of McFadzean's dictum, I could not carry on with the Planning job and I would have to resign. Brouwer urged me to carry on and work towards change . . . It would take time to change people's minds and get new ideas accepted." In 1968, Ashley Raeburn was asked to consider the year 2000 and to speculate what it might look like. The CMD also asked Karel Swart to do a study of the future. Essentially, there were enough CMD members feeling uneasy about a general stance of stability and control across Shell. The CMD therefore asked for a variety of views from different perspectives in the organization. Swart made his final presentation to the CMD based on what he and his team learned on February 25, 1969. Davidson commented: "We were still stuck with the UPM system, and it generated reams and reams of paper with useless forecasts and every attempt to change it through 68 and 69 was blocked by McFadzean who was Managing Director."

Davidson and others patiently continued to wear down the CMD by showing them case after case in which their forecasts could be dangerously wrong. Finally, in 1970, McFadzean was able to agree that a different sort of planning system was worth exploring. In part, it was Swart's presentation on the Year 2000 that had an important effect, as well as the fact that McFadzean "could see the writing was on the wall . . . He was an extremely bright, very intelligent chap." Swart was promoted to the role of Managing Director and Member of the CMD on January 1, 1970 and four days later, Davidson recalled: "On January 5th, 1970, I had the first useful discussion on the CMD and how we might change the planning system." Finally, a real interest in alternative planning approaches could be explored.

Davidson said that his knowledge of scenarios came from Newland, when he was working in Exploration and Production. He became very concerned about uncertainty in the business environment as far back as 1966. He had visited UPM and met Ted Newland who started talking to him about scenarios and how they could be used to manage uncertainty and risk. But because Davidson didn't know how to construct scenarios, when he took over for Group Planning, he had to find someone to manage that role. Given the practical focus he would face from the CMD, Davidson was also keenly aware of the need for another talented individual who could connect the scenarios to corporate strategy.

## Pierre Wack Comes to Group Planning in London

Pierre Wack joined Shell Francaise in April 1961, due to the flexibility offered for employee leave. He was hired as Chief Economist and quickly became Director of Economics under Andre Benard, who was then President of Shell Francaise. According to his wife Eve, "He liked the fact that Shell was an Anglo-Dutch company with two cultures (rather like Alsace)." Wack spent nine years working on various economic forecasting models related to national development and planning for both Shell Francaise and the French National Plan before he started on scenarios: "Benard asked me to do a lot of management studies. But planning, again was based on the number crunching you know, the consequence of what we do, which were done by someone else and I'm very happy because I have not this type of mind." It was during these years that Wack continued his fascination with Japan and India—taking his holidays at the more comfortable times of the year. He had found his guru—Svamiji Prajnanpad—that same year (1961) in Channa after a bit of searching. Wack was content to be living in Paris, working on Shell and the French Plan. A few years later, in the mid-1960s Wack learned about Herman

Kahn who was looking at future planning a bit differently, and went to visit him a few times in the US. By chance, he encountered another Shell colleague at several of Kahn's meetings —Ted Newland. The two became friends and it was at these meetings that Newland stressed the amazing growth of the Japanese economy, suggesting it would be the strongest overall for the next decade and should be considered in Shell's planning.

## Horizon Year Planning at Shell Francaise

In 1968, as part of the CMD's requests for a few different views of the long-term future, they asked for a study that became known as the Horizon Year Planning Exercise. A few key operating companies around the world were asked to be involved, including Shell Francaise. The project needed to look out to 1985, and as Director of Economics, Wack led the Horizon Year Planning efforts for Shell Francaise. This was his first experiment with scenarios. Having already met Herman Kahn, the exercise in "thinking the unthinkable" was familiar for Wack, and with a bit of overhaul, he thought it might be useful in corporate planning. He provided a detailed account of the project and what the team learned in a manuscript Wack would write many years later called "The Gentle Art of Re-perceiving":

> France, at that time, operated under an oil regime that favored French national companies and severely limited Shell's market share there. France, however, had just joined the Common Market and might have to change its oil regime to conform to EEC policy. There were therefore two options: France's oil regime would remain largely unchanged; or it would liberalize, after the transition period provided by the Treaty of Rome. Combining these two alternatives (Chart II) with the major uncertainty on gas availability gave us four scenarios.

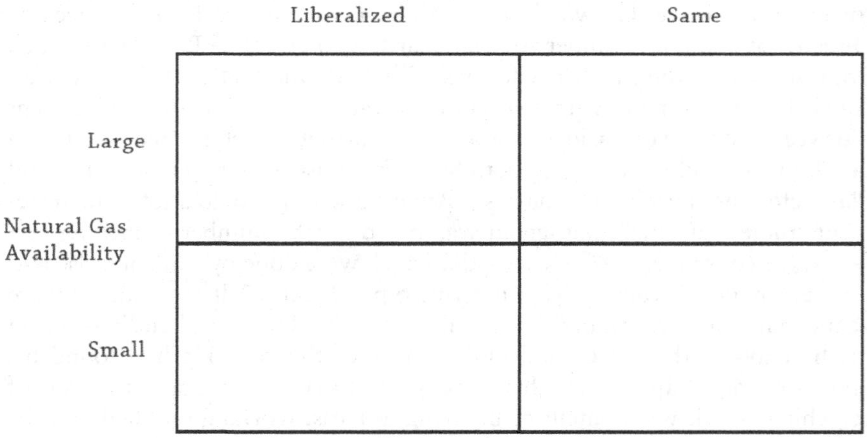

|  | Liberalized | Same |
|---|---|---|
| Large | | |
| Natural Gas Availability | | |
| Small | | |

*Chart 3.1* French Oil Regime**

Here is where we began to make some discoveries.

(**Incidentally, this set of scenarios is one of only two in which Wack used what would later become known as the 2x2 scenario matrix. The "matrix" is one of many approaches to scenario practice in which participants work to define two critical uncertain factors out of which they create a 2x2 matrix. The resulting four quadrants yield four different scenario frameworks)

The results of the Year 2000 Study and the Horizon Year Study led to the same conclusions: The oil industry was about to see significant change. In short time, the various studies showed the CMD that they could choose to prepare for unexpected shifts in the industry, or remain committed to forecasting techniques and accept the heightened risk. Further, the consequences that resulted when their forecasts failed would be increasingly devastating.

Davidson recalled: "Now I had been trying to get Pierre Wack released from Shell Francaise since 1969 onwards. At that time Andre Benard was the Managing Director of Shell Francaise and just wasn't willing to let Pierre go because Pierre was too useful to him." Wack recalled being visited by Karel Swart on at least one occasion, but he did not have the impression of being invited to London. Further, Wack was very happy at Shell Francaise, working on the French Plan and generally enjoyed his life in Paris.

There were two reported events that led to Wack's acceptance of the position in London. First, Wack did not want to put Indra (his Afghan dog named after the Hindu God of Wind), in quarantine for six months in moving from Paris to London. Shortly after he was offered the position in London and refused, Indra unfortunately passed away. Wack's wife, Eve recalled: "I heard two versions of the cause of his death. The first: he had been hurt by a wild hog and had suffered an internal hemorrhage not detected by the veterinarian. The second: Pierre had called Indra during his run and turning his head toward his master he'd run into a tree—head fracture."

Second, Davidson simply suspected that Benard wasn't willing to let Wack go because of his importance in Shell Francaise. Wack had been making progress, working on Shell's activities in France. In 1970, Benard was promoted to European Regional Coordinator, "and then he agreed that I could have Pierre Wack," said Davidson. Wack later clarified, "It was because of Indra's death and Benard's promotion that I agreed to go to England to direct Group Planning." Wack further recounted his transition to London:

> Jimmy lured me. He put me in a very good hotel—an extremely luxurious hotel, and treated me very well. I was a little bit desperate at the quality of the people . . . The only one who was really outstanding, but was feeling not very happy there, was Ted Newland. The others came afterwards, Napier . . .

Davidson also recalled: "Wack was a very dear friend of mine. He was an absolute prima donna. He had a wonderful imaginative mind, a very excellent grasp of macroeconomic interplay and interrelationship of human forces."

Wack officially joined Shell International in London in January of 1971, but he had negotiated the previously mentioned year sabbatical in Japan with Benard before his promotion: "And I told him [Andre], 'Look, you should send me to make the reverse trip the Japanese make when they come to the West. You should give me as a target: What can we learn from Japan? And he said 'OK. Next time you change jobs you will have a sabbatical.'"

Wack arrived at the Shell Centre in London in January of 1971. He would travel to and from Japan many times over the year, spending most of it in Japan. He studied how Japanese executives were planning for the future, Japanese gardening and Zen meditation (he was a master at combining his passions and his work). Wack was apprised of what was happening in Group Planning over 1971, and returned to London as needed for important presentations.

## Ted Newland's Path to Scenarios

Edward (called so only by his wife, Elena) "Ted" Newland had been at Shell for years. It is increasingly clear that Newland was a critical complement to Wack, without whom, we would not be telling this story. According to Wack, "The one who really deserves much more credit than he has is Ted Newland. Really Ted is a key man, there is nobody in the organisation which has contributed comparable to Ted." Newland had initiated several studies outside Group Planning and was working on his own experiments in applying Herman Kahn's ideas. Newland first met Kahn on a visit to California in 1966 and made frequent visits to the US for Kahn's meetings in New York City after that, where he would frequently encounter Wack.

Newland was born in Madrid, Spain, spent 10 years in Switzerland, and took a career-long roller coaster ride through England, Argentina, Colombia, Venezuela, Nigeria and back to Europe. He spent approximately five years in each of these locations, piecing together his education along the way, eventually attending Manchester University to study Personnel Management. Upon his return to England in the 1940s he enlisted as a pilot and flew throughout the end of World War II. Newland's career was based in the Western Hemisphere, whereas Wack's experiences drew largely from time spent in the East.

Newland had been running operations for Shell in Nigeria: "I was Administration Manager in Nigeria during the period in which the country gained its independence. There was chaos in Nigeria. There were no civil servants, no viable police force. The first thing that struck me is that it was a huge market decline, to be able to get structure into the country to allow us to go on operating and slowly integrate smoothly . . . That seemed to me highly dubious without some major calamities on the way."

Newland began to foster stability in the Shell camp by privatizing a hospital and slowly creating infrastructure. He worked with people in the compound to bring in surgeons, build houses and integrate food supply systems around 1964: "Basically what I did was to privatize the heavy overhead charges that would result from oilfield operations in an independent country." At the time, it was not permissible to use fencing as a security boundary around the compound, so Newland suggested they dig a moat: "So I said why don't we join up these links and things and have a perfect moat? Everyone said, 'oh yes, well that's maybe not such a bad idea. They can swim across.' I said, 'Well we can always put crocodiles in.'" Newland was able to lead the establishment of security in the Shell compound and garnered a reputation as a creative problem solver among his superiors. He was brought to London to work on planning in 1965: "I was placed in a little cubicle on the 18th floor and told to think about the future with no real indications of what was expected of me."

In 1966, Newland met Herman Kahn at the Hudson Institute in the US. Kahn had previously worked for the Rand Corporation, which was a leading military think tank focused on issues related to the Cold War. Kahn left Rand in 1961 and formed his own shop called the Hudson Institute. Kahn's most famous work continued to explore the implications of nuclear escalation toward the year 2000. Kahn saw the world at the beginning of a new era of prosperity and growth and Newland found the scenarios Kahn was working on to be fascinating. Kahn's ideas would find their way into some highly optimistic scenarios for Shell many years later. The pair would continue to develop their friendship over the years.

Based on Kahn's ideas, in 1967 Newland undertook his own Year 2000 study of current trends extrapolated indefinitely which they shared with colleagues in Exploration and Production. By analyzing status quo oil demand growth over 35 years, the result showed it would reach 110M B/D by the year 2000, which seemed impossible at the time. The teams considered the implications upstream and down. As Newland reflected: "The study was, therefore, fairly successful and was a precursor of what was to come. The CMD had for the first time allowed a planning group to produce a document about the long term future. Up to then it had been a sort of 'rain dance.'"

Following this work, Newland suggested that further detailed study was needed. He began to look at global political power dynamics, oil production requirements and related supply and consumption positions over the short-term future—5 years. All this occurred in 1970, when the oil industry was dealing with the Teheran negotiations. Newland remarked, "It became obvious to me that very shortly a situation would arise in which the power would shift to the producing countries."

## Cornelius Kuiken

Cornelius "Cor" Kuiken was "a real kind of deep thinker," according to Davidson. He was already part of UPM in 1968 when Davidson took over and the unit was renamed Group Planning. Kuiken was head of the

Technical Research Division and "a really outstanding mathematical econo-mist, chess player, pianist and extremely modest person." He was also a tremendous supporter of the proposed changes to UPM—he could see insta-bility rapidly emerging in the oil industry. According to Wack, "He was a very remarkable man, but he was a quiet man, a silent man. Basically, he was an advisor of Jimmy's . . . He was a man with whom I could speak." Kuiken had a reputation as someone happy to work behind the scenes and without interest in fame or recognition. He loved his job and was a deeply analytical and incredibly thoughtful member of the team.

## Harry Beckers

Davidson recalled that "Harry Beckers was a brilliant scientist, mathemati-cian and engineer. He later became Group Research Coordinator and Head of the Group's worldwide research in 1969. When I first knew him, he was heading up the Applied Mathematics Division." Davidson was able to con-vince Lord Victor Rothschild, who was then Coordinator, to release Harry to come to Group Planning for a couple of years: "Harry Beckers was a giant not only intellectually, but also physically. He was large." Essentially, Davidson had been able to negotiate the release of both Pierre Wack and Harry Beckers, so they could join Group Planning at the same time.

Then came the difficult decision of which new star would lead the sce-nario work and which would be given the task of linking scenarios to strat-egy. Many years later, Wack described the situation: "Harry Beckers was an operations research man. I had some difficulty with him . . . Now Harry Beckers, he was very strong . . . we were a little bit competitive. At the beginning, Jimmy didn't exactly know who would lead. I was interested in the scenarios and not at all in strategy. Apparently Harry Beckers also. But I don't know, I think it would have been a total disaster." Beckers and Wack tried to find common ground. They simply saw the world differently and their minds worked differently. According to Davidson, "Pierre really seemed the most suited to scenario work and he expressed a stronger prefer-ence. So he went off on the scenario work. It could easily have been Harry Beckers if he had expressed a stronger preference."

Beckers was put in charge of evaluating policies and investment strategies against the background of the scenarios produced by Wack and his team. Wack further recalled: "It would have been a catastrophe if I had gotten Harry Becker's job and Harry would have my job . . . I would have refused the other job, because I had a weakness I recognized—I knew practically nobody . . . I would have said no, immediately."

## Napier Collyns Joins Group Planning

Napier Collyns was born December 23, 1927 in a small village on Exmoor called Dulverton. Collyns was home schooled until the age of seven when he went to a traditional all boys' school where "the headmaster beat every-body all the time and everyone was terrified." Once his mother found out, he transferred to another boys' school called Abinger Hill, based on the voluntary Dalton System, in which students would choose their studies and compose a plan based on their interests. Collyns was captain of the cricket team. He stayed there until 1940 when the threat of the war meant that most of the wealthy parents took their children to Canada. Without classmates, Collyns changed schools again, enrolling in an elite boarding school called Marlborough. After six years there (and becoming head boy and playing cricket for the school at Lord's), he enlisted in the British Army. This was not a success: "I hated the Army. Absolutely loathed it, everything about it: the discipline, the bossing, the authority from the top down, and the titles—all things I still hate." Collyns left the officer track and went into the educational corps.

He was sent to Egypt and then Kenya, where he participated in teach-ing Swahili to the soldiers and hoped they would learn English after that. Collyns also ran a school for African children in Kenya before returning to England in 1948. He studied economic history at Cambridge and led a bicycle tour of Europe for 20 American students one summer. As a result, he went to Brooklyn to chase one of the young ladies he fancied: "I got into all sorts of trouble, and her father (who was a famous scientist in the States) refused to let me speak to his daughter after that." Upon returning to Cambridge, Collyns realized he really wanted to study in America and found himself increasingly attracted to the importance of technology. He went to Brown for two years where he met an old friend from Marlborough who was studying at Harvard. The friend proposed a road trip across America one summer and at the last minute, asked if it was okay to bring a woman with him. Collyns agreed as long as he could bring a lady, too. After checking with all of his American female friends, none of whom he could convince to go on the adventure—"It was very inappropriate to go off in a car with men for the summer"—he recalled an English woman named Pat who was studying at Smith. She agreed to the trip, and the experience was certainly a positive one, as they were married a year later.

They lived in a small apartment on the Upper West Side of New York City (which at the time was quite an unruly place but is now one of the most fashionable parts of the city) until they decided to move back to England in 1956. Employment back in England was difficult to come by and the pair struggled for a few months. Collyns kept applying for various opportuni-ties. After selling mutual funds to US military people for a short time (under questionable circumstances), he applied for positions at two companies—Shell in London and Rolls Royce in Derby. He was invited to an interview with Shell and met another former friend from Marlborough who advised him not to take the position. Collyns accepted and recalled: "I told Shell I'd start on April 1, 1957 (April Fool's Day!)."

On joining Shell's Economics Division, Collyns essentially calculated correlations of oil demand to economic growth for two years. He was then assigned to work on the dynamics in Latin America where he first met Ted Newland in early 1959, who was coordinating Shell's activities in Brazil. Both had offices in London and worked on the economic variables for Shell under the assumptions of relatively stable growth. Shortly after, Collyns was given responsibility for planning Shell's activities in the western hemisphere and had the opportunity to travel to Colombia to explore the possibility of building an oil refinery at Buenaventura, Colombia. While travelling, his youngest son died at four months. In the circumstances Shell decided to post him back to New York where he worked as an economist at the time that OPEC was started and the Russians began exporting significant quantities of oil again. He worked out of Shell's New York offices for two years, and was then sent to Nigeria, where he crossed paths with Newland again.

Nigeria was at a particularly volatile point in its history. Collyns was essentially an executive assistant to Shell's chief executive and after a year in Port Harcourt he was transferred to Lagos where he also represented the oil industry to the Chamber of Commerce and Shell's financial relations with the Federal Government. After a couple of years in Lagos where Shell went through a series of political murders and bloody coups, they finally ended up in a civil war—it was a turbulent time. Once the war broke out, most Shell expatriates were evacuated but about 20 of the rest who worked in Port Harcourt except for Collyns, were held under house arrest.

It was a difficult time but they had persuaded one of the Managing Directors—Frank McFadzean—from London to come to Lagos and see if he could get them out. He managed to get to Enugu, the new capital of Biafra and persuade General Ojukwu that Shell would be unable to continue paying royalties and taxes to both regimes. All expatriates then left the country but Collyns stayed on in Lagos. When he left at the end of the year the oil ministry threw a huge party, and the head of the petroleum ministry who headed OPEC said, "It's a very sad day losing Napier because of all the oil people who have been here, he's the only one who's really been able to understand us, be with us as if he's one of us." Collyns further recalled:

> I was then transferred to Venezuela—the Cardon refinery—which completed my oil industry education. Suddenly I was asked to go to London in the last 3 months of 1969 to join a team at Shell Center in London that was looking at possible diversification from oil and natural gas. My topic was mining and minerals. That was the first time I have ever heard the term "scenario", a term developed by Herman Kahn while he was working for the Rand Corporation on the possible consequences of developing the hydrogen bomb while he was living in Santa Monica the home of the movie business whose term it was. He was thinking in

scenarios long before anyone. The term was also used by Paul Ehrlich when he was writing *The Population Bomb* as a biologist at Stanford. As part of the work I did on mining and minerals we looked at what Shell's investment in the mining entry might be. Our very early scenaric thinking led to the possible purchase of a company called Billiton, a relatively small mining company founded in 1860 by the grandfather of the then managing director of Royal Dutch the parent company of Shell. After studying alternative scenarios it seemed wiser to buy a relatively small mining company rather than one like Rio Tinto Zinc which had grown very successfully in the previous ten years. We showed that with similar rates of investment Billiton could itself grow in to a large successful company which it has become as the largest mining company in the world in recent years.

Collyns was back in London in 1969 working on Shell's "New Enterprises" which focused on diversification of the company. Metals were selected as the target for exploration and Collyns was put in charge of the study by Swart—then the Managing Director with responsibilities for both Planning and Diversification. He reported directly to Swart throughout 1971. In the spring of 1972, he was sent to join Group Planning. He was eager to work closely with Newland as they had met many times before but never really worked together directly. Collyns had not yet met Wack and first heard of him when he was summoned to London to help:

> Then one day my boss called and said, "I've got this crazy Frenchman who they think should go to London to do our planning there, named Pierre Wack. The reason I'm telling you this is because I want you to go and understudy him because I want to be sure that someone we know is there if he walks off." I said, "Well, where is he?" He said, "He's in Japan. He refused to take the job until he'd spent a year in Japan."

## Two Scenario Role Archetypes—Two Pieces of Jade

The synergy between Wack and Newland is regarded by many as one of the most important factors in the development of scenarios at Shell. Wack is remembered as a particularly unique individual. However, even the most unique person cannot do it all on their own. Elvis needed a band; Jobs needed a Wozniak. There is something ineffable about these types of connections that create unprecedented innovation. The affection with which Newland spoke about Wack made it clear that their relationship was a driving force in getting scenarios accepted. Newland and Wack had a marvellous and uncommon synergy. Newland commented: "It was a union ordained in heaven—we could read each other's minds and never a harsh word was spoken. We just intuitively understood each other. It was a true partnership."

Wack frequently used the story of two pieces of jade to describe their relationship and Newland retold it as follows:

> The Chinese have a peculiar addiction to jade. Jade as you know is created through ages in the putrefaction of insects inside trees and turns into a very beautiful substance which they say is more precious than diamonds. So, that's the quote—it comes from that corner—"You can only polish jade with jade, but it must come from another mountain." And that I think is very, very important in the scenario construction process—just to have one guru designing—it can happen but it's not creative enough. You need another able to communicate. That was me and Pierre.

Given their histories, Wack and Newland clearly came from different mountains and yet, within a remarkably short period of time, were able to connect their mountains through mutual interest, fascination and respect. Newland went on to say that really living in different cultures and seeing the world from a variety of points of view was essential to the scenario process. Wack's experiences came mostly from Japan and India, and eventually the Middle East, while Newland's history had exposed him quite deeply to North and South America and Europe.

Newland most wanted to reflect on his relationship with Wack and the roles they played. Both he and Wack were able to disconnect themselves from whatever problem they were looking at and put a very broad perspective on how they thought about it:

> This is not multi-culturalism—that is something different—if you want to do this [scenario planning] you must find people who live in different cultures, not adopt them or understand them, but actually live in them. And that was my side of the jade, which was extremely useful. When we came together and it was largely a coincidence, I was picked because I had changed a few things in Africa. Pierre was selected by one of the French managing directors—and he was put out on a string and told to get on with it.

Newland went on to say:

> It all sounds rather conceited, but it's the contribution and the obligation that anyone designing or thinking of scenarios must have in mind if they want to use them effectively or use them at all. I would switch the light onto the archetype of creator and presenter, if you want. The first thing to say is the presentation of scenarios is at least as important as the creation of the scenario and the process. I'm talking at the highest of effective levels, not down in the engine room of the planning department. You've got to have the right mix of talent in presenter and creator if you want to launch something that is—as the American's call a game changer.

## Shapeshifter

Newland also described how Wack tended to take on the appearances of the places he visited: "When he came back from a visit to Japan, he looked like a samurai, when he returned from Thailand, he looked Thai, when he arrived from Nepal, he appeared as a Sherpa. He had a mysterious ability to quickly take on the characteristics—even physical characteristics, of the places where he spent time."

Of course, ultimately, it was Davidson masterminding and supporting the whole project behind the scenes from the start that enabled such a team to be assembled. "These three, Pierre, Harry Beckers and Cor Kuiken formed a formidable team which I felt very privileged to head up." And now that the team was coming together, the revolution was underway. Having established the case for this evolution in future studies, Davidson was able to unleash the creative power of the CMD. With such strong and often divergent personalities, there were bound to be challenges. Yet the ultimate outcome—the highly productive, truly mind shattering approach—would be well worth the effort to bring this group together.

## Chapter 3 Sources (in order of use)

Hansford, S.H. (1950). *Chinese jade carving*. London: Humphries.

Rawson, J. (1995). *Chinese jade*. London: British Museum Press.

Manning, G. (2005). *Airliners of the 1970s*. Hinckley, UK: Midland Publishing.

Wilkinson, A., & Kupers, R. (2013). Living in the futures. *Harvard Business Review*, *91*(5), 118–127.

Wilkinson, A., & Kupers, R. (2014). *The essence of scenarios: Learning from the Shell experiences*. Amsterdam: Amsterdam University Press.

Kleiner, A. (1996). *The age of heretics: Heroes, outlaws, and the forerunners of corporate change*. New York: Doubleday.

Kleiner, A. (2008). *The age of heretics: A history of the radical thinkers who reinvented corporate management* (Vol. 164). New York: John Wiley & Sons.

Cornelius, P., Van de Putte, A., & Romani, M. (2005). Three decades of scenario planning in shell. *California Management Review*, *48*(1), 92–109.

DuMoulin, H., & Eyre, J. (1979). Energy scenarios: A learning process. *Energy Economics*, *1*(2), 76–86.

Kolk, A., & Levy, D. (2001). Winds of change: Corporate strategy, climate change and oil multinationals. *European Management Journal*, *19*(5), 501–509.

Wack, P. (1986). *The gentle art of re-perceiving*, Doc No. PL-86-R21. Amsterdam: Shell Int'l Petroleum Co.

Kleiner, Art, James C. Davidson telephone interview: Spring 1993. (n.d.). 21 pp. The annotated transcript of a telephone interview between Art Kleiner and James Davidson regarding the development of Shell's Group Planning Department. Retrieved from the Art Kleiner Archive, University of Oxford.

Kleiner, Art, Pierre A. Wack interview in Curemonte. (n.d.). 53 pp. The annotated transcript of an interview between Art Kleiner and Pierre Wack regarding the development of Shell's scenario planning. Retrieved from the Art Kleiner Archive, University of Oxford.

Excerpt from personal communications with Ted Newland. Author held interview and discussions in 2014–16.

Excerpt from personal communications with Napier Collyns. Author held interviews and discussions in 2014–16.

Excerpt from personal communications with Eve Wack. Author held interviews and discussions in 2014–16.

Wack, E. (1998). *Pierreve: 1977–1997*. Curemonte, France, Unpublished manuscript.

Ghamiri-Tabrizi, S. (2005). *The worlds of Herman-Kahn: The intuitive science of thermonuclear war*. Cambridge, MA: Harvard University Press.

Wack, P. (1985a). Scenarios: Shooting the rapids. *Harvard Business Review*, 63(6), 139–150.

Wack, P. (1985b). Scenarios: Uncharted waters ahead. *Harvard Business Review*, 63(5), 73–89.

Wack, P. (1985c). *Scenarios: The gentle art of re-perceiving*. Harvard Business School, Unpublished manuscript.

Wack, P. (1984). *Scenarios: The gentle art of re-perceiving*. Harvard Business School Working Paper 9–785–042, December 1984.

Wade, D. (1994, May). *Long and medium term global scenarios: 1971–1992*. Taped interview with Ted Newland, Cybard, France, Unpublished manuscript.

Eidinow, E. (2002). Some random reminiscences [interview and story of Napier Collyns]. *Netview*. Copy in possession of the Pierre Wack Memorial Library, University of Oxford.

Excerpt from personal communications with Napier Collyns. Author held interviews and discussions in 2014–16.

Ehrlich Paul, R. (1968). *The population bomb*. New York: Ballantine.

Excerpt from personal communications with Ged Davis. Author held interviews and discussions in 2014–16.

*Review of this chapter and corrections on details regarding Herman Kahn provided by Bretton Fosbrook.

# 4 Getting Scenarios off the Ground (1971–73)

*Pierre returned from Japan with a lot to say. He prepared a seminar to highlight his experiences studying Japanese companies. Most from the Planning group were in attendance, including Harry Beckers, Hans DuMoulin, Ted Newland, Guy Jillings, among others. Also in attendance was a Japanese man named Eizo Kobayashi, or "Kobi" as they called him, who had been working in Shell's economic office for Harry Beckers. As usual, Pierre's presentation was enthralling; he spoke about the Japanese economy, the people he had met, and how different their ideas about planning were. He actually started to look like a samurai as he delivered his presentation with a practiced skill. He proceeded to expound about various cultural and historical aspects of Japan which he believed were key to their development. The audience was spellbound as usual. Towards the end of his presentation, Pierre began to draw some basic distinctions between the approaches common in Shell versus those he observed in Japan and said, "We Westerners have a linear approach to situations. We tackle them by solving a succession of problems, one after another. The Japanese, on the other hand, think of the whole complex at once." At this point Pierre turned to Kobi and asked: "What do you think Kobi? Do you agree?" Kobi replied, "Terribly sorry, I don't understand." The room erupted in laughter. It was never learned if Kobi was defeated by the English language or simply disagreed with the assessment of his home culture.*

When Wack arrived at the Shell Centre in London in early 1971, he was ready to work. Eight days after his arrival, Davidson gave him a copy of the latest Group Planning book on the external environment. And then there was an early version of the Club of Rome book, *Limits to Growth*, before it was actually published a year later. These were already important documents. They represented the existing efforts, the processes and thinking already underway within Group Planning. They were provided with the intention of helping get Wack familiar with these efforts. After looking the documents over for about a week, Wack returned to Davidson and said he wanted to go a different way and use a different approach: "This was about eight months before my first presentation before the managing directors.

I came back for Christmas. It was very early January. There was no sense of urgency at all . . . I couldn't contain my adverse reaction: they must have seen I was not enthusiastic."

After being briefed on his role and the planning work in process, Wack headed to Japan on the sabbatical he had been promised. Throughout most of 1971, Wack was in Japan studying Japanese corporations with occasional visits back to London for important presentations and meetings. Davidson held several meetings with the CMD, but was not able to make much progress gaining support for scenarios. Wack was apprised of the situation: "I was in Japan knowing what was done, knowing that I would have to play the next stroke with who were extraordinarily stimulating people and a very stimulating company."

## The 1971 Scenarios

With the support of Jan Brouwer, Davidson was able to keep the possibility for scenarios alive. On July 20, 1971, Wack returned to London to accompany Davidson and Newland to the CMD. Their purpose was to present three alternative oil prices based on the work developed by Newland and Henk Alkema. Beckers followed up with what the implications might be on the strategy side but the effort still did not dislodge the CMD's commitment to systems already in place. In fact, at the conclusion of this presentation (according to Davidson), McFadzean is reported to have said he could do as well on the back of an envelope.

Davidson took the heat: "I had to try and get the CMD to listen sympathetically to Pierre's presentation. And this first one wasn't a great success, and as the Head of Group Planning I was promoting his efforts. I had to face a certain amount of scorn and criticism."

The strategy side was not doing any better. Davidson took Beckers to the CMD again on the 28th of July, 1971:

> We attempted to show how the balance of group investment between principal activities might be changed over a longer term . . . We were still completely, heavily committed to oil. And the longer term didn't look too good. But the CMD wanted to know, they wanted convincing reasons as to what they should do . . . Anyway this wasn't a very convincing effort with the CMD and we knew it wasn't but it was part of a kind of learning process.

Then, on November 3, 1971, Wack made another presentation to the CMD that included expanded implications for oil consumption and revenues in the Middle East. Again the presentation was based on Newland and Alkema's previous work, albeit with continued revisions, and again the impact was minimal. Wack had become familiar enough with the updated set of 1971 scenarios to present them to the CMD but recognized some shortcomings which he felt he would only be able to help with over time. While the scenario presentation still did not convince anyone, Wack was warming up to the role and his presentations were improving.

Davidson again suffered some criticism: "There was an awful lot of difficulty over this. Of course the scenarios, when they first came out met with a terrible lot of skepticism. The big operating companies and coordinators said 'what do we do with these? Tell us which is most probable.' One couldn't prepare three or four or five different sets of plans. We were trying to figure out how to do it."

There really is no better way to capture the experience than to present the content—in Wack's own words—of these first generation scenarios. What follows is a passage taken from "The Gentle Art of Re-Perceiving." Here, the original scenarios presented to the CMD are provided in their entirety:

### The 1971 First Generation Scenarios

The Horizon Planning exercise indicated that the existing rate of growth for oil demand couldn't continue indefinitely; some break would have to come before 1985. Accordingly, 1985 was chosen as the horizon for the 1971 scenarios. Another significant date would be 1976, because the Teheran Agreement of 1971 (which established the level of oil producer-government taxes for OPEC) was to be renegotiated at the end of 1975.

*Scenario 1:* A surprise-free, consensus scenario virtually lifted from the concurrent UPM work. It assumed median economic growth and led to an estimate of free world energy demand in 1985 of 154MM B/D oil-equivalent. While this was slightly higher than the 1971 UPM estimate of 150MM B/D, it fitted well with managers' expectations at the time, because the UPM had been consistently underestimating energy demand. (For orientation, 1971 free world energy demand was 78MM B/D).

*Scenario II:* Postulated a great increase—a tripling—of host-government tax take on the occasion of the renegotiation of the Teheran Agreement at the end of 1975, and further increases later. These assumptions of much higher oil prices would result in lower economic growth and energy and oil demand levels than those seen in the surprise-free scenario.

*Scenario III:* Treated the other obvious uncertainty: very low growth. Based on the recession years of 1970 and 1971, and a proliferation of already evident "me-first" and nonwork-oriented values, this slow-growth scenario premised an economic growth rate only half that under Scenario I. International trade would also slow down due to the lower growth and because the same attitudes would manifest themselves as nationalism and protective tariffs. Low oil demand would limit any oil price rises, and producer government take would increase less than in the surprise-free scenario.

·  *Scenario IV:* Postulated that demand for coal and nuclear energy would grow at much increased rates, mainly at the expense of oil. Other premises were kept similar to those in the surprise-free scenario.

The scenario team quickly concluded that few paid any attention to the 1971 scenarios. In fact, the presentations were considered failures. They came to realize that no strategic action, decision or thinking could be formulated based on the material. This was the same problem Wack had in his experiments with scenarios in Shell Francaise. The results were mildly positive with some members of the CMD, though few were really on board. McFadzean had gone from hostile to neutral, but was still not impressed. However, there was strong agreement between Wack and Newland that the scenarios could be useful as backdrops for more serious analysis, but significant revisions and new angles were needed.

As a result of their initial scenario set and the failure to gain traction with the CMD, the team realized that the purpose of any initial set of scenarios is learning and understanding. So they went back to the scenarios in search of less obvious factors that could yield insights after a deeper analysis. The team started to consider possible oil-producing country actions in light of the four high-level 1971 scenarios and created another matrix with "absorptive capacity" on one axis and "reserves" on the other (Chart VII). This was the second and final 2x2 matrix Wack ever used in his scenario work.

With Davidson's continued protection of the scenario team and masterful patience, the scenario work was allowed to continue. Newland and Alkema continued to study government take variability as well as possible stances for producer countries. Given the likelihood of increasing oil prices across the board, Swart pushed for a study of coal and nuclear energy options over the long term. Collyns was selected to lead the project until he would join Group Planning in 1972. Wack later recalled:

> We were beginning to understand the forces driving the system. Could we now tackle the 1971 scenarios again and devise a set of scenarios that would catch the decision maker's attention, and help him cope with the coming discontinuity and focus usefully on its uncertainties? We now felt we could design scenarios that might provide a proper framework for decision making, but we realized that we would have a formidable communications task.

It is not well known, but on review of the facts it is clear that Wack had little to do with the two iterations of the 1971 scenarios: "In 1971 I spent 2/3 of my time in Tokyo. Not in London. So I was not deeply working on these first generation scenarios." The 1971 scenarios were essentially completed by Newland and Alkema when he returned from Japan more permanently. Wack clarified: "At the end of 1971, I spent two months working with Group Planning." Once Wack was more permanently stationed in

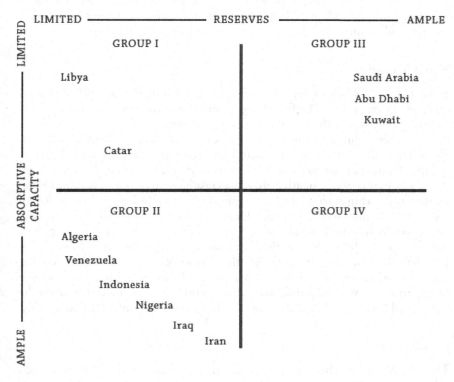

*Chart 4.1* Major Oil Exporters

London, the Wack and Newland synergy could begin to express itself. In late 1971, he purchased an apartment in London's posh Lennox Gardens.

## Experiments

Nick Pettinati was a new recruit to the scenario team in early 1972. He recalled Wack's early experiments in approaching scenarios, and the instance in which Wack assigned the same task to two different teams:

> He set up two teams with identical terms of reference—find out how much money Saudi Arabia can spend (wisely) in a given year and then divide that by the current level of production to arrive at the oil price, or divide the same finite sum (of money) by the current oil price to arrive at the level of production. Pierre's only request was that neither team should consult with the other. And so we set off and a month later duly reported our findings. The remarkable thing is that both teams came to very similar conclusions, but the reasoning process was completely

different. And, being a true intellectual, Pierre quickly became fascinated in the mechanics and logic of each answer and rather bored with the end result!

## Fiona Youlton

From the time Wack arrived in London until 1980, Fiona Youlton would serve as his assistant: "The first thing I noticed was his burning of joss sticks. Certainly, he was different. He never wrote down very much apart from maybe notes to himself, but he never wrote reports. He looked half Nepalese or Japanese something—you could immediately remark upon it." Stressing that he never took too much effort to write things down, Fiona recalled it was not that it was beneath him, it was just he viewed it as a waste of time. He had other things to do and think about: "He would sit and think for an awful lot of time and meditate." Fiona recalled one morning she walked into Wack's office to find him on the floor: "I thought he had actually passed out flat on the floor. He was there across from the door, but I thought for sure he'd had a heart attack!" Another instance involved a fly, bouncing again and again at the window of his office. She prepared to swat it with a newspaper, but Wack stopped her: "Pierre said 'No! Don't—don't touch the fly!'" And Wack gently gathered up the fly, opened the window, and let it fly.

## In the Green

This era was also when the two pieces of jade began to complement each other. Newland's archetypes of scenario creator and scenario presenter began to emerge, and each settled into his role comfortably, yet intuitively understood the other.

Shell Francaise owned a monastery in the South of France—Lurs—that was used for various functions, although at this time it was empty and unused. Wack thought it would be a great place to get away and think deeply about the future with his team. Newland recalled the general purpose: "If you want to get answers, frustrate a very intelligent group of people and they will find them." He went on to say if they were able to frustrate people enough—for a span of about four or five days—the subconscious would take over and they would come to realize the scenario is there. Newland regarded the subconscious mind as "a thousand times more powerful than the conscious mind," but they could not get the subconscious to intervene until a high degree of frustration had been reached. To achieve such frustration, Wack had a plan:

> The whole team went in the green. We had seven and we were in the South of France in an old monastery. I'm not sure if there was a telephone, but there was certainly no television and we were really hard-working putting this thing together. If we would not have come up with

something spectacular, it would certainly have been the end of this way of scenario planning at Shell.

Wack went on further to describe that it was important not to limit the amount of time in the green. Completing the task in four days or five days was fine, but it was critical to function without a time limit. The intensity was important—as was the process of increasing that intensity without breaking. The team worked until two in the morning if necessary. The first day was well structured—designed so that team members would come away with scenario building blocks. Each day thereafter was less structured and was intended with development and free thinking in mind. Wack recounted that the end of the second day was usually met with a degree of dissatisfaction—and that this was absolutely required. Fighting was commonplace—particularly on day three. Wack recalled Gareth Price and Hein Tausk "really fighting physically."

While Wack never articulated a scenarios process, it is clear that isolating the team in an environment in which they could think deeply was critical: "If you can really go into the green, be it only for two days, outside the office, in a secluded place, where the tension can grow, and where you are not going to sleep until you finish your thing—it's an enormous advantage." The team took the opportunity to revise the 1971 scenarios and focused their efforts on expanding the proposed dynamics in a direction that would most certainly capture the CMD's attention. A new particular focus was the predetermined elements.

## Predetermined Elements

Wack frequently used the stories of rivers (he used both the Ganges and the Nile) "to introduce a notion of predetermined elements. It is not the obvious predetermined which you might call something in the pipeline, the most important are the system predetermined which are not obvious at first. And you discover then when you do exploratory scenarios. That is why you do exploratory scenarios—to find the system predetermineds." The story of the Ganges as told by Wack is one of his most famous:

> I happen to know the Ganges pretty well, from stream to mouth. It's a very extraordinary river. Now, if you know that it had a monsoon rain at the upper part of the basin, you can be sure that within two days, some extraordinary floods are going to happen at Rishikesh, which is at the foothills of the Himalayas. And three days later in Moradabad, which is northeast of Delhi. And again four or five days later in Benares. This is not fortune-telling. This is not crystal-ball-gazing. This is merely describing future implications of something which has already happened. So the first thing we do, is to find our predetermined elements. And not the obvious predetermined only. And this was the great advantage of several exploratory scenarios. That you find out interconnections.

The story about the Nile is more complicated:

> The Nile takes a little longer to explain. But it is a very long river that, and it's the only river which has floods in summer where there is absolutely no rain. It's miraculous. And it was very important for the people to be capable of anticipating if there would be floods because this was the basis of their power. And you had Nilometers to measure the height of the Nile. If the flood was below a certain level, people had the right not to pay taxes. It was quite serious. So there was a caste of priests who had been trained in Sudan, outside Egypt to watch the color of the Nile. At this time the Nile was made of 3 colors—the white Nile [which] goes to swamps from Lake Victoria and then you have another Nile, the blue Nile which comes in from the mountain of Utopia and it's not blue, it's dark red. And this [color] it gets from the monsoon type of situation. And then you have a third one which [joins from] the River Atbarah. Again [it] comes a different time and it's a mix of those three and it's a different color. The priests could tell first when the flood would start by making signs of fumes during the day and a fire during the night. They could warn several days in advance when the flood would start. Now you know when there is no rain and suddenly to be capable of saying the flood will start and so on, it's quite something. The second thing they could say is it would be a heavy flood or not heavy flood. And the heavy flood is very important for the immediate, because this gave rise to the seven bad years and heavy floods were breaking the dams and then would bring pestilence and for seven years it would be just absolutely horrible. So heavy floods were even more dangerous than low floods where you had no taxes to pay. So there were priests trained to be capable of seeing the things which matter. Not to make any reasoning, just seeing, but being capable of reading what might occur.

Wack gave the example of Iran as a predetermined element in their early scenarios. It was not obvious that Iran would increase its oil prices until the team understood the extent to which they would come to be depended on for their oil supply under a potential crisis and how much reserve they had.

Predetermined elements became a fundamental and foundational building block for planning scenarios in the early days. Wack came to believe that one of the true arts of good planning work was to separate what was predetermined from what was truly uncertain. This was no easy task and the major finding was that the first round of scenario work often resulted in identifying the predetermineds. Then, more concentrated work could be aimed at exploring and working to understand the uncertainties.

## On the Term "Scenarios"

According to Newland, "Just about everybody in business and politics talks scenarios nowadays. In those days it was unheard of—the word wasn't even known. It was considered opera—good opera. You must take in the whole stage—not just one thing that you see." In mid-1972, Wack used the term "scenario" to describe Group Planning's work exploring varied futures. The term stuck. A prominent earlier use of the term with a similar context was by Paul Ehrlich in his book *The Population Bomb* in 1968. Ehrlich was a biologist, and he used the term "scenarios" to describe various future events concerning global overpopulation. Of course, Kahn had also used the term and it was floating around several US government quarters in late 1968 and 1969. On the military side, a document published in February 1967 by the Rand Corporation titled "Political-Military Scenarios," written by H. A. DeWeerd used the term. On the label "scenarios" he wrote:

> The use of the term "scenario" in connection with these matters is of relatively recent origin. There is no entry for the term "scenario" in the Dictionary of U.S. Military Terms prepared by the Joint Chiefs of Staff in 1964. I vividly recall the surprise with which I first heard the term used in connection with a military event. It was in the summer of 1944 at the Headquarters of Army Ground Forces. As a lowly major serving as an associate editor of INFANTRY JOURNAL I heard Lieutenant General Ben Lear ask for the "scenario" of a recent military event. Because up to that time I had heard the term used only to cover radio or movie scripts, I thought the general was being facetious. A defense research scenario can be one of many different things. It may be as brief as two or three sentences or as long as a book. It may be fanciful, representing nothing in the real world, or it may be modeled with great faithfulness on existing conditions. The requirements for scenarios change with the purposes involved and they change with the times.

Wherever Wack actually picked up the term is not clear, but once he used it, their craft had taken on a name.

## The 1972 Scenarios

The 1972 scenarios were, by all accounts, a significant turning point for scenario planning at Shell, although it was not a fait accompli and their effects would unfold over the course of a year. Wack, Newland and Davidson had an opportunity again to present to the CMD on September 19, 1972. This time, things were different—a confidence was emerging. Wack was developing his skill as a persuasive and talented presenter: "We insisted on the whole morning—they can leave if they are not interested. I don't mind if they leave, but if they are interested they must be able to stay the whole morning. And we got it!" Wack went on to describe how unusual the situation was: "Nobody gets a whole morning from the Managing Directors. It had not yet been done. So there was some risk. So before, I went to see the Managing Directors and I told them, 'look we have a good story' and I gave them some bites to raise their appetite . . . but I knew that we may have had some people leaving and it was a chance. But nobody could have asked for a whole morning."

Wack proceeded to give what many recall as a particularly enthralling, compelling and consuming presentation, followed by a series of questions which he answered as though he had somehow known the questions and prepared his responses in advance:

> In September 1972, we presented to Shell's top management an array of possible futures, gathered in two families, A and B. All of our analyses had pointed with great likelihood to the early surfacing of a major discontinuity, namely, the impeding scarcity of oil and an ensuing sharp increase in its price. What appeared "uncertain" was its timing (although it couldn't be too many years away) and, more particularly, how different actors would respond to it.

The presentation lasted approximately four hours and the basis was a chart depicting a river forking into two, and then three streams. This now famous "river chart" would frame scenarios at Shell for years to come.

The 1972 scenarios are summarized from Wack's "Gentle Art of Reperceiving" here:

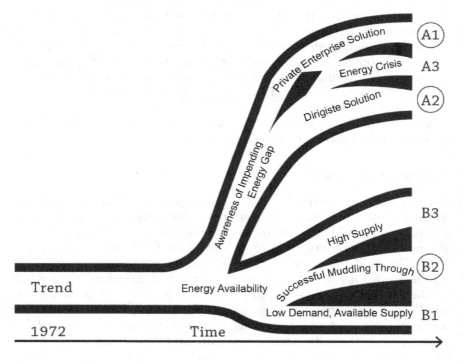

*Figure 4.1* 1972 Scenarios

## The 1972 Scenarios—A-Family

*The A-family of scenarios* postulated the discontinuity and then examined three ways in which circumstances might develop:

A1 would be a private-enterprise *solution* to the emerging energy shortage;

A2 would have governments intervene to solve the problem, the dirigisme *solution*;

A3 presupposed that solutions would not be found early enough, and an *energy crisis* would result.

The A-family of scenarios fixed the timing of the discontinuity at the end of 1975, coincident with the scheduled renegotiation of the Teheran price agreement. In reality, the discontinuity came in the fall of 1973—not yet caused by demand outrunning supply, but when the oil embargo was imposed after the outbreak of the Israeli/Arab war in reaction to US assistance to Israel.

Moderate economic growth was assumed through 1976, with growth thereafter threatened by a possible scarcity of energy. Most oil-producing countries would be reaching the technical limit of their capacities by 1976, while the others would be reluctant to increase output further due to their inability to absorb the additional revenues. Accordingly, producer countries' oil prices would increase substantially at the end of 1975. Consuming countries, confronted with the possibility of physical shortages of energy supplies and with greatly increased oil import bills, would experience shock waves.

The essential point in the A-family of scenarios was discontinuity. Shell would have to prepare for a sudden change in the behavior of both producing and consuming countries that would result from their awareness of an impending imbalance between demand and supply of oil. The discontinuity might arise from a situation of tension, created by the producing countries imposing a limit on the amount of oil they produced. It might also come about if these nations announced a gradual decrease in the rate of production growth, or if they gave advance notice of such a policy. In any case, the awareness of an impending energy gap constituted only the first stage of the process. The most important consideration, it was felt, was the timing and direction of the "active responses" to such awareness.

## The 1972 Scenarios—B-Family

*The B-family of scenarios.* With hindsight, the critical assumption of discontinuity for the A-scenarios looks rather obvious. At the time, however, it was seen as quite the reverse. We believed in the A-scenarios, we put them forward very strongly as the most likely direction of events. But they did represent a major revolution in thinking for an oil company—and many Shell managers (like their counterparts in other companies) still wanted to believe in futures without discontinuity.

The B-family of scenarios therefore described how discontinuity might be avoided.

*B1* was a protracted *low-economic-growth scenario*, requiring at least 10 years of low growth to force a demand fit to the oil supply presumed available. While low growth had seemed plausible in the downturn of 1971, by 1972 we could see signs of a coming economic boom. We did not know, of course, the extent of this period of above-average growth, or that growth in 1973 would be the most spectacular since the Korean War. But we could already see that our low-growth scenario, B1, was extremely unlikely: It would require an immediate and sharp drop in the growth rate of the world economy, which we had no reason to anticipate. Moreover, the negative cultural trends of the late 1960s in industrial countries were waning. Governments and the public perceived that rising unemployment was a problem and were consciously seeking growth. So, the B1 scenario, premising very low growth for a long period, had low credibility. However, it performed its function of highlighting the major discontinuity most effectively, simply because it was not a likely way to avoid the discontinuity.

*B3*, a more important alternative, postulated a very *high supply of oil*. We called it the "three miracle" scenario, because it required three extremely unlikely situations simultaneously. First, it required an exploration and production miracle. Our original surprise-free scenario had predicted a certain level of demand for oil. To meet that demand, rapid development of Middle Eastern reserves and extensive new discoveries were necessary. Our Exploration and Production staff believed that there was a 30 percent likelihood of finding the necessary reserves in each of the oil provinces individual, but that there was only a very small percent change of finding the necessary reserves in all the areas. Meeting the forecast 1985 demand would require not only 24MM B/D from Saudi Arabia, but also 13MM B/D from Africa and 6MM B/D from Alaska and Canada. Many new discoveries would be needed for these figures to become reality.

The second miracle demanded by the B3 scenario was a sociopolitical one: All major producing countries would be happy to deplete their resources at the will of the consumer. Countries with low absorptive capacities would agree to produce huge amounts of oil and put their money in the bank, exposed to erosion by inflation, rather than keep their oil in the ground for future generation. This scenario projected onto the oil-producing countries the values of consuming countries—a kind of Western cultural imperialism that was extremely unconvincing once examined rationally.

The final miracle of B3 started with the recognition that there would be little, if any, spare capacity over projected demand under the high-supply scenario. Previously when minor crises developed in the Middle

East, there had always been additional oil available to meet sudden, short-term needs. (For instance, in 1956 during the Suez crisis, Texas and Louisiana helped out with their spare capacity. Similarly, during the June 1967 Middle East conflict, Iran called on its spare capacity to meet consumers' needs.) Under Scenario B3 there would be no spare production capacity. The miracle, then, was that there would be no need for it—no wars in the region, no acts of God, no cyclical peaks of demand higher than anticipated. Again, nothing short of miraculous.

The B3 scenario also performed its function very well by demonstrating that the high-supply assumption was extremely unlikely. Its essential role was educational.

B2, a totally artificial construct, was a *middle-of-the-road* scenario premising that despite all the problems, a muddling-through approach could be more or less successful. A widespread sentiment, particularly among the Anglo-Saxon managers, is well expressed by William Ogburn: "There is much stability in society . . . social trends seldom change their directions quickly and sharply . . . revolutions are rare and evolution is the rule." We couldn't really justify this scenario, but we knew that the worst outcome is not always the one that develops, and we imagined a situation in which the most positive outcomes were the norm. Oil-producing countries would take a live-and-let-live approach in order to obtain military and other concessions. Consuming countries, with great foresight, would take immediate steps to curb the rapid growth of oil consumption by encouraging energy saving.

## Beginning to Take Hold

Although they were essentially completed and first presented in 1972, the process of developing and disseminating the 1972 scenarios spanned well into 1973. Therefore, the scenarios were officially circulated inside Shell as "Scenarios for the 1973 Planning Cycle," though Wack referred to them as the 1972 scenarios in his writing. The document became known as the "Blue Book." Another book titled "The Impact on the World Economy of Developments in the Market for Oil" was compiled and released in May, 1973, which Napier Collyns, Guy Jillings and Joe Roeber were given responsibility for writing.

## The Impact on the World Economy of Developments in the Market for Oil

This supporting analysis became known as the "Pink Book." It was Collyns's first major task on joining Group Planning. The report was constructed on the basis of a single scenario that highlighted the looming changes and laid out the effects on oil-consuming countries. The introduction to the report states:

> This paper analyses the implications of a possible scenario covering development in the energy and oil industry in the next fifteen years or so. No attempt is made to forecast precisely the possible future outcome, but rather to draw attention to a possible sequence of events if there is no reaction from those involved—in particular the consumer governments. There are of course many possible alternative scenarios of the way in which the future may unfold, but the proposed scenario merits particular attention because it involves a threat to the economic well-being and progress of this industrialised world. This is an extreme assumption. Nevertheless it serves to highlight the issues of energy policy to which governments should be directing their urgent attention.
>
> The demand for energy worldwide over the period 1970–85 is conservatively expected at least to double. With only a modest increase in supplies expected to be available from other energy sources during the period, the demand for oil would also have to double by 1985. This would involve a large volumetric increase in demand and place pressures on limited sources of supply. It could also lead to a sharp escalation of prices instead of their relative stability during the 1950s and 1960s.

The report went on to fill in details of the world market for oil essentially under the A3 crisis scenario from the 1972/3 set. The report detailed various reactions by countries around the world and concluded that a "do nothing" approach was likely to result in oil price collapse and a global energy crisis.

Davidson continued to protect the team and eventually McFadzean, who had been the one most vocally opposed to modifying Shell's planning system, came around. A letter dated May 14, 1973 documents his reaction to "The Impact on the World Economy of Developments in the Market for Oil":

MR. SWART

1.  Leaving aside one or two small points—for example if energy demand doubles in 1970–85, oil demand will *more* than double and it is more accurate to state that Middle East oil reserves are approximately 60% of the world total rather than "over half"—I regard the booklet produced by Group Planning on "The Impact on the World Economy of Developments in the Market for Oil" as one of the best and most thoughtful I have read on the subject. The real question is what do we do with it?

2.  I do not know who has been concerned with its preparation but I suggest it should be circulated to all Co-ordinators and the Managing Directors should have a joint meeting with them to discuss its

contents. In particular, I would like to have the views of Tox on the atomic energy, fuel cell and magneto hydro-dynamics aspects raised toward the end of the document. If we can reach agreement on its final content we should then give consideration to submitting it at a high level to the main consuming governments, together with measures to mitigate an oil supply scramble. I have only seen a summary of Group Planning's views on the latter and suggest the longer note should also be circulated. It is also for consideration whether we should submit the papers at the next McCloy meeting since I sense that Exxon, for instance, do not fully share our views on these topics.

*14th May, 1973.*
c.c. Managing Directors
Mr. Davidson

The positive reaction from the CMD to the 1972/3 scenarios and positive regard for Wack's increasingly unique presentation style led to a more in-depth analysis of the various oil prices that were depicted. Over several debates with internal and external economists, figures that all agreed to be plausible were finally settled. This led to the approval for using the scenarios in the central offices. Further, following McFadzean's yielding and recommendations, a series of presentations was made to the governments of the major oil-consuming countries that began in October of 1973. Wack started to travel extensively—reporting on their scenario work across the globe: "I went every year, Japan, Australia, Shell Oil, usually we had the Philippines, for all small companies around the Far East, Germany, France—France I hated to do . . . Because I just couldn't speak in French about scenarios, I was used to speaking in English."

Wack also visited Toronto and Houston with Davidson and Beckers in 1973. Reactions were mildly positive in Toronto but Houston was particularly resistant. In fact, Wack was never able to break into the higher levels of leadership in Shell Oil (Shell Oil was a 69 percent owned affiliate in Houston, Texas). Managers were not impressed by his presentations. In fact, years later Ted Newland was sent to Houston specifically to try and convince the operation in Houston to adopt the scenario approach, but no traction was achieved. According to Wilkinson and Kupers, the firm resistance from Shell Oil in Houston led to the insight that the scenarios may not fit individual countries and reinforced the idea that tailoring and focusing the scenarios to specific regions and their dynamics may be required.

Newland and Alkema continued their work on increased government takes, coal and nuclear opportunities, as well as Middle Eastern oil cartels and inevitably rising oil prices:

Wack reacted to the tasks associated with the evident acceptance of the 1972/3 scenarios:

Within Shell, the next step was to present the A and B scenarios to the second echelon of management. For most of them, it was their first exposure to scenarios. The meeting was in stark contrast to the traditional UPM meetings which dealt with forecasts and trends and premises—all with an avalanche of numbers. Scenarios focused less on outcomes and more on understanding of the forces that would compel the outcome; less on figures, and more on insight. This meeting was positive and unusually lengthy, and the audience clearly appreciative. We thought we had won over a large share of them.

In the next few months, Group Planning would find that while they had finally convinced the CMD and despite a generally positive view from Management, very few managers were actually using their scenarios and planning for the discontinuity they saw coming. It was widely recognized that the scenarios had created intellectual interest but the connection to decision making was still lacking and stood in the way of more widespread use. This is when Wack discovered the importance of mental models and microcosms of decision makers. He realized that if the scenarios did not impact managers' mental models, they would not question their inner model of reality and be able to change it.

## A Major Turning Point

Wack's discovery of mental models, microcosms and the importance of connecting scenarios to decision making changed the way he thought about his role—and it was a profound insight. Wack took it as a shock that so few were actually using the scenarios inside Shell, when he thought the team had explicitly spelled out the details of what was to come. From this point, for Wack, scenarios became about changing the minds of managers rather than about the book or the presentation. This was a fundamental shift—he previously felt if he laid out the dynamics well, people would know what to do with the information. Once he had this insight, it was evident, quite quickly, that this was not the case.

It was also around this time that the "two pieces of jade" fully took to their roles. Wack stated that after 1972 it was only he who presented to the CMD on scenarios. Newland was active with many presentations inside the Operating Companies, but not with the CMD. Wack's ability to persuade (with the use of metaphors, vivid historical examples, and generally the "way" about him) made him a particularly effective presenter of scenarios.

Finally, Wack began to fully recognize the ineffectiveness of the methods so far—equating them with the ultimate utility and efficiency of a vacuum cleaner:

> A vacuum cleaner, for example, has an effectiveness of 30 to 40 percent; the rest is heat and noise. Future studies, particularly when they point to discontinuity, have an effectiveness below that of a vacuum cleaner.

He later stated this may have been an exaggeration, but it was clearly frustrating that the scenarios and the efforts of the team had not reached as deeply into the minds, behaviors, and actions of Shell managers as they had hoped. Wack's realization that the mental models were the true targets of scenarios became a foundation for scenarios from then on. Meanwhile, Group Planning did not simply rest on its newfound support from the CMD. The team continued to think about the future and almost immediately, amidst many presentations around the world, got to work on the 1973 scenarios—"the Rapids."

## The "Rapids"

"The Rapids" were an evolution of the 1972 scenarios based on a more detailed and plausible analysis of their facts and figures. The title "Rapids" was suggested by Gareth Price and Wack began incorporating it into his presentations. And, of course, the famous "river chart" carried the metaphor further. Because the team was able to discredit the B-family of scenarios from the 1972 set, the focus for the Rapids became a detailed development of the A-family of scenarios. According to Wilkinson and Kupers, "The scenarios were divided into two time frames—the 'Rapids' (that is, the period through 1980) and a 'New Habitat,' which evolved after 1980." When they were presented to the CMD, a new level of support and interest had been achieved.

Wack also documented the details of the "Rapids" in his own work. The following description is excerpted from "The Gentle Art of Re-perceiving:"

### The 1973 Scenarios—The Rapids

"It was ordained at the beginning of the world that certain signs should prefigure certain events," Cicero noted twenty centuries ago. All the signs at the end of 1972 and early 1973, as we set about preparing the next set of scenarios, still pointed to that major oil discontinuity.

We had done new analyses that again told us that a very tight supply-demand relationship would exist during the coming decade. Even in 1973, '74 and '75 (before the anticipated renegotiation of the Teheran agreement), demand could be expected to push right up to available production capability. And that supply would already be stretched, since it predicated that certain countries, such as Saudi Arabia and Kuwait, would produce contrary to their logic

Now we saw even discontinuity as total PREDETERMINED. Prices, then, would rise rapidly, and oil production would be constrained, not because of a true shortage of oil, but for political reasons—taking advantage of the very tight supply-demand relationship. Discontinuity would thus be our surprise-free scenario. What was not known was *how soon* the discontinuity would occur, *how much* of a price increase there would be, and *what the reactions* of the various players would be. Our company was like the canoeist who hears the white water around the next bend, and now needs to prepare for "THE RAPIDS" he will soon have to negotiate.

To reframe the outlook of our managers, we portrayed the situation for the 1973 scenarios as in Chart XI. From the calm up-river of the TRADITIONAL ENVIRONMENT, we would be plunged into the turbulence of THE RAPIDS, and have to learn to live in a NEW HABITAT for oil producers, for oil consumers, and—especially our concern—for oil companies.

The alternate branch of the river (the B-challenge scenarios of 1972) had now been dammed off. The "No Growth-No-Problem" possibility (B-1) now seemed completely noncredible as economies, fully recovered from the recession of 1971, boomed. "Three miracles" (B-3) still seemed just that—three supply miracles. And from our discussions to warn governments about impending crisis, we concluded that any reaction from governments would be *after the event*. (Obviously, we hadn't yet learned how to impact the microcosms of governments either!)

Another technique we used in the 1973 scenarios to keep the B-branch of the river dammed was to allow for delay in the onset of the discontinuity. In Phantom Scenario I we assumed a delay of five years; in Phantom II, fifteen years. (These, respectively, were typical times for bringing a new oil facility into service and for its amortization.) What we sought with these phantom scenarios was to measure the "regret" we would experience if Shell planned for the discontinuity but it did not in fact occur during the phantom years.

In the booming economy of late 1972 and early 1973—with growth exceeding any period since the Korean War, trade expanding at a record clip and oil consumption higher than even our bullish reference line—it was particularly difficult to convince an oil company having an affair with expansion that now was the time to slow down, to hold off on expanding refineries to stop building tankers and so forth.

And the phantom scenarios *did* measure a considerable "regret" if expansion continued and we didn't go with it. But, again, only two developments could delay the discontinuity, enabling business-as-usual to continue for any period of time; and both seemed so implausible that discontinuity soon had to be regarded as a PREDETERMINED. (The two situations allowing for a continuation of the existing pace of oil demand increase and which were ruled out, were: the discovery of new Middle East-size oil reserves in an area with no absorptive capacity problem; and, the dominance of producer countries by consuming countries through some sort of political or military intervention.) The phantom scenarios acted, therefore, to reinforce the unpalatable message we were sending.

Finally, the team was getting somewhere. The scenarios had finally begun to achieve a level of impact that was in line with expectations. Perhaps the hardest road had been travelled. It had been five years since the formation of

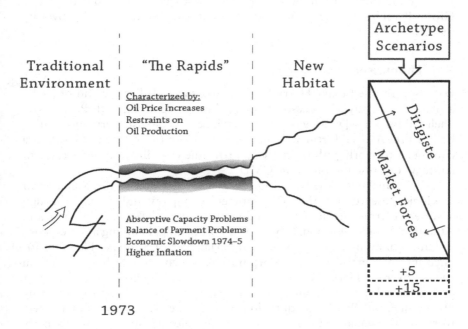

Chart 4.2 1973 Scenarios

Group Planning under Davidson's leadership, yet the group was only now recognized as contributing significant value.

Here we can point only to the simple matter of time it can take to change the minds of decision makers in powerful positions. Some CMD members clearly thought it was important to look at different ways of thinking about the future as far back as 1967. But again, it took five years to find the critical chink in the armor of the CMD. They were attached to embedded systems, and each member of the CMD "grew up" professionally in a time of unprecedented economic stability. While some were immediately more receptive than others, the previous stability created deeply entrenched world views. No wonder it took time!

## Scenarios and Strategy

Beckers had been making progress on the strategy side, too. "Gradually, Harry Beckers, who was really an exceptional man, managed to develop a system for analyzing the effects of the groups' investment plan against the risks," Davidson said. Working with his team and particularly Gerry Wagner, Beckers introduced a process for preparing an annual report of the groups' policies and related strategies against the scenarios. This report required input from both the scenarios and strategy teams, and it was up to Group Planning to finalize the report. Eventually, it required approval by the CMD.

## Ray Thomasson

Davidson recalled that "Harry Beckers was succeeded at the end of 73 by a man named Ray Thomasson whom I'd recruited along with Pierre from Shell Oil [in Texas] who was a very imaginative geologist. Very outstanding ball of fire. And he fortunately developed a close rapport with Pierre, and continued to work with trying to improve the coordination of investment strategy for presentation to the CMD".

Ray Thomasson joined Shell Oil in 1959. He began as the Manager of Geologic Research for Shell Development Company and worked through a variety of roles in the US, including Manager of Texas, Louisiana and Atlantic Offshore Division, Manager of Forecasting, Planning and Economics, and finally in 1973 he became the Manager of Strategic Planning for Shell International Petroleum Corporation, which brought him to London to take over for Harry Beckers. Wack had visited Houston earlier that year and observed one of Thomasson's presentations. He did not say anything at the time, but Wack was quite impressed. When it was time for Beckers to retire, the replacement had already been selected by Wack who simply reminded Davidson about the talent in Houston. Thomasson recalled: "Pierre was very impressive as an intellect, as a speaker and as a human being. He obviously played a role in having me selected to come over to work with him. He was head of scenario planning and writing and I was head of another group that 'mashed the numbers.' We both worked directly for Jimmy Davidson."

The pair quickly became friends and worked well together. They shared a deep interest in spiritual matters, and Thomasson took advice from Wack: "Pierre's concern was when I was reading various sources of information on the occult. Yes, he gave a warning based on his experience that I should steer clear of this area because it can have extremely dangerous results for an individual. I took his advice."

## The 1973 Oil Shocks

In October of 1973, the first world oil shocks began to occur. Because the scenarios had foreseen these events, leaders became keenly aware of their potential power and utility. Davidson stressed the point: "Finally everyone saw then that the scenarios, if they had used them would have been enormously useful—they saw they would have made other investment decisions." Suddenly, the credibility of scenario work skyrocketed and Group Planning was considered a huge success and a valuable asset. By the end of 1973 Group Planning was on solid ground and was about to embark on a flurry of scenario activity, developing the method and experimenting with shortened time frames.

The major shift was based on the fact that the scenarios enabled managers and directors to see the situation from the various oil-producing countries' points of view. Then, able to engage in exercises about anticipating reactions by all the major players involved, Shell managers and directors were ahead of the game. Thinking through the possible actions and reactions, as well as the side effects and consequences (both intended and unintended) allowed decision makers to rehearse the future in ways they had never before been able to do.

Regarding the oil shocks, Thomasson recalled:

> When I got into the US job the two groups reporting to me were preparing for a presentation in November to the president and two executive vice presidents. I was shown a graph depicting oil supply in the US headed downward starting in 1970 and oil usage rising steadily, creating a giant gap. I asked where that oil was going to come from. The answer was the Middle East. I asked how much it would cost and the answer was, "we don't know," so I instructed them to find out. It turns out the United States could not afford that kind of cost and so I suggested that we would necessarily have to conserve more in this country and produce more in this country. Having been introduced very briefly to scenario planning, we created a conservation scenario that predicted by 1980 we would be able to conserve a sufficient amount of energy that we could afford to import the volumes of oil necessary.

## Exploratory and Focused Scenarios

The other major discovery in the early evolution of scenarios was the difference between exploratory and focused scenarios. Wack even called these "mini-scenarios" later on. He further emphasized that they were faster to create and easier to work with than the more macro exploratory scenarios. But Wack was clear that if you jump directly to the focused scenarios, you miss key elements—particularly the predetermineds. This led Wack to a tiered scenario approach—you start with the exploratory learning scenarios and then zoom into the focused decision scenarios. This ensures you do not miss major factors in the external environment and preserves the major dynamics that most certainly shape strategic decision making. Wack had realized that: "If scenarios didn't engage the mental model of the decision maker, they would be like water on a stone." He began experimenting with interviews to help make them stick.

The sets of scenarios developed in 1971, 1972 and 1973 were necessary gateways—though by all accounts they still had not become fully embedded in Shell's long-range planning and decision making. Further, while those scenarios served to gain approval from the CMD for continued use (particularly after the events of autumn 1973), the task had shifted toward understanding and tailoring to manager's mental models. A major insight in 1973 for Wack was that the 1971 and 1972 scenarios were sets of exploratory, or first generation scenarios. Again, the point of doing the exploratory scenarios was to find the system's predetermined elements. The 1973 scenarios became the first effort to really understand managers' deepest concerns. Wack summarized:

> The early scenarios were exploratory. From this we had what we called the time study. Now you speak to anybody in planning, they will know what the time study is. What will be the future behavior of each of the major 3 actors on the energy scene in each of the four exploratory scenarios . . . We use exploratory scenarios but really to see how each of the actors will behave under each of those scenarios. And what we could learn from those we derived in the second generation of planning scenarios.

The team had discovered the need for and utility of more specific and focused scenarios. This development was starting to change the game, yet again it was only through a process of team learning that would lead the thinking down this path.

## Facing East

Throughout 1971–73, Wack was frequently travelling to Japan and India. He visited Japan because he loved the aesthetic of the country and had many contacts there as well as Shell scenario presentations to deliver. He visited India specifically to meet with his guru. No doubt Wack continued to refine his ability to "see" as he called it, and he credited his time in the East studying Buddhism and meditation as fundamental to his scenario work. Wack visited Svamiji Prajnanpad every year for extended meditation sessions either in November or in February. It is without question that Wack's interest in spirituality, his level of disciplined thinking, his ability to focus and his evolving ability to "see," contributed significantly to his scenario work. He regarded himself as the "eyes of the pack."

In London, the most familiar indicators of Wack's frequent visits to the East were the ever present sticks of incense that burned in his office (#1129 on the 11th floor of the Shell Centre) whenever he was there. It was detectable the moment one stepped out of the elevator. It helped his concentration and focus. He preferred incense from the famous Japanese shops of Shoyiedo and Yamada-Matsu which were made of entirely natural ingredients.

According to his assistant, Fiona Youlton, he usually arrived at the office early, often before anyone else. He meditated in his office before work; a daily practice of focus, reflection and meditation as suggested by Svamiji allowed Wack to create a habit of looking for patterns and gave him a way to deeply understand complex systems by leveraging his intuition. It did not matter whether the subject of his focus was his personal life, the oil industry or nothing at all. His practice of quietly generating insight is difficult at best to explain, but it made him who he was and without question, contributed to the magnificent scenario insights at Shell. And the scenario work was just getting started.

## Chapter 4 Sources (in order of use)

Roussopoulos, G. A. (1998, September 18). [Letter to Eve Wack]. Copy in possession of Eve Wack.

Meadows, D. H., Meadows, D. L., Randers, J., & Behrens III, W. W. (1972). *The limits to growth: Club of Rome: Crisis of humanity report.* Tokyo: Diamond.

Wilkinson, A., & Kupers, R. (2013). Living in the futures. *Harvard Business Review, 91*(5), 118–127.

Wilkinson, A., & Kupers, R. (2014). *The essence of scenarios: Learning from the Shell experiences.* Amsterdam: Amsterdam University Press.

Kleiner, Art, Pierre A. Wack interview in Curemonte. (n.d.). 53 pp. The annotated transcript of an interview between Art Kleiner and Pierre Wack regarding the development of Shell's scenario planning. Retrieved from the Art Kleiner Archive, University of Oxford.

Kleiner, Art, James C. Davidson telephone interview: Spring 1993. (n.d.). 21 pp. The annotated transcript of a telephone interview between Art Kleiner and James Davidson regarding the development of Shell's Group Planning Department. Retrieved from the Art Kleiner Archive, University of Oxford.

Royal Dutch/Shell Oil. (1971). *The 1971 scenarios.* Unpublished internal document. Copy in possession of the Pierre Wack Memorial Library, University of Oxford.

Wack, P. (1985a). Scenarios: Shooting the rapids. *Harvard Business Review, 63*(6), 139–150.

Wack, P. (1985b). Scenarios: Uncharted waters ahead. *Harvard Business Review, 63*(5), 73–89.

Wack, P. (1985c). *Scenarios: The gentle art of re-perceiving.* Harvard Business School, Unpublished manuscript.

Wack, P. (1984). *Scenarios: The gentle art of re-perceiving.* Harvard Business School Working Paper 9–785–042, December 1984.

Wade, D. (1994). *Long and medium term global scenarios: 1971–1992.* Taped interview with Ted Newland, Cybard, France, Unpublished manuscript, May 1994.

Pettinati, N. (1998, February 13). (1998, June 24). [Letter to Eve Wack]. Copy in possession of Eve Wack.

Excerpt from personal communications with Fiona Youlton. Author held interviews and discussions in 2014–16.

Wilkinson, A., & Kupers, R. (2013). Living in the futures. *Harvard Business Review, 91*(5), 118–127.

Wilkinson, A., & Kupers, R. (2014). *The essence of scenarios: Learning from the Shell experiences.* Amsterdam: Amsterdam University Press.

Cornelius, P., Van de Putte, A., & Romani, M. (2005). Three decades of scenario planning in shell. *California Management Review, 48*(1), 92–109.

DuMoulin, H., & Eyre, J. (1979). Energy scenarios: A learning process. *Energy Economics, 1*(2), 76–86.

80    *The Shell Years*

Kolk, A., & Levy, D. (2001). Winds of change: Corporate strategy, climate change and oil multinationals. *European Management Journal, 19*(5), 501–509.

Kleiner, A. (1996). *The age of heretics: Heroes, outlaws, and the forerunners of corporate change.* New York: Doubleday.

Kleiner, A. (2008). *The age of heretics: A history of the radical thinkers who reinvented corporate management* (Vol. 164). New York: John Wiley & Sons.

Transcript of tapes 1, 2 and 3 from GBN Scenario Planning Seminar 19 April 1993 [transcription by Peggi Oakley, 2 copies]. Document retrieved from the Pierre Wack Memorial Library, University of Oxford.

Transcript of tapes 4 and 5 from GBN Scenario Planning Seminar 19 April 1993 [transcription by Peggi Oakley, 2 copies]. Document retrieved from the Pierre Wack Memorial Library, University of Oxford.

Transcript of 'Wack @ Curemonte' from Tape 1/Side A to Tape 5/Side A [94 pages, 2 copies]. Document retrieved from the Pierre Wack Memorial Library, University of Oxford.

Wack, P. (1994). *Speech & interviews* [37 pages, 2 copies]. Document retrieved from the Pierre Wack Memorial Library, University of Oxford.

Photocopied pages from Srinivasan. (1987). *Talks with Swami Prajnanapada,* pp. 114–137. Document retrieved from the Pierre Wack Memorial Library, University of Oxford.

Burt, G. (2006). Pre-determined elements in the business environment: Reflecting on the legacy of Pierre Wack. *Futures, 38*(7), 830–840.

Burt, G. (2010). Revisiting and extending our understanding of Pierre Wack's the gentle art of re-perceiving. *Technological Forecasting & Social Change, 77,* 1476–1484.

Ehrlich, P. (1968). *The population bomb.* New York: Ballantine.

Ehrlich, P. (1970). The population bomb. *New York Times,* p. 47.

Ehlrich, P. (2015). *The population bomb. Thinking about the environment: Readings on politics, property and the physical world.* London: Routledge

Ehrlich, P., & Ehrlich, A. H. (2009). The population bomb revisited. *The Electronic Journal of Sustainable Development, 1*(3), 63–71.

DeWeerd, H. A. (1967). *Political-military scenarios* (No. RAND-P-3535). Santa Monica, CA: Rand.

Excerpt from personal communications with Napier Collyns. Author held interviews and discussions in 2014–16.

Excerpt from personal communications with Ged Davis. Author held interviews and discussions in 2014–16.

Royal Dutch/Shell Oil. (1973). *Scenarios for the 1973 planning cycle.* Unpublished internal document. Copy in possession of the Pierre Wack Memorial Library, University of Oxford.

Royal Dutch/Shell Oil. (1973). *The impact on the world economy of developments in the market for oil.* Unpublished internal document. Copy in possession of the Pierre Wack Memorial Library, University of Oxford.

Excerpt from personal communications with Ray Thomasson. Author held interviews and discussions in 2014–16.

Wack, E. (n.d.). *Quelques dates et événements de la vie d'un "homme remarquable": Pierre Wack* [draft; 12 pages with note by Eve Wack]. Document retrieved from the Pierre Wack Memorial Library, University of Oxford.

Wack, E. (1998). *Pierreve: 1977–1997.* Curemonte, France, Unpublished manuscript.

Hindle, T. (2008). *The economist guide to management ideas and Gurus*. New York: Bloomberg Press.

Guru: Pierre Wack. Adapted from: Hindle, T. (2008). *The economist guide to management ideas and Gurus*. New York: Bloomberg Press. Published online: http://www.economist.com/node/12000502/ Accessed August 26, 2016.

Hines, A. (2015). *Exploratory and decision scenarios*. Blog post: http://www.andyhinesight.com/tag/pierre-wack/ Accessed September 3, 2016.

# 5 Regrouping and Modifying the Scenario Method (1974–77)

*Pierre asked Fiona to order him the standard lunch (for whenever he ate in his office), which was smoked salmon, brown bread and butter, a small side of coleslaw, a glass of white wine, and an orange for dessert. It had been a busy morning. As he finished his lunch, he pored over the documents, newspaper clippings and magazines he had collected over the last three months. A global economic storm was brewing. He proceeded to try to get his head around the materials that absorbed the small table at which he preferred to work. His desk was usually too full to be of use. Pierre glanced over at one of his favorite sumi paintings, which hung on the wall behind his desk, framed by vertically striped orange and white curtains that went from ceiling to floor. He was looking for inspiration. How would he convince others? He recalled that Svamiji told him exactly that—his task was not only to "see" things as they really are, but also, and perhaps more importantly, to convince others to "see" as well.*

The scenario team at Shell was already an impressive set of innovative thinkers, but more importantly, they had synergy. Pierre Wack, Ted Newland, and Napier Collyns were in place. Wack and Beckers built their teams quickly by adding consultants. While the efforts of Wack and Newland made unique contributions that bolstered scenario work and its acceptability among the CMD, Beckers was making progress on the strategy side, too. His task was to integrate the insights from the scenarios into the tactical side of the business.

## Turning the World Upside Down

The culture of the scenarios team was solid and developed quickly. Wack and Newland "were like Tweedle Dum and Tweedle Dee," according to Newland. They rapidly came to appreciate each other's talents and unique ways of looking at things, but it was too early to know how important their synergy would be. Once Collyns was added to the team and gained success with the "Blue" and "Pink" books, he became a critical part of sustaining and solidifying the use of scenarios inside Shell. He recalled:

We were turning the world upside down. In a way, you had to be very courageous to do it. I reckon it took me about six months really to cope with it. But once you've learned how to think, then the rest of your life is completely changed and you always think scenarically. No matter of fact person could have coped with it: they would find it very confusing.

The excitement around what was developing was tangible. Wack, Newland and Collyns knew they were onto something important and were learning how best to articulate their new approach. As the team was growing, personalities were also evolving. As with any team, there are personalities, perspectives and mental models that are not always immediately compatible.

While Wack, Newland and Collyns had formed a trio; (perhaps the three musketeers is an appropriate comparison), additions to the team sometimes struggled to find a place. Wack was known to avoid trite conversation and chitchat. According to Peter Schwartz, "He was a man who spoke little and did a lot. He believed in the power of silence and the carefully spoken few words rather than the babble of ordinary conversation." Some even described Wack as being quite shy. He was an intellectual and deeply introspective man. It was further clear that Wack's prior work in modelling at Shell Francaise gave him perspectives he valued deeply. He entered Shell Francaise when he was 38 years old as Chief Economist. He worked on forecasting and was asked to manage the planning function from top to bottom. But planning against the numbers and the models was not something he found interesting. His wife Eve again reflected on this theme: "He didn't want to feel trapped . . . ever. Not by people in his life, not by companies, not by economic models . . . he wanted to be free. That was his greatest pursuit." His experiences with modelling in the early days at Shell Francaise led him to conclude: "Forecasts and models are simply someone else's judgment, crystallized in a figure, that substitutes for thinking on the part of the user," and "computer models are the enemy of thought." As the teams brought on more economists, trained in models, there would be disagreements on how to "see" the world.

## The Team

Wack was always clear about the importance of the team, yet he was increasingly seen as the leader of scenarios. "What you do in this field so enormously depends on the quality of your team," he said. In his work published in the *Harvard Business Review* he always used the terms "we" and "our" when referring to the scenario work and its insights. And his accounts of the work they were doing suggested that all members were required to make unique contributions, or they quickly found themselves in other positions. Wack had little tolerance for non-contribution and he often tested individuals for their abilities to add value. If they could not . . . well, there were no free-riders in Group Planning at Shell under Wack's leadership.

According to many accounts, Wack did not actively seek individual credit for the work of the team, but accepted the requirement that scenarios have a leader. Because of his deep passion for what they were doing—he often said he would have paid to do it—he accepted the role and performed it to the best of his ability.

Overwhelmingly, people described Wack as being introverted at his core. He had to learn how to take on a stage role, create an extroverted part of himself and deliver the presentations he became so famous for again and again. Collyns recalled the way Wack would withdraw, become silent and take on a whole new persona in the minutes before a presentation: "He always had a habit before he spoke of going almost into a kind of trance. You know, he had a special kind of body, and he would shiver with his body for about five minutes before he would speak. Which I happen to know, but he always did that type of thing in private, obviously." It was a real transformation.

In Davidson's recollection years after retirement, he commented: "Now Pierre of course by the nature of his presentation and public appearances was the most visible, and his success in formulating gradually more convincing scenarios was really beyond my greatest expectations. He was a natural for the job." Yet, without question, it was a job he needed to learn, and it took years for him to hone his expertise in communicating scenarios.

## Michael Jefferson

Michael Jefferson joined Shell as its first Group Chief Economist in January, 1974, having been recruited from the outside as the 1973 "oil crisis" broke. Jefferson was initially hired on a three-year contract. His background in the Middle East, economic and social history, and a family connection to a former Chairman of Shell were all advantages.

Of course, the 1973 scenarios—the Rapids—had already been developed and were being presented around the company. According to Jefferson, the "Rapids" was a scenario framework that emerged earlier than most report. In fact, the label surfaced in 1973—January to be specific, and Wack's account agrees on this. The title had been conjured up by Gareth Price. The "Rapids" was a larger framework on which more specific scenarios could be built, and reflected the thinking about detailing more narrow sets of shorter-term scenarios that became known as decisions scenarios. In 1974, the scenario team was beginning to work on the short to medium-term using more decision-focused scenarios, but they were not yet a fully understood practice.

When Jefferson arrived, he immediately went to work on the planning assumptions of the Operating Companies following the 1973 "Rapids" scenarios and early weeks of the "oil crisis." He felt the work missed critical elements related to inflation and recession impacts. For him, these were important omissions from the original scenario set. Pointing to a weak analysis of macroeconomic implications contained in the 1973 scenarios, Jefferson worked diligently to fill in the wide-ranging effects. His efforts were intended to bring a scope of realism to the scenarios that needed more detailed economic figuring. While the scenario effort was gaining traction within Shell and the CMD—even the managers were starting to use them— Jefferson recognized significant missed opportunities.

The Operating Companies' planning assumptions in late 1973 and early 1974 referred to expected short-term annual inflation rates (ranging up to 5 percent) and continued GDP growth, while there seemed to be a consensus that OPEC-member countries would not be able to absorb their additional oil export revenues. Jefferson disagreed with all three points, indicating that short-term inflation rates could rise up to 15 percent, GDP could be up to six percentage points lower than some assumed, and OPEC countries would have no problem "recycling" their additional revenues. This caused ripples in some quarters. The original set of 1973 scenarios did not contain any attention to inflation rates or how the potential spike would affect the key countries involved. Jefferson reflected: "The topic of inflation so interested the then Co-ordinator of Group Planning, Jimmy Davidson, that he backed the writing of a history of inflation going back 2000 years."

## In the Green—1974

As the team was working to expand the 1973 scenarios, they needed once again to go "in the green" and spend some time thinking through the major plots and their implications. In 1974 the team went back to Lurs—the monastery—to deeply engage with each other and debate the possibilities of what was coming. Collyns was involved this time and recalled a set of very "upset tummies" as they considered what was on the horizon. Wack recalled, "We came back in [Napier's] little Volkswagen bus, a very nice trip, and it was a very nice place. We were not disturbed by anything. It was a beautiful little village where you have a wide view on both sides. That was a turning point." Wack continued to weave his interests in unconventional thought into the off-site sessions and introduce ideas from vastly different perspectives. He would increasingly invite outsiders to the "in the green" sessions as a means of challenging and breaking the team's own oil mental model. In this way, Wack's travels and relentless curiosity for alternative points of view directly influenced scenario planning at Shell. He literally brought his worldly travels to the scenario development sessions. He also stressed getting the team away from their routines and into alternate spaces. According to Newland, "Pierre always sought encouragement for the team by promoting existential inspiration, for example, visits to Picasso country and extraordinary landscapes." He would choose the locations with the aesthetics he thought would be conducive to scenario development.

On the return drive to London the team detoured through a massive gorge. Excitement was high among the eight brilliant thinkers in the VW bus. The team had realized the potential of scenarios, and they spoke excitedly about setting up their own scenario planning consultancy. Their conversation was so engaging that Collyns, who was at the wheel, recalled taking his eyes of the road to engage with his colleagues and they almost went over the side, deep into that gorge.

Jefferson also recalled the 1974 Lurs session:

> Shell's scenario team in the 1970s would meet in various locations for five or six days "in the green." There would be seven to nine participants, guided by Pierre Wack. Meetings would start around 8.30 in the morning and carry on until lunchtime. Then there would be a long break until 4.00 or 4.30 pm, when a late afternoon session would carry on until about 7.00 pm. After that it was time for a good dinner, washed down with some good quality wines.
>
> The most memorable places where the scenario group met were Lurs, in the Alpes-de-Haute-Provence; and Villequier, in Normandy. Lurs is situated among the Luberon hills and itself on top of one of them. A village full of ancient buildings, the scenario group met in a former Seminary, which the Bishops of Sisteron had built and long maintained for the training of clergy but by the 1970s had come into the ownership of Shell Francaise. In the afternoons, for those who cared to do so, there were lovely walks—one along the Promenade des Eveques being particularly memorable, and several having fine views over the River Durance. In the evening we repaired to the local auberge for a very satisfactory supper.
>
> The members of the scenario team for most of the 1970s included Ted Newland, Gareth Price, Napier Collyns, Hans DuMoulin, Michael Jefferson, and later, Graham Galer. Their number was added to from time to time by other Shell planners and some of Wack's "remarkable people."
>
> At the 1974 meeting in Lurs two long-term scenarios were produced: a "World of Internal Contradictions" and a "New Belle Epoque." The latter was issued in October, 1974—a full year after the first oil 'crisis' had begun, and created more dissent within Group Planning than elsewhere, because it was perceived by some to be far removed from reality. It had its source in the work of the Hudson Institute and the influence of Herman Kahn, faithfully transmitted by Ted Newland.

Indeed, the scenario team was not immune to disagreement and the inability to reach consensus, but Wack never advocated for consensus. Jefferson and DuMoulin were clearly "seeing" the environment differently from Wack and Newland. Jefferson and DuMoulin viewed the "Belle Epoque" scenario in particular as overly optimistic and unable to stand up if subjected to their analysis. This tension would continue to grow, though all involved recalled a degree of respectful disagreement that categorized those early meetings.

## Samadhi

Shortly after returning from Lurs in 1974, Wack received word that Svamiji Prajnanpad had died. The guru entered Samadhi on Sept 24, 1974. Samadhi is a term used in reference to a specific state of being. Samadhi refers to a deep state of meditation, absorption, or trance known to monks and yogis. It is often referred to as a one-pointedness of mind. In India, it is common to refer to someone who has died as someone who has entered Samadhi.

Patanjali's eight components of yoga conclude with Samadhi. The eight components, sometimes referred to as "paths" or "limbs," include: (1) Yamas (non-violence, truthfulness, non-stealing, fidelity and non-possessiveness), (2) Niyamas (clearness of mind, spirit and body, acceptance of others, perseverance, self-reflection, contemplating a "True-self"), (3) Asanas (yoga postures—literally, "posture holding still, breathing always normal"), (4) Pranayama (control of breath), (5) Pratyahara (withdrawal from external objects / materialism, and a focus within), (6) Dharana (focusing the mind on an inner state), (7) Dhyana (contemplation and meditation) and finally (8) Samadhi (combining with a whole, harmonious trance).

By accounts of his disciples, Svamiji had faithfully practiced the eight limbs of yoga throughout his adult life. His practices as documented by Roumanoff make it clear that Prajnanpad did not preach, did not force his views on others, only met with his followers one at a time, and made no great leaps to unreasonable demands that can be common with many so-called "masters." Indeed, Wack and Svamiji were great friends for over a decade and it was a relationship of great importance to Wack, but a true master like Svamiji would surely have remained without attachment.

It was this very topic that Wack would recall in his "four pages", transcribed in the Foreword and it became one of the few things he actually wrote about. His pages were originally written in French for inclusion in Roumanoff's book and years later, Collyns ask his wife Eve to translate them while they were going through his documents after he died. Wack famously did not care for his thoughts to be taken down on paper for the public to read. On this occasion, he wrote his story for inclusion in Roumanoff's tribute and biography of Svamiji Prajnanpad in 1993. No doubt Svamiji's passing profoundly affected Wack—his guru was gone. Records and personal histories indicate Wack did not seek to find another, and arguably he was becoming a guru himself.

Wack did not have a specific or emotional reaction to Svamiji's passing. According to Eve, much like his account of Chantal's death years earlier, Wack tended to speak of it without emotion. It was a fact of life, and emotions were a signal of not seeing the situation "as it is." To accept the events of life was the basis of Wack's entire tutelage with Svamiji.

## Scenarios for the 1975 Planning Cycle

The results of the off-site work in Lurs became known as "Scenarios for the 1975 Planning Cycle (October 74)." These were presented and circulated starting in late 1974. The set consisted of two scenarios that played out unique and fundamentally different futures that would become the foundation for several additional scenario books in the coming years. While there was some basis in the previous sets of scenarios, the work in Lurs generated some new direction even though Jefferson and DuMoulin were not fully on board. The resulting scenarios were titled "New Belle Epoque" and "World of Internal Contradictions." The report summarized:

1   Main Themes
    Recent discontinuities in the evolution of the oil and energy market only serve to reinforce the main themes of last year's scenarios:

- growth in demand for energy and especially for oil is constrained due to high prices, international balance of payments considerations and desire for national security.
- while the totality of the oil business grows at a much reduced rate into the eighties, internationally traded oil is likely to peak out in the late seventies at levels little above those of 1973.
- surplus capacity in many phases of the traditional oil business especially in refining and tanker capacity will give rise to structural strains and less attractive profitability prospects.
- extension of participation and constraints on exploitation of natural resources by multinationals is increasingly pushing the private oil industry into the roles of offshore buyer and contractor.
- fairly high levels of inflation in conjunction with political desire to limit rents and windfall profits give rise to continuing controls over prices and profit margins.
- the risk profile on energy investments in these circumstances shifts adversely and calls for the emergence of new institutional arrangements.
- encouragement of alternative energy sources involves a massive diversion of resources but is inadequate to prevent a very tight supply situation from developing in the next decade.
- both in this and the next decade a large potential market for energy conservation emerges.
- this supplements the more evident but risky new markets for supplying new forms of energy such as international trade in coal.
- the most dynamic element in the growth in international trade lies in capital goods, energy related equipment and complex triangular trade arrangements favouring certain Third World countries.
- the major customers of the oil industry will increasingly be the governments of producing and consuming nations. While capital will remain essential, corporate legitimacy will lie progressively in problem solving capacities.

- human resources and in particular knowledge-based skills are the new 'mining rent' of the multinational corporation, especially in the energy sector.

The summary descriptions of both scenarios are as follows:

A  World of Internal Contradictions (WIC)
   Instead we have concentrated first on a world that struggles to grapple with the challenges of turbulence and stress created by the apparent ending of the post-war era. The problems that posed threats to the international system in 1974 are slowly overcome in a world in which national and regional self-sufficiency is slowly made to work. Economic growth rates are held back by the resultant costs of increasing local protection, economic distortion and trading bilateralism and decline from the 4.5–5.0% averaged over 1960–73. The main features of this 'lower growth' world are:

- Persistent conflicts on social objectives inhibit capacity to grow.
- Unsatisfied expectations as 'takers and dreamers' exercise a more influential role.
- Problems tackled in terms of national and regional self-sufficiency.
- Recycling problems contained by lower growth and bilateral agreements.
- Trade grows by 6% p.a., doubling by 1985 but focused on bilateralism.
- High inflation despite considerable government intervention.
- The energy sector is bypassed as an agent of change and evolved on public utility lines.

B  New Belle Epoque (BE)
   Although a lower growth world could result from persistent currency crises, inadequate demand management and unresolvable regional conflicts in the Middle East, the techniques of economic growth are being steadily mastered, the desire for higher standards is a dominant force in world aspirations and increasing numbers of technologists, scientists and communications media give every sign of maintaining the underlying strength of the progressive international growth multiplier.
   After a modest check in 1974/75 a 'New Belle Epoque' is envisaged as emerging on the basis of the US-led recovery and strong growth in the Pacific and Mediterranean basins and in resource-rich territories, backed by effective recycling mechanisms from oil producing countries to both the industrialised and Third World countries. The main features of this 'higher growth' world are:

- New phase of economic mastery, growth ethic and self-confidence.
- Recycling problems overcome, partly by active development of lesser developed countries.

- Trade grows by 10% p.a., almost tripling by 1985 to create a 'one world economy'.
- GWP grows by 5.5–6.0% p.a., doubling by 1985.
- Persistent high inflation rendered acceptable by high growth in market oriented economies.
- The energy sector is a major new catalyst and motor of growth.

The scenario team was still in the process of proving its utility to the CMD and the managers within Shell. Wack, Newland, and Collyns firmly knew and understood their roles, and each became even more expert at playing them. Toward the end of 1974, Collyns went to The Hague as a planner for Shell's European companies and Newland went to Shell Oil in Houston. Both continued to promote scenarios in their planning work.

Some new additions to the team advocated for the modelling benefits, and others worked to bolster the connection to finance. Neither of these were top priority for Wack and the resulting dissonance created challenges. As the primary figurehead for an increasingly important effort within Shell, Wack's opinions took precedence. His towering strengths in the use of metaphor, ease of communication and elegance in presentations worked to reinforce his position as leader within the organization.

There was no manual, no 2x2, no process for creating scenarios. In fact, Wack later stated that he could not actually articulate the "how" of scenario planning. His method of teaching new recruits was simple: They had to join the scenarios team over the course of a year and participate in various projects. It was a true apprenticing experience—consistent with everything we know about teaching practices of the Eastern arts, particularly Japan. Practice, repetition and repetition of the repeated with increasing intensity are the key features of learning Japanese arts. Wack took this approach to teaching scenarios—a mentorship that is time consuming and for which he saw no step-by-step process.

## Jefferson Reflections

As he considered his early days in this era of scenario planning, Jefferson identified several challenges. He recognized the tensions that had been growing:

> In particular, there was serious failure up to early 1974 to understand fully and take due note of forces "already in the pipeline"; failure to draw on past experience—from economic and social history, from past financial crises, from the operation of business organisations and industrial cartels, from past military and religious conflict; from the history of the Middle East (especially the Gulf); and failure to assess sufficiently the risks of taking ones' eye off the short and medium term for whatever reason.

Two key issues stood out to Jefferson about the 1973–75 scenario work, namely (1) that the scenarios had not adequately thought through their recessionary and inflationary aspects, and (2) there was a failure to recognize that OPEC could stay intact for many years, and member countries would easily be able to spend their oil revenue reserves.

Jefferson also perceived a tendency toward overly optimistic outlooks, particularly in a few of the scenarios such as "Belle Epoque," and later "The Carter Miracle" and "Californian Mirage" that "were clearly overly optimistic and unreal." They just didn't fit with what was known about the economic figuring at the time. Further, he felt that far too many resources were put into those scenarios without a stronger connection to reality, again citing the recession, inflation aspects and his reading of social and economic history as well as behavioral economics. After Jefferson repeatedly raised his concerns to Wack, he was invited to join the scenario team officially in October 1974, and transitioned from a three-year consulting contract to permanent employee status.

Jefferson questioned the benefit of Wack's travels around the world to find remarkable people. He had no doubt these individuals were interesting people, but they knew nothing about oil. Further, Wack's dedication to meditation and Eastern philosophy did not deliver anything significant in Jefferson's eyes, and Wack's interests in the Californian "voluntary simplicity" promoted by the Stanford Research Institute bore little relation to the basic realities Jefferson had been studying.

The tensions described by Jefferson provide insight into the dynamic people involved who had preferences, biases and tendencies, just as any of us do. While the majority of people who knew him had a high regard for Wack, some recall a potential for dismissal, and a lack of interest in things he did not find important. He could be difficult. Davidson recalled, "If things didn't go his way, he would tend to get up and walk out." It is obvious Wack did not get along with everyone. Wack's later wife Eve recalled, "When he had something to say, he just said it. When you are angry, when you explode you have the cover too long on the pan . . . so it explodes. Because he always said what he wanted it was much easier for him, he did not put the cover on the pan." This open way of communicating was not always easy for the people around him. The accounts of this history further demonstrate that while mental models were the focus of scenario efforts in Shell, no one is immune to the fact that mental models get stuck, leading us to reject ideas, things and unfortunately, people. Luckily, such tensions among the different personalities in the work group actually led to better scenarios, as Jefferson's recollections indicate.

Another challenge was that, at times, the Managing Directors dictated what figures the scenario books could and could not contain. There was a political nature to it all, and if some outsiders knew all the details of the thinking going on inside Shell, they would have panicked. There were several cases in which the CMD instructed Group Planning to bring down their estimates of demand, price and other variables simply because they thought policy makers outside Shell would be too shocked if they ever found out about the conversations going on internally and the numbers they were throwing around.

## Breathing In and Out

According to Newland, it was around this time (late 1974) that Wack generated more metaphors and included concepts from eastern philosophy to describe the scenario approach. For example, he used the term "breathing in" to refer to all of the data gathering, the "in the green" sessions, and seeking out and meeting with remarkable people. With a constantly expanding network of such individuals around the world, he had access to many different points of view, and could justify his travel as part of his "breathing in." Youlton recalled:

> His love of travel was legendary. He never went straight to a place and back home again. We would spend ages trying to find out the best route for visiting the most places en route to his main destination and on the return. He was often gone from the office for several weeks. But of course, he did his best thinking in out-of-the-way places. The most irritating thing about these arrangements was that he frequently changed his mind about where to go or which airline to use. And he sometimes went back to the original plan, but I became used to it!

"Breathing out" referred to the presentations he would make to the CMD and inside the Operating Companies, as well as the reports they generated. Of course, the "breathing in" took significantly more time, effort and resources. His use of these terms and the way he talked about planning added to his mystique and lent an air of intrigue to the scenario team's activities. Newland later commented—with a smile—that if one paid attention, Wack almost always smelled of sulphur, a clever reference to the fact that Wack often had the persona of a magician, which he sometimes promoted.

## Four Year Industry Outlook 1975–78 (February 1975)

After the "Scenarios for the 1975 Planning Cycle" were developed and circulated, additional support exercises were undertaken. It is important to note that from this point forward, many of the various scenario books are not actually held in the Pierre Wack Memorial Library at Oxford. Further, according to Wack's assistant Cheryl Aldons, when Shell moved Group Planning to The Hague in 1987, many of the scenario archives were lost or destroyed. However, Doug Wade compiled a listing and summary of scenario work from 1971–92. In the cases where the actual document could not be found, Wade's comments are provided. The "Four Year Industry Outlook" essentially explored the short-term implications of the 1975 scenarios.

"World of Internal Contradictions" was a finer look at the same previous scenario by the same title, with specific attention to economic and energy oil factors through 1978. "Depression Contingency" covered oil demand specifically, as well as the configuration of OPEC, though stated that a breakup of OPEC was not likely to occur. These were nested, focused scenarios using the previous scenarios as the global framework.

## Short-Term Scenarios

In the aftermath of the first oil shock in 1973, Wack and the team came to another important insight. The scenarios presented in 1974 concerning the "Rapids" held the major shakeup of the oil industry as a predetermined element. The uncertainties were related to how certain groups would react (producers, consumers, governments). Once the discontinuity had arrived, Wack wrote: "everyone's attention was focused on the short-term economy and its cyclical fluctuations. Such short-term fluctuations would pattern not only economic growth, but oil demand and inflation rates, currency and interest rates, and the sensitive OPEC supply-demand relationship and its politics." The test was now to see if the scenario method could have utility with shorter timelines. The best insight into this discovery is covered in "The Gentle Art":

### 1975 Scenarios for the Rapids—The Uncertain Part

We had spent a lot of time developing the PREDETERMINEDS. The bridge we had built was now firmly anchored in our decision-maker's experience, since we had gone back far enough to include those events which had already unfolded and of which they were painfully aware. We also took care in this rooting process to develop those matters which, while not yet evident, would almost certainly occur. Reflation of economies would be the expression of the "Predetermineds." What was unknown was the timing of the recovery and the nature of it.

We designed two recovery scenarios:

> *Boom and Bust*—a vigorous recovery which had within it the seeds of its later destruction.
> *Constrained Growth*—A kind of muddling-through recovery but fundamentally different than earlier business cycle recoveries.

The two scenarios are depicted in Chart XIV. We allowed, too, for the possibility that reflations might not happen (for whatever reason), but including a *Depression Contingency*; it seemed so improbable, however, that it was not considered relevant for planning.

*Boom and Bust* described a world which develops in cycles of greater amplitude and shorter duration than those of the 1960s, more characteristic, in fact of the 1950s. It was clear that the longer the recover was deferred, the more likely this scenario would become as governments turned to panic measures to reflate their economies.

## Japanese Flowers in London

In 1975, Wack met a Japanese woman named Yuko Iwanade. He had put an advertisement in the London newspaper looking for someone skilled at Ikebana (Japanese flower arranging). He offered room and board at his flat to someone who could compose a series of Ikebana arrangements for him to be used in a variety of settings. A young Japanese woman by the name of Yuko Iwanade responded and soon came to take up residence with Wack. It wasn't long before their association turned romantic. A few years later, in order to marry her, he would have to pass an "exam" with her father. This was one of the few occasions in which Wack described himself as being particularly upset. According to his later wife Eve, he did not see why he should have to be presented to her father, but Japanese customs required it. Wack was not often angry, but this was an occasion reflecting his intolerance for what he viewed as unimportant formalities.

## Scenarios for the Eighties: An Update (January 1976)

This document was developed for use in the 1976 planning cycle. The summary from the report highlighted these general points:

- The framework scenario concepts of "Belle Epoque" and "World of Internal Contradictions" are still considered valid.
- Global economic growth is projected to average 5 percent per annum for the "Belle Epoque" and 3 percent per annum for the "World of Internal Contradictions" through the 1980s.
- Inflation is expected to be about 6 percent over the 1980s, but is a major uncertainty.
- Little change is expected in the current mix of activities which make up GNP.

The report was an update to the earlier Four Year Industry Outlook generated in 1975 and played out several other variables with updated economic figuring.

## Scenarios for the Rapids: A Review (May 1976)

This report was an update to the Scenarios for the Rapids set. The document presented the "Constrained Growth" and "Boom and Bust" scenarios with updated figuring, and added a third scenario called "Recovery Turns Sour." The summary from the introduction to the report stated:

> The turn-around of the major OECD economies in 1975 is giving rise to concerted growth in early 1976. The stability and strength of this recovery, however, is largely uncertain and has therefore been analysed in terms of three possible patterns of future development:
>
> • Constrained Growth (CG), a scenario of moderate economic cyclical growth;
> • Boom and Bust (BB), one of pronounced oscillation in growth rates, and;
> • Recovery Turns Sour (RTS), in which the initial boost from pump priming and inventory restocking peters out in the face of weak consumer demand, erratic trade prospects, adverse investment prospects and political accidents."

The report went on to summarize various environmental drivers (oil price, tankers, cut of the barrel, chemicals, coal, natural gas, etc.).

## A Visit to Shell Oil in Houston

In 1976 Wack took another trip to Shell Oil in Houston. At the time, Newland was stationed there trying to get the 69 percent-owned affiliate in Houston, Texas, to adopt scenarios. They had been there three years earlier with no success. This time, Norman Duncan had recently joined the planning team and their focus was what was happening in the social change domain. A few months earlier, Duncan's boss had visited London and it did not go well. After spending a few days in Houston, it is not clear if any further progress was made.

However, given the scenario focus on social change, Newland, Wack, and Duncan took off on a tour of Chicago, Seattle, San Francisco, and New York to "breathe in" what they could about social change. They visited Sears in Chicago, Weyerhaeuser in Seattle, and Hewlett-Packard and the Electric Power Institute in Silicon Valley. They also made a stop at the Institute for the Future and met with Roy Amara and Ted Lipinski. They came to major insights on interview questions and techniques. Amara and Lipinski shared their views about an approach for the potential to access mental models. This brought on a new set of interesting questions. They took a tour of Lake Tahoe and drove through Yosemite National Park.

## The Seven Questions

The meeting with Amara and Lipinski led to an innovation that began to change the nature of Shell's scenarios. Wack already understood that scenarios needed to be closely connected with managers' mental models, but how to achieve this connection was not clear. He picked up a set of questions from The Institute for the Future, one of which became a favorite question for the rest of Wack's life—the Oracle question. Wack revised the questions over the years, and within his personal documents is a single page titled "The Seven Questions." Unfortunately, there is not a date associated with the document. Still, it is meaningful to see the questions as Wack used them.

## THE SEVEN QUESTIONS

(not fixed but modified and evolving)

1   *The Oracle*   If you could visit with someone who really could foretell the future, are there any questions that you might like to ask?
2   *Good World*   What is your perception of an optimistic, but realistic world future, and its implications for Shell?
3   *Bad World*   What is your perception of a pessimistic, but not catastrophic world future, and its implications for Shell?
4   *Corporate Culture*   Where would your perception of the culture Shell will need to develop in the future differ from what now exists?
5   *Looking Back*   What have we not done well, where we had the information to do better, and what can we learn from this?
6   *Critical Choices*   What are the critical decisions which the Group is preparing to take, or should prepare to take, over the next 5–10 years?
7   *Personal Vision*   If you could personally choose the vision for Shell, is there anything further that you would wish to contribute? (This question has evolved from 'For what would you personally like to be remembered?).

Wack never provided any guidance about exactly how to use the interviews, and he certainly had no elaborate data analysis process. Based on what we know about the way he tended to operate, it is almost certain that he used these interviews as windows into the concerns of the people who would be using the scenarios. He coupled this information with his remarkable people, intuitive abilities and his gifts for understanding relationships, systems and interdependencies.

## Willis Harman and SRI

After their fruitful time at the Institute for the Future, and as part of continuously, "breathing into" the scenario work, Wack, Newland, and Duncan made their way back to San Francisco. They stopped for one more meeting in the bay area. Wack's interests had evolved beyond his guru in India (who had passed away a few years ago) and monks in Japan and now included anyone he heard was unique or unconventional—particularly those with somewhat provocative reputations.

Wack became aware of Willis Harman and wanted to stop and see him. At the time, Harman was leading the Futures program at the Stanford Research Institute. Formerly a Professor of Engineering at Stanford, Harman had a series of experiences that led him to deeply question his view of knowledge. He became aware of many emerging ideas through a combination of curiosity and the recommendation of close friends and colleagues. At one particular meeting, he recalled:

> I realized that the discussion leader, a dignified and scholarly professor of business and law, was convinced of the reality of various psychic phenomena that I "knew" reputable scientists had debunked. For the next few months I spent all the time I could in the Stanford Library, reading avidly about topics I had barely heard of before—psychotherapy, mysticism, even parapsychology. It was a great shock to my ideals of scientific objectivity and neutrality to realize that there was far more research in this area, and of far better quality, than any of my science courses had ever led me to suspect.

Harman was deeply interested in things like bio-feedback, guided imagery in healing and auto-suggestive techniques to reduce stress. He concluded that all new ideas begin as blasphemy and came to a point that he realized even our modern reining champion—"Science" itself—was born the same way:

> Surprisingly, in the case histories of scientists, we found that not only many specific scientific discoveries but the very foundations of science itself were built on breakthrough experiences, later backed up by empirical investigation. It is ironic that science, the institution that has most strongly branded these kinds of experiences as daydreams, delusions, or hallucinations, appears to have been born in just such a state—in a fever dream, in a flash to an individual who could not solve the problem with the conscious portion of the mind.

Consciousness was something that grew in importance for Harman and he was eventually asked to join the Institute for Noetic Sciences as President in 1977. Harman pointed out on numerous occasions that language is also a key indicator linked to the mind in ways we do not fully understand. For example, the term "inspire" literally means "inner breath," and the term "insight" literally means "looking within."

It is easy to see why Wack would want to meet him. They were both fascinated by the human mind and agreed further understanding was needed. Wack wrapped up his tour of the US with Newland and Duncan at SRI, spending time with Harman and his colleague Arnold Mitchell. Harman had a young and impressive staff of extremely motivated and bright people who would also pique Wack's interest.

Harman would go on to extreme experiments with psychedelic drugs and their effects on the brain. It was common in the mid 1970s in California. Newland even recalled a particular project at SRI in partnership with the US Central Intelligence Agency focused on mind reading. According to Schwartz, Wack viewed the use of drugs as a false consciousness and an inauthentic approach to exploring the human mind. He viewed thinking about the future as a deeply rigorous mental discipline, a very serious endeavor, not something to be fooled around with.

## A Young Man in California

On the same trip to California in 1976, after meeting with Harman and Mitchell, Harman took Wack across the hall to meet a young man named Peter Schwartz. Schwartz had just finished working on a scenario exercise for the Environmental Protection Agency in the US. Schwartz gave Wack an overview of the project—literally in a spontaneous "blackboard presentation." Wack asked a few questions and politely gathered his things and left. Schwartz recalled his immediate impressions of Wack:

> He was quite cryptic. Had a vaguely Asian look, a heavy French accent—but we immediately hit it off. We had several common interests, particularly the idea that the human mind was capable of remarkable leaps of perception. As a result, we formed an intellectual bond, but he certainly seemed strange to me. I had not had much experience with business executives as I was 29 years old at the time. He did not fit my image of what a corporate executive should look like. He seemed very interested but he was very difficult to get a read on.

Two days later, Schwartz received a telex from Shell and Wack asking him to come to London for two years: "I turned it down, thinking 'this is nuts'—I don't know this man and I have no desire to up and move to London." Schwartz continued to work at SRI and later reflected that if he had gone to Shell for those two years he probably would not have been selected as Wack's successor. Schwartz wanted to hone his own scenario skills and carve a path of his own. In the end, he got the best of both worlds. Wack kept him on his menu of remarkable people and often invited him to various functions, meetings and several of the famous "in the green" sessions.

The scenario work continued with a stable but flexible scenario team. Various interpretations of what the 1980s would bring were bouncing around Group Planning and given the resources, different scenario packages were being built, often using the "World of Internal Contradictions" and "New Belle Epoque" scenarios as foundations. Wack began interviewing managers as the first step of scenario work after his return from California and discovery of the so-called "seven questions." He began working with the interviews as a way to understand the mental models he was trying to impact. He also hired Peggy Evans to take charge of writing the scenario books. Wack felt they lacked style and from this point on, the scenarios took a more narrative form.

## Meetings in Yoga Postures and Bidding at Christies

Amidst all of this scenario work, Wack was making his way through the various roles he needed to play. It is no secret he was not the usual "Shell Man." Ever the eccentric, it is not clear if he performed all of his antics intentionally or it was just who he was. Another anecdote captures the kind of thing that was so common for Wack but so surprising to others. Robert Tsenin came to planning to interview in 1976. He was Australian:

> I was being interviewed for a job and had met a procession of grey-suited and very serious Shell executives, that is until my last interview which happened to be with Pierre Wack. On entering his office, I was immediately hit with a smell of incense and Pierre in a complicated yoga position on the floor. He conducted the meeting from that posture!"

Another incident from that year is a story from Keith R. Williams—a short time member of the scenario team:

> One morning Pierre came into my office and said that he wished to bid on a piece of Native Southeast Asian art at Christies but had to appear before the Committee of Managing Directors when the auction was due to take place. Would I go and bid on his behalf? This I readily agreed to as it sounded interesting, so armed with Pierre's blank cheque, I went off and duly acquired this large object for less than Pierre's limit.

## Not Only Magic

Wack's travels continued as usual and were as varied as ever, though his meetings were not always with mystics or people on the fringes of society. Often, they were quite practical and obviously related to his role at Shell. Some did not feel Wack's travels around the world bore any contribution to scenarios at Shell, but where to draw the line? The people he met in more common roles were equally remarkable, and frequently, his meetings took him into other large corporations. In 1976, Wack met with Ian Wilson at General Electric. Wilson wrote:

> One day in the fall of 1976 I arranged a meeting between Pierre Wack, who at that time headed Royal Dutch/Shell's Business Environment component, and some of my colleagues in General Electric's strategic

planning staff. The focus of our discussion was to be on the role of scenarios in corporate planning. At that time, GE had, arguably, the most elaborate and sophisticated strategic planning system in the corporate world, and Shell was enjoying an international reputation for its pioneering scenarios work. Yet in each case, something was missing. Wack was convinced that his scenarios needed a tighter linkage to strategic planning and decision making if they were ever to engage operations managers seriously and continuously. And GE, still shaken and puzzled by the fallout from the first "oil shock," needed to ground its strategy in an assessment of the future that acknowledged, more explicitly, the inherent uncertainties that then marked the future of the business environment. The two parties thus came to this discussion from differing points of view, but focused on the same central need: linking perceptions about the future to current decisions.

Wilson went on to write that the meeting marked a turning point for him, highlighting the absolute necessity of connecting scenarios and decisions. There is no question that Wack took away the same feeling, which he would articulate more clearly a few years later.

## In the Green—1976

Wack and Jefferson continued to have disagreements and their relationship could be described as complex. But Jefferson's ultimate frustration with Wack came in the belief that from March 1976 the Shah of Iran would fall from power and a second "oil crisis" would occur.

In October 1976, when the scenario team met again in Lurs, there was a sharp division of opinion—but this time, more seriously within the scenario team. Jefferson recalled:

At the second meeting in Lurs, in September, 1976 there were now firm signs that the "voluntary simplicity" ideas of the Stanford Research Institute (SRI) were taking a hold of Wack and some of his colleagues. SRI's 500th Report: "Life Ways and Life Styles" had appeared in November, 1973, and had begun to exert some influence. In the opposite corner were me and DuMoulin, both of us considered such societal vagaries were taking the team's eyes off the ball. I recall I even pointed out that the term "voluntary simplicity" had been around since 1936 and was reflected in the Quaker beliefs of its author. Of more direct importance was my concern that the Shah of Iran's regime was profoundly unstable, and the key issue was what the consequences of his downfall were likely to be, including the real possibility of a second oil "crisis." DuMoulin backed me, but there were no other takers and some disappointment ensued.

Jefferson pleaded that the potential fall of the Shah of Iran and its consequences be highlighted in the scenario package and DuMoulin agreed. Months later the next scenario book issued in January, 1977 referred to such events as infeasible. However, Wack agreed to make some Middle East "crisis" a case, but refused to elevate it to the level of the scenario book. Jefferson cites this as a tremendous missed opportunity. If the scenarios had reflected those events, Group Planning would have had another documented case of foreseeing future events.

Jefferson has been clear that the Shell scenarios approach featured a heavy reliance on a few key individuals, namely Pierre Wack and Ted Newland. Yet Jefferson has also fully recognized Wack's abilities to communicate brilliantly to his audiences in what he described as "riveting, powerful and elegant presentations" making full use of a remarkably engaging Gallic style.

## Exploratory Scenarios for the Long Term (January 1977)

This longer-term report played the scenarios out to the year 2000. Again, based on the "World of Internal Contradictions" and "Belle Epoque" scenarios, this document took a longer view of elements such as societal change, consumer logic, lifetime of the oil industry, tanker tonnage, among several other variables. The introduction to the report states:

- This year's long term scenario booklet is issued specifically to meet the Group's planning timetable requirement, although two main exercises underlying the scenarios are still being developed separately in PL. They are mentioned in this document and have already been used to some extent in the preliminary energy quantification. They are:

  1. The Societal Studies.
  2. The Market Vulnerability/Lifetime of the Oil Industry Studies.

- The planning horizon has been extended on an exploratory basis to the year 2000 (Chart 1).
- The economic structure of this year's scenarios has been constructed around the two framework scenarios Belle Epoque (BE) and World of Internal Contradictions (WIC). Following a thorough review of the political and economic assumptions underlying them the scenarios have been revalidated and they remain conceptually similar to those of previous presentations.
  In addition to the diverse societal assumptions underlying BE and WIC, a scenario of substantial change in the societal environment—the Transformed Society—has also been proposed, for critical evaluation and as a tool of understanding (Charts 2 and 3).

Notable in this report is the attention to the societal shifts and transformations to which Jefferson had objected. This is the first time the scenario books reported a specific emphasis on the importance of societal values and the implications of major change in consumer markets.

## Tea, Bar-B-Que and Cotton-Eyed Joe

In late 1977, Norman Duncan visited London from Shell Oil in Houston. He was meeting with Wack at his Lennox Gardens apartment to discuss how the scenario work was coming along in Houston. He recalled a few anecdotes about Wack and his preferences:

> I am about to drink my tea clear. "Do not do that," said Pierre. "There is something very harmful in the theine and you must neutralize it with a little milk." I believe there is some reference to something he learned in India. At any rate, I have *always* taken a little milk with my tea ever since.

A few months later Wack went to Houston again to follow up and Duncan wanted to introduce him to some local Texas culture. They went to a small place shaped like a boat called "Captain Benny's." It was a crowded seafood place, where you stand and eat at the counter. It could be a little rough in the Texas kind of way—all in good fun. When asked what he would like to drink, Wack first went for a glass of wine, but was informed, they only had beer. "A Perrier?" he asked. "Mister," the bartender said, "We only got Tap-ier."

No doubt Wack was surprised by the Texas culture. He had a first experience with barbeque there with Duncan. When Duncan described what it was, "meat, thrown on a fire and left there a long time, smothered in sauce," Wack looked horrified but admitted it tasted much better than in sounded. After this, they went to hear some Texas Country music where the band started playing "Cotton-Eyed-Joe." There is eventually a pause in the song and everyone shouts, "Bull Shit!!" Within this scene, Wack and Duncan were approached by a couple of women who asked them to dance. Wack was a little embarrassed and declined, to which his suitor replied, "Come on, you're not too old!"

## Scenarios for the Rapids (May 1977)

Again drawing from Wade's summary, these scenarios detail recession recovery possibilities in scenarios called "The Carter Miracle," "Convalescence" and "Relapse." "The Carter Miracle" was focused on exactly what it sounds like—President Carter would be able to restore confidence in international trade. "Convalescence" suggested a slow and below normal recovery, and "Relapse" held that Middle Eastern conflict fueled a Saudi resistance to increasing production. These scenarios were more detailed analyses of the "Rapids"—again, a focused set of scenarios within a global one.

## In the Green 1977

The scenario team continued to go "in the green" and develop scenarios aimed at a variety of business issues across the company. The locations were always changing as Wack continued to seek out inspirational and scenic locations. Jefferson described the 1977 meeting:

> The scenario team met in 1977 in University College, Oxford, sleeping and mainly eating in the College. By this time Graham Galer had been responsible for covering societal developments for a year, and the team were joined by Peter Schwartz, who would be Wack's successor five years later. Schwartz had co-authored with Arnold Mitchell the SRI Report: "The Art of Exploratory Planning," which had appeared in December, 1976. There was again tension over the emphasis on societal and individual value changes when some members of the team considered there were much greater short—and longer-term vulnerabilities for Shell's business.

## Exploratory Scenarios for the Long Term: Further Developments (October 1977)

Wade's listing again provides some help with the contents of this report. According to Wade, it was a collection of deeper analyses related to the "Belle Epoque," "World of Internal Contradictions" and "Scenarios for the Rapids" sets. Elements such as market vulnerability and commercial prospects were examined.

With all of the reports and scenario efforts, it is clear that 1974–77 saw a flurry of scenario activity. Many refer to this as the "Golden Age" of scenario planning at Shell. The success coming out of 1973 as the first oil shocks began to occur allowed Shell to react faster than their competitors and significantly improve their market position. As a result, the next several years saw continued investment in scenarios as a critical resource to stay ahead and track the environment. The expanded resources for Group Planning allowed for a degree of experimentation. Again, because of the success of the scenarios in anticipating the 1973 oil crisis, the team now had license to experiment with shorter scenario timelines under the full support of the CMD.

## At the Source

In 1977, January 21 to be specific, Pierre Wack met Eve Baudoin. Wack was at the peak of his career at Shell leading the scenarios program, and he was heavily invested in his work. Eve recalled their first encounter:

> The door opens, I only see the look in his eyes. I don't see the rest of his face. I don't know if he is handsome or ugly. Not very handsome.

Better than that. I am hypnotized by the man's intense look mixed with certain warmth, certainly a smile. My heart beats fast. I hope he likes me, and I am glad I took the time at the hotel to put on make-up and dress elegantly, rare for me. My hair is short. I'd had my long red braid cut off to break with the past. In the last few months I make people call me Eve and no more Evelyne. It is January 21, 1977, I am 32 years old, and Pierre is 54. "Good evening, I am happy to meet you." He is happy, I am seduced.

They spent the rest of their first evening sampling a variety of whiskeys as Wack had just returned from Scotland where he was meeting more remarkable people. She described his apartment in Lennox Gardens as having the feeling of a temple—incense burning, a Japanese painting of a Zen landscape hanging on the wall and low furniture. They go for dinner at an Indian restaurant in London. "English cooking is without interest," he tells her.

Throughout 1977, they saw each other in Paris and in London whenever they could—"About 10 or 12 visits," said Eve. Based in Paris, Eve had no phone at the time but she had given him her office number. She waited patiently and hoped . . . and then one day:

At the office, I hear "How are you?" This sentence would become a ritual. He never identified himself; he leaves it up to the person at the other end to recognize his voice. The formal "vous" was so like him. At all our meetings, he would use the formal "vous" for the first quarter of an hour. He kept his distance.

Baudoin suspected he was a charmer. Most did not regard Wack as a particularly physically attractive man, but his magnetic quality could be extremely seductive. Early on, one morning she discovered a pair of Japanese slippers in his flat, which he explained belonged to a friend who had returned to Japan.

Wack would invite her to London with little notice and these impromptu invitations seemed like challenges to Eve. She was proud of herself for overcoming the various obstacles; "baby sitters, transportation, especially during the holiday season . . . when the planes were full, I took a boat."

They drove to Devon and other locations in the south of England, always taking the little side roads in his Citroen DS. They had all kinds of adventures:

In France, Pierre took me to Le Touquet where, barefooted, eating strawberries, we walked to the market at Berck. About 8 KM, with stops in the dunes—the wind blowing through our hair and the smell of the ocean. At the end of the beach, we had lunch in a restaurant where I was fascinated by the manner in which Pierre devoured a crab. He loved this seafood, and not to lose a gram of the meat he broke every little piece of shell and licked his fingers with a surprising sensuality.

Because his apartment in Paris was being rented, he would often meet her at a hotel. He always left strawberries on the nightstand: "These strawberries, which afterward became a rite at each of our encounters, were reassuring. This beautiful red fruit was a symbol of an uninterrupted affair." She hoped it was intentional and that he was a romantic. On their long drives he would tell her about his work, that he was in Group Planning at Shell and that "My work is my yoga." He told her about Gurdjieff, Svamiji Prajnanpad and his interests in Japan and other spiritual endeavors. He passed along important rules he learned from Svamiji, for example, one always takes a little milk with tea to counteract the cancer-causing theine. He recommended books and said, "Each time I buy a book, I force myself to throw away another one." Surely, it was a magnificent year—both swept up in the excitement of new love: "People, objects, animals, everything that surrounded Pierre, everything that earned his love appeared totally exceptional. He never had a sense of guilt, nor regrets, and turned even the worst events to his advantage." She saved a set of sheets only to be used with him.

Their relationship would last the year over their 10 or 12 memorable meetings and then Wack broke it off until they would meet again 14 years later. On their reunion, they would be together for the rest of Wack's life. In recalling what may have been most powerful about Wack, we turn to another French word: "regard." Eve recalled that the way Wack looked at her—the way he regarded her, meaning the way he 'saw' her was particularly powerful: "It was an unforgettable gaze, as though he could see right through to the core of who I was."

## Chapter 5 Sources (in order of use)

Excerpt from personal communications with Fiona Youlton. Author held interviews and discussions in 2014–16.

Wilkinson, A., & Kupers, R. (2013). Living in the futures. *Harvard Business Review, 91*(5), 118–127.

Wilkinson, A., & Kupers, R. (2014). *The essence of scenarios: Learning from the Shell experiences.* Amsterdam: Amsterdam University Press. Scenarios for the 1973 Planning Cycle.

Royal Dutch/Shell Oil. (1973). *The impact on the world economy of developments in the market for oil.* Unpublished internal document. Copy in possession of the Pierre Wack Memorial Library, University of Oxford.

Excerpt from personal communications with Peter Schwartz. Author held interviews and discussions in 2014–16.

Kleiner, Art, Pierre A. Wack interview in Curemonte. (n.d.). 53 pp. The annotated transcript of an interview between Art Kleiner and Pierre Wack regarding the development of Shell's scenario planning. Retrieved from the Art Kleiner Archive, University of Oxford.

Transcript of tapes 1, 2 and 3 from GBN Scenario Planning Seminar 19 April 1993 [transcription by Peggi Oakley, 2 copies]. Document retrieved from the Pierre Wack Memorial Library, University of Oxford.

Transcript of tapes 4 and 5 from GBN Scenario Planning Seminar 19 April 1993 [transcription by Peggi Oakley, 2 copies]. Document retrieved from the Pierre Wack Memorial Library, University of Oxford.

Transcript of 'Wack @ Curemonte' from Tape 1/Side A to Tape 5/Side A [94 pages, 2 copies]. Document retrieved from the Pierre Wack Memorial Library, University of Oxford.

Wack, P. (1994). *Speech & interviews* [37 pages, 2 copies]. Document retrieved from the Pierre Wack Memorial Library, University of Oxford.

Photocopied pages from Srinivasan. (1987). *Talks with Swami Prajnanpad*, pp. 114–137. Document retrieved from the Pierre Wack Memorial Library, University of Oxford.

Excerpt from personal communications with Ray Thomasson. Author held interviews and discussions in 2014–16.

Kleiner, Art, James C. Davidson telephone interview: Spring 1993. (n.d.). 21 pp. The annotated transcript of a telephone interview between Art Kleiner and James Davidson regarding the development of Shell's Group Planning Department. Retrieved from the Art Kleiner Archive, University of Oxford.

Excerpt from personal communications with Michael Jefferson. Author held interviews and discussions in 2014–16.

Jefferson, M. (2016). Energy realities or modelling: Which is more useful in a world of internal contradictions? *Energy Research & Social Science, 22*, 1–6.

Jefferson, M. (2012). Shell scenarios: What really happened in the 1970s and what may be learned for current world prospects. *Technological Forecasting & Social Change, 79*(1), 186–197.

Jefferson, M., & Voudouris, V. (2011). Oil scenarios for long-term business planning: Royal Dutch Shell and generative explanation, 1960-2010 (No. 27910). Munich: University Library of Munich.

Jefferson, M. (2011). Weaknesses in past Shell scenarios: How they might now be put right. *European Business Review* (May–August), 46–47.

Jefferson, M. (2000). Long–term energy scenarios: The approach of the World Energy Council. *International Journal of Global Energy Issues, 13*(1–3), 277–284.

Jefferson, M. (1982). Historical perspectives of societal change and the use of scenarios at Shell. In B. C. Twiss (ed), *Social forecasting for company planning*, pp. 188–209. London: Palgrave Macmillan.

Excerpt from personal communications with Ted Newland. Author held interviews and discussions in 2014–16.

Kleiner, A. (1996). *The age of heretics: Heroes, outlaws, and the forerunners of corporate change*. New York: Doubleday.

Kleiner, A. (2008). *The age of heretics: A history of the radical thinkers who reinvented corporate management* (Vol. 164). New York: John Wiley & Sons.

Roumanoff, D., & Prajnânpad, S. (1993). *Biographie* (in French). Paris: La Table Rhonde, pp. 262–266.

Excerpt from personal communications with Ged Davis. Author held interviews and discussions in 2014–16.

Patanjali, B. (2015). *The yoga sutras of Patanjali*. BookRix: Online.

Eliade, M. (1975). *Patanjali and yoga*.

Royal Dutch/Shell Oil. (1974, October). *Scenarios for the 1975 planning cycle (October 74)*. Unpublished internal document. Copy in possession of the Pierre Wack Memorial Library, University of Oxford.

Excerpt from personal communications with Eve Wack. Author held interviews and discussions in 2014–16.

Royal Dutch/Shell Oil. (1975, February). *Four year industry outlook 1975–1978 (February 1975)*. Unpublished internal document. Copy in possession of the Pierre Wack Memorial Library, University of Oxford.

Wack, P. (1984). *Scenarios: The gentle art of re-perceiving*. Harvard Business School Working Paper 9–785–042, December 1984.

Wack, E. (n.d.). *Quelques dates et événements de la vie d'un <<homme rearquable>>: Pierre Wack* [draft; 12 pages with note by Eve Wack]. Document retrieved from the Pierre Wack Memorial Library, University of Oxford.

Wack, E. (1998). *Pierreve: 1977–1997*. Curemonte, France, Unpublished manuscript.

Royal Dutch/Shell Oil. (1976, January). *Scenarios for the eighties: An update (January 1976)*. Unpublished internal document. Copy in possession of the Pierre Wack Memorial Library, University of Oxford.

Royal Dutch/Shell Oil. (1976, May). *Scenarios for the rapids: A review (May 1976)*. Unpublished internal document. Copy in possession of the Pierre Wack Memorial Library, University of Oxford.

Duncan, N. (1998, February 14). [Letter to Eve and Jean-Pierre Wack]. Copy in possession of Eve Wack.

Royal Dutch/Shell Oil. (1977, January). *The seven questions: Typed document with the name "Pierre Wack"*. Unpublished internal document. Copy in possession of the Pierre Wack Memorial Library, University of Oxford.

Harman, W. W. (1976). *An incomplete guide to the future*. San Francisco: San Francisco Book Company.

Harman, W. W., & Rheingold, H. (1984). *Higher creativity*. New York: JP Tarcher; Distributed by St. Martin's Press.

Harman, W. W., McKim, R. H., Mogar, R. E., Fadiman, J., & Stolaroff, M. J. (1966). Psychedelic agents in creative problem-solving: A pilot study. *Psychological Reports, 19*(1), 211–227.

Harman, W. (1994). The scientific exploration of consciousness: Towards an adequate epistemology. *Journal of Consciousness Studies, 1*(1), 140–148.

Markley, O. W., & Harman, W. W. (Eds.) (1982). *Changing images of man*. Oxford: Pergamon Press.

Youlton, F. (1998, June 24). [Letter to Eve Wack]. Copy in possession of Eve Wack.

Williams, K. R. (1998, February 11). [Letter to Eve Wack]. Copy in possession of Eve Wack.

Wilson, I. H. (2000). From scenario thinking to strategic action. *Technological Forecasting and Social Change, 65*(1), 23–29.

Wilson, I. H. (1992). Teaching decision makers to learn from scenarios: A blueprint for implementation. *Planning Review, 20*(3), 18–22.

Wilson, I. H. (1978). Scenarios. *Handbook of Futures Research, 84*, 240.

Wilson, I. H. (1998). Mental maps of the future: An intuitive logics approach to scenarios. In L. Fahey & R. Randall (eds), *Learning from the Future: Competitive Foresight Scenarios*, 81–108, New York: John Wiley & Sons.

Royal Dutch/Shell Oil. (1977, January). *Exploratory scenarios for the long term (January 1977)*. Unpublished internal document. Copy in possession of the Pierre Wack Memorial Library, University of Oxford.

Duncan, N. (1998, February 25). [Letter to Eve and Jean-Pierre Wack]. Copy in possession of Eve Wack.

Royal Dutch/Shell Oil. (1977, May). *Scenarios for the rapids (May 1977)*. Unpublished internal document. Copy in possession of the Pierre Wack Memorial Library, University of Oxford.

Royal Dutch/Shell Oil. (1977, October). *Exploratory scenarios for the long term: Further developments (October 1977)*. Unpublished internal document. Copy in possession of the Pierre Wack Memorial Library, University of Oxford.

Senge, P. M. (1992). Mental models. *Planning Review*, 20(2), 4–44.

Review of this chapter and corrections on details regarding Willis Harman provided by Bretton Fosbrook.

# 6 Evolution of Scenarios inside Shell (1978–82)

*The Monastery in Lurs was cold and wet. The rooms were small and the stone walls did not insulate well. Actually, the place had the feeling of a prison. There wasn't even a phone. Going "in the green" was not a comfortable activity by any means, although Wack and Newland agreed it was necessary for the scenario process to maximize its effectiveness and get people to do their best thinking. They needed to frustrate the team until their subconscious minds would take over and then they could get to the essence of a few scenarios. It had been a long day and while the inside of the monastery was rather plain, the scenery outside was inspirational. They had already been at it for two days. Wack anticipated that tomorrow would be the day they would be at each other's throats, and then they could start to make some real progress. Still he knew he would not sleep well; it was raining hard outside and the roof of the monastery leaked.*

Wack continued to develop his network of remarkable people, but his use of the term "remarkable" is often misunderstood. In many ways it is helpful to look to the French language in understanding Wack. His use of the term remarkable is meant from the French origin of the word, *"remarqur,"* which became *"remarqable"* meaning "to take note of." As Kleiner noted in his chapter about Wack, the French word can also be interpreted to mean people with unconventional insight—people with deep curiosity. An appropriate English interpretation could be "worthy of attention, especially as being uncommon or extraordinary." Wack clarified his own definition of remarkable, which many often think he borrowed from Gurdjieff's *Meetings with Remarkable Men*, but that is not the case: "By remarkable, I mean someone outstanding, someone unique and remarkable people were people who were extremely acute observers and were very interested in things. Not the conventional type—it had nothing mystic . . . had nothing to do at all with the sense of Gurdjieff."

Wack's greatest compliment was to call someone remarkable, though it caused anxiety for some—what if you weren't remarkable? You weren't in Wack's inner circle and probably not someone to whom he paid much attention.

Wack was collecting different points of view throughout the world. He cultivated comprehensive thought and cognitive diversity. He challenged his own mental models by continuously interacting with those he thought were interesting people—interesting meaning those he judged to think differently than he did. How many of us do that with such intention today?

The late 1970s saw another period of significant scenario development. The scenario and strategy teams run by Wack and Thomasson were at their peak, involving many in the exciting ideas related to exploring the future in unexpected ways. Wack's team once reached 52 people and Thomasson had a staff of 17. The successes of the early 1970s had already become legendary and the legacy around scenario planning inside Shell continued to grow. But the 1980s were coming and early signs suggested things were going to change wildly again.

The scenarios of the late 1970s continued with three major efforts: "Scenarios for the Next Five Years," "Scenarios to 1985," and "Scenarios for the Long Term." These works continued to explore uncertainties and predetermined elements into the 1980s and beyond.

## Scenarios for the Next Five Years, 1978–83 (June 1978)

This report detailed a set of mini-scenarios within the "World of Internal Contradictions" framework. Societal change, energy development and economic development were major themes that cut differently across three scenarios, namely, "Successful Restructuring," "Constrained Growth" and "Extended Relapse." "Successful Restructuring" featured positive political leadership in a variety of countries and posited growth through new enterprises and technology. "Constrained Growth" recognized the difficulties with achieving the economic milestones that would be required for recovery, and suggested sporadic and inadequate overall political leadership. Finally, "Extended Relapse" showed a significant loss of consumer confidence and more protectionist policies across a variety of powerful nations.

## In the Green—1978

As its primary process for scenario development, the team continued to move out of the office to secluded but inspiring locations selected by Wack. Wack and Jefferson continued in their debates about the importance of dramatic social change and the dynamics of the Middle East:

> By the time the scenario group met in Villequier, in Upper Normandy, in the autumn of 1978 there was some wider recognition that the way ahead could be a bit rocky. Close by the River Seine, the team stayed in a former manor house and ate in a small local restaurant. There were afternoon walks near the Seine, an opportunity to catch up on the life and works of Victor Hugo who had spent much time there, and visits to nearby Caudebec, with its beautiful late Gothic church, and Fontenelle

Abbey, in the village of St. Wandrille. The team had the opportunity to listen to exquisite singing of Gregorian chants.

Among the participants this time was Shell Manufacturing's Planner Gilbert Wawoe. He took the warning signs which some of the scenario team's members were voicing, and asked what the personal investment options might be in such circumstances. The price of gold had already started edging up, by 29% in 1978 over 1977, but it rose 121% in 1979 over 1978. Wawoe was pleased he had followed the signal. For those who still doubt that Shell's scenario planning in the 1970s had financial rewards, here is a further piece of evidence.

## Getting out of the Tanker Business

Scenario team members were always paying attention to any evidence of their impact. Newland was eager to recall a few instances of scenario effectiveness in the late 1970s. The technique was still new, still evolving, and any wins were big wins:

> First we got out of the tanker business early. I was at a board meeting in 1978 when the likelihood of another shock was being presented to them. Gerry Wagner found the case proven and turned to McFadzean who had just ordered five VLCC's and said something to the effect "well, don't worry about it—we all make mistakes" . . . My point is that we got out of the tanker business much faster than other companies. We stopped dead and this made a great difference to our position vis-à-vis our competitors.

This is a specific instance of how scenarios can function as warning systems and guide decision making. Even though McFadzean had ordered the tankers, it was reversible, and Shell, on the whole, halted its orders long before the competition.

## Scenarios to 1985 (April 1979)

According to Wade, by mid 1979 the Group realized that the world was evolving similarly to the "World of Internal Contradictions" scenario and developed four more medium-term scenarios to cover the possibilities. They were "Unrestrained Producer Logic," "Gradualism," "Stabilisation" and "Imposed Consumer Logic." These scenarios highlighted the relationship between the US and Saudi Arabia as well as developments in Iran and perceptions of struggling democracies in developed countries.

## Jefferson's Last Involvement with Scenarios

Jefferson moved to The Hague at the beginning of April 1979, so he was already "moving on:" when the April scenario book was being produced:

"The last Note I have relating to some of this is dated February 20th, 1979. Its title: 'The Wider Implications of Recent Disturbances in Iran.' The changed circumstances expected to shift the Saudi position to one of being a price hawk is one of the numerous elements discussed in this Note."

Jefferson began his new post as Head of Oil Supply Appraisal and Evaluation in Shell's European Organization on April 1, 1979, (taking over from David Varney). He later became Head of Planning in the European Organization in October 1979, (taking over from Napier Collyns). And he carried the scenario work with him: "In November, 1979, I introduced the 'Hard Times' scenario into Shell's European Operating Companies, which proved an accurate reflection of the next seven or so years." While the scenario work in April 1979 was the last that involved Jefferson's direct input, his contributions over the years were significant and clearly shaped the legend of scenarios at Shell. Further, his willingness to challenge Wack leaves us with stories and insights that even legendary teams have their frictions. Perhaps such frictions are required for the work of teams to earn a legendary title.

## Scenarios for the Long Term (October 1979)

Two scenarios—"Restructured Growth" and "World of Internal Contradictions—Revisited"—were developed to provide a better understanding of the business environment evolution into the 1980s. The "Restructured Growth" scenario was built on the assumptions of additional oil shocks and continued price increases. "World of Internal Contradictions—Revisited" described low growth and continued inability to respond to the changing environment, making for minimal progress in transitioning to self-sufficiency for large oil companies.

## Cheryl Aldons

In 1980, there was a shift in the administrative support for Wack and he was to receive a new assistant. Wack had the opportunity to interview a variety of potential aides, which was a new experience for him. Cheryl Aldons was selected and became Wack's assistant from 1980 until his retirement. Aldons recalled the story of how she came to work with him:

> It was January of 1980 when I applied for an interview. I went to meet Pierre and there was an Australian gentleman Alan Crowe who worked in strategic planning. I had a long chat with him and I remember thinking it was quite strange because it was just a general chat and it wasn't an interview. I remember thinking "Where is Pierre?" and after about half an hour Alan said to me "Pierre is very shy, so he asked me to have a chat with you." So eventually Pierre arrived in the doorway and said he was ready for me and I went in. He sat there looking rather sheepish and he said, "You know I just don't know where to start because I've never

recruited a secretary before. My previous secretaries I inherited, so if you were me, what would you do?" And I said, "I think I would choose someone you felt you could work with," and he said, "Ooh I'm sure I could work with you," and I felt it was, you know, typical French charm. We talked nothing about experience or skills or anything like that—I think he thought because I came through the Shell system I would be able to do the job. By the time I went back across the river my boss said, "We're going to be losing you—they've just rang to offer you the job."

Aldons clearly identified Wack as a unique character within Shell. She further recalled her impressions of Wack as she started working with him:

He was extremely unconventional—not like most other Shell managers. He was very indulged because of the creativity and the insights that he brought. He was pretty much given a free reign to follow his interests, to do as much travel as he liked. The budgets didn't apply to him. We would sit down and try to work out the budgets for next year and basically the main question would be "where do you think you might travel next year" so that we would try to build a large enough travel allowance, but again restrictions didn't apply to him. If he heard there was an interesting person in Japan or Singapore or wherever he would just go off to meet them.

Two more scenario books in the late 1980s would be Wack's last. They were "Links from the Medium to Long Term Scenarios, 1980/85 to 1990," and "The Restructured Growth Scenario, 1980/85 to 1990."

## Scenario Impact in Early 1980

Always attentive to showing how scenarios informed decision making, Newland kept a list of the major events related to how their scenario work played out in reality:

We were the first company to upgrade our facilities, particularly in Europe, and this put us ahead of the game by some years. This was worth billions of dollars especially in the early 1980s. The feature of this was that Manufacturing under Jan Choufer made the decision themselves after seeing the scenarios and without planning's help. The probably would never have made this decision without the scenarios.

The impact is hard to argue with here—the scenarios showed the Mangers in Manufacturing just how volatile the future could be and they could make an investment that would advance operations under any of the dynamics they were considering. Further, because they saw the opportunity and had tested it with their scenarios, they could make the move faster than their competitors.

## Up or Out

Wack was initially hopeful to take over for Davidson on his retirement. According to Davidson:

> Pierre expressed to me his desire to succeed me, but I had to point out to him that his value to the Group as a specialist and expert in his current field of activity was far greater than that of being the Coordinator of Planning. He was indeed so very exceptional. At first this was understandably a disappointment for him, but after discussing it with him, his intelligence and reason enabled him to accept this. I arranged that his salary promotion would proceed as one of the Group's most valued specialists.

During his conversations with Davidson, Wack must have realized the administrative implications of becoming Coordinator of Planning. It is likely to have reminded him of his early position in L'Institute des Sciences Politiques, which became an administrative bore. Being promoted to run a division would mean taking on the bureaucratic systems for which he had such intolerance. According to Aldons, he even refused to give performance evaluations to members of Group Planning. As his international reputation as a scenario expert grew, he knew there would be options. His disregard for administrative activities could only mean one thing—it was time to consider options outside Shell.

## Links from the Medium- to Long-Term Scenarios, 1980/85 to 1990 (September 1980)

According to Newland, these were the last scenarios to which Wack made any serious contribution. Building on "Restructured Growth" and "World of Internal Contradictions—Revisited," this report quantified the dynamics of these scenarios under the steadily increasing prices of the 1980s. The report highlighted the potential for further oil accidents fueling a crisis for OPEC, but also the fact that a crisis may pave the way for later recovery under the "Restructured Growth" scenario.

Throughout 1980, Wack's travels continued to contribute to his group of remarkable people and constituted a sort of "intelligence network"—a very unique information gathering system. It may seem elementary to us today, but in the absence of computers, the Internet and social media, Wack's technique for actively seeking wildly alternative and unconventional views was beyond cutting edge for the time and required considerable commitment. And he was able to gain the resources required. Few others (inside and out of Shell) were actively investing anywhere near the level of resources and curiosity in attempting to understand the world differently through finding remarkable people.

The cultivation of a network of remarkable people became the basis of Wack's abilities to understand and integrate far reaching and seemingly unrelated dynamics. It became, as he put it "an addiction; my own luxury," and was certainly a challenge for his assistants who were required to book all of his increasingly complex travel plans. Often, Wack's travels brought unexpected visitors to Shell. Aldons described the frequent results of Wack's visits around the world:

> He would call these people remarkable—"Pierre has met another remarkable person," and he would invite them to come and work with us for a few months. And he wouldn't ever tell anyone, so suddenly, you would find someone arriving in the office and there was no office, no designated space for them. I had to rush around looking for somewhere for them to sit and get them off to HR to have a contract drawn up, but all these little details were just of minor significance to him. What was important was that he got someone to come in and share his original insights with the rest of the group.

## Cherry Trees

This era of scenario work reflects significant evidence of the tiered approach to scenarios. Having used the "Restructured Growth" and "World of Internal Contradictions—Revisited" scenarios as the macro frameworks, many rounds of decision scenarios were constructed related to more detailed issues. Wack would later develop the metaphor of cherry trees to describe this insight. He said you need a trunk, but the blossoms form on the small branches, equating the global scenarios with the trunk and the more focused scenarios with the branches. The blossoms, of course were the insights that came from carefully studying the dynamics.

## Transition and Two-Year Reflection

In late 1980, Arie de Geus asked Wack to spend some time documenting what he had learned about the use of scenarios over the years. After all, Shell had invested considerable resources in scenario planning. Wack was also beginning to think about his activities after retirement from Shell. As a part of his extensive travel, Wack started to work out his reflections on scenarios and what they had come to mean for him and for Shell. He was outside of London extensively in 1981, and frequently attending conferences, meeting with university professors, visiting think tanks, as well as continuing on his own personal adventures. His mind was endlessly curious and he began trying to summarize what he had learned. Wack was given an understudy by de Geus—a Shell insider named Kees van der Heijden, who would try to capture as much knowledge from Wack as he could. Van der Heijden recalled:

I took my job as understudy very seriously and I wanted to pick up what he thought about these things it was not very easy—it was very difficult to get a hold of him, particularly when he was travelling around speaking to all these experts, which he did frequently. I tried to join in, but my own work was not allocated fully for this.

## A Significant Trip to Japan

A particularly fortuitous trip occurred in 1980. An economic conference in Hakone, Japan, (sponsored by Shell—to which Wack invited Yuko, Napier Collyns and his wife Pat, and Peter Schwartz with his wife Frances) would have considerable future implications. Schwartz recalled:

> Shell sponsored various economic conferences as annual events. They were extravagant and quite expensive events—really wonderful. They would bring a group of economic thinkers from around the world and spend three or four days having briefings on oil, energy, etc. . . . in attempt to be influential. It was very stimulating. Pierre invited me as a delegate one year—1980. Napier was there and it happened to be in Hakone Japan. It was absolutely beautiful—just gorgeous. Pierre and Yuko were not yet married at the time. First, we went to Isa, then Kyoto, a village on the coast, maybe Nara? We visited temples, art, gardens and all the unique things Japan has to offer. Pierre loved the food. It was quite wonderful. We stayed at traditional Japanese Ryokan. Having Yuko made it all possible as she spoke Japanese. In those days it was much more difficult to get around Japan if you couldn't speak Japanese. It was a very special visit to Japan and Pierre wanted to share some of his favorite places. We stayed on about a week after the conference.

The trip was a great success, yielding insights that would be valuable for scenario planning at Shell, and solidified already strong relationships among three very important people to scenarios. The trip would also have implications that would be revealed about nine months later.

## Succession Planning

Such adventures were not just random occurrences. There was always intent—Wack had begun to think about his successor. He was searching for someone remarkable to take his place—someone he had been cultivating over the years:

> Pierre often gave me advice. We spoke about things before Shell and after, however it didn't become apparent to me until well into our friendship and collaboration that he had become a real mentor and he had been consciously developing me over the course of the years. He had invited me to participate in a variety of kinds of situations. There

were so many elements, some about interesting people, some about gathering information.

The pair continued to develop their friendship based on mutual interests in the human mind and in Buddhism. And both were steeped in applying these kinds of concepts in a constant search for insight, open to the possibility of understanding that could come anytime, and "all at once."

## Reframing

Van der Heijden recalled that as he travelled with Wack in 1981 and 1982, Wack often carried a little book called *Reframing* by Bandler and Grinder: "The one word I take away from Pierre is reframing. A little bible—it's called reframing. All this work—it is only productive if you can use it to reframe the way you are thinking. Suddenly you see something you didn't see before—and suddenly scenarios become so powerful." The little book sheds some light on Wack's thinking about the uses and processes associated with scenarios. The introduction proceeds:

> A very old Taoist story describes a farmer in a poor country village. He was considered very well-to-do, because he owned a horse which he used for plowing and for transportation. One day his horse ran away. All his neighbors exclaimed how terrible this was, but the farmer simply said "Maybe." A few days later the horse returned and brought two wild horses with it. The neighbors all rejoiced at his good fortune, but the farmer just said "Maybe." The next day the farmer's son tried to ride one of the wild horses; the horse threw him and broke his leg. The neighbors all offered their sympathy for his misfortune, but the farmer again said "Maybe." The next week conscription officers came to village to take young men for the army. They rejected the farmer's son because of his broken leg. When the neighbors told him how lucky he was, the farmer simply replied "Maybe." The meaning that any event has depends on the "frame" in which we perceive it.

As part of his deep interest in mental models, and commitment to using scenarios to challenge how people tended to "see" situations, Wack saw the concept of reframing as a perfect fit. The task increasingly became how to show people different ways of framing or seeing a situation. This was the crux work of scenarios and the team was getting better and better at it.

## An Addition to the Family

Approximately nine months after the tour of Japan, a baby boy was born. It was June 20, 1981. Yuko had decided to name him Jean-Pierre. She planned to call him JP—intending that his initials stand for Justice and Peace. Wack was so private about his personal life that his assistant, Aldons, had no idea, although she did recall him asking her a few months before about the name Jean-Pierre: "

> I didn't even know they were going to have a baby. I remember he said to me once, he came into the office and stood beside me and he said, "What do you think of the name Jean-Pierre?" I said "Oh—it's a nice name, why?" And he just sort of grinned and he said he thought so too. I thought it was a strange question and he went into his office. And then Yuko used to ring up quite frequently. Apparently what they were doing was testing if she went into labor how quickly she could get hold of him. "

In September of that year, they were finally married according to all the Japanese customs—things that Wack sometimes disliked, but clearly accommodated in this case.

## Peter Schwartz Comes to Group Planning

When it came time for Wack to recommend someone to take his place, he urged the others at Shell to hire Peter Schwartz. Schwartz had the savvy, the skill, the knowledge, the background, the "everything"—to take the scenario planning helm at Shell. What separated Schwartz in Wack's mind was their mutual interest in Buddhism and Eastern philosophy:

> It was a particular slant at Buddhism—it was not very spiritual, to be honest, it was more of an intellectual and mental discipline. He was not a believer in Hindu gods or Shinto gods, or other as far as I know. What he did believe was that the human mind was a remarkably sophisticated instrument that we didn't understand very well and that it also had very deep connections to the universe and our understanding of reality. As you know, Pierre had early connections with a variety of mystics, Gurdjieff, and others, on up through the times we knew each other. And as it happens, so did I. In my case it was a combination of Tibetan Buddhism and Zen Buddhism, both of which were very active here in the bay area. In particular, there was one connection that was quite important because it was personal. Don Michael was a great friend of Pierre's and he was influential on Pierre and vice versa. Don was studying Tibetan Buddhism with Tarthang Tulku, Lama of Nyingma sect of Tibetan Buddhism in Berkeley. Don suggested I take a course with Tarthang—and that was another connection to Pierre.

The connection through Buddhism for understanding the human mind made Schwartz an ideal successor capable of furthering the scenario institution that had been established in Shell. Plus, Schwartz had been a part of many "in the green" meetings—he already had insights into how Wack generally went about leading the scenario team. Wack had been quietly and intently training him for years. So, the wheels were set in motion to offer the position to Schwartz. Schwartz had his interviews in late 1981 and was made an offer. This time, he did not turn it down. Schwartz made the change from SRI to Shell and began a new era of scenarios at the start of 1982.

## Dinner at the Wack's

When Schwartz arrived in London, he was eager to get started. The large corporation and its complicated dynamics needed some understanding. Schwartz recalled a particularly insightful evening with the Wacks at their apartment in Lennox Gardens:

> One of the more consequential and interesting moments came over dinner one night with Yuko. We were having dinner, and we were talking about something, and I mentioned that I was dealing with a guy who was very interesting, but I thought he wanted to use me for something and therefore I was pushing him away. And Yuko said "What's the matter, aren't you strong enough?" And she made the point "If you are strong enough and somebody wants to use you, you can let them and you're not going to be subsumed by them. Maybe there is something you ought to do together but you are the master of your own fate, rather than being the victim. If you are strong enough and can take that." It was very interesting and led me to ask some tough questions about how I related to leadership, management, among others. It was a highly consequential, influential and quite memorable conversation for me.

Yuko was obviously a strong woman. She had no trouble telling Wack what she thought and for all Wack's brilliance she was known to be willing and able to put him in his place. She had some tough advice for Wack's protégé as well. Her words had a lasting impact on Schwartz and helped him find an additional perspective on navigating the waters he would swim for years to come.

## Schwartz' First Scenarios

As Schwartz took over the scenario team, Wack continued on his travels and reflection. The two remained close, and whenever Wack was in London, he preferred to work in the office. Rarely a day would go by that the pair wouldn't share notes over lunch or some other meeting. Schwartz had been busy working on his first set of scenarios and when the time came to test them with Pierre, he set a meeting. Schwartz described his first effort at presenting scenarios directly to Wack behind closed doors:

About two thirds of the way through the scenarios, I put together a bunch of slides and went to test it with Pierre. He almost laughed me out of the room, because it was so cumbersome and complex—so little of the essence of the story—a big tangled mess. Basically about halfway through he stopped me and essentially threw me out of the room and said "go start over again." It was a very painful experience and lesson and I remember it very clearly to this day. He had this sort of conference table and we had gone through the slides one by one. They were hand drawn—I wasn't projecting them. One of his gifts was getting down to the essence of what you were really trying to say to the management and getting rid of extraneous stuff that didn't support what you were really trying to accomplish. The scenario books that he produced were very elegant and straightforward in their essence in terms of what kind of consequence. Mine was exactly the opposite of that.

For the rest of 1982 Wack was travelling around the world, giving presentations and meeting people. But he would come to the office when he was in town and it was there he tended to write and work. It wasn't unusual for Schwartz to run into him as his office was just down the hall: "When he was in town he continued to coach and mentor throughout his time there, and beyond."

## "World of Internal Contradictions" and "Hard Times" Emerge in Reality

Further evidence of scenarios and their anticipatory power is easy to find these days—particularly in the reflections of those who led much of the scenario work at Shell. And of course, hindsight helps. Newland continues to eagerly recall the work they did and how it allowed them to really see ahead:

> We also got the economic implications right in terms of the effect of the first oil shock on the world economy. For example, the WIC scenario highlighted the very nasty period of inflation that would follow the price rises. This surely had an impact on the Group strategy. In a subsequent scenario round, we predicted that Europe would experience a period of poor growth and this proved correct. In 1981/82, we had the "Hard Times" scenario that was incredibly pessimistic about the world economy. Now, the "Hard Times" scenario was written in Shell some two to three years before the industry accepted that this was reality.

Wack later reflected that it was really 1981 and 1982 that were crazy for oil companies, and it was the scenarios in 1978 and 1979 that were actually quite important for Shell. However, he had an agreement with Shell that he could not speak or write about anything in the previous five years so the importance of these scenarios did not make it into his works. Nonetheless, the flurry of scenario activity throughout the mid to late 1970s is generally regarded as the key to Shell's survival and success. Interestingly, these scenarios were constructed on shorter timelines, which Wack also saw as an important development. He said: "If you have to wait 20 years to see the results, you have no credibility base." Because the world was changing so fast, and the shorter-term scenarios of the late 1970s could be assessed in terms of their accuracy, Group Planning gained even more credibility as Shell leaders prepared for the shake ups that were about to occur.

In fact, in Newland's presentation on the "Hard Times" scenario in 1982 he began with the now legendary introduction, "Humpty Dumpty sat on a wall, Humpty Dumpty had a great fall." His use of the rhyme was intended to signal the coming collapse of oil prices that eventually bankrupted three of the seven large oil companies. Shell's scenario team also accurately anticipated the second major oil shock in 1982 and in the next three years the industry would consolidate, inflation would spike and Shell was prepared for it all.

## Final Presentations to the Operating Companies

Toward the end of 1982, to conclude his reflections, Wack made a series of eight presentations to Shell's different Operating Companies. Kees van der Heijden, in his role as understudy, attended the final presentation given to the Manufacturing Function. Fortunately, he recorded and later transcribed it. It is among the gems to be found in the Pierre Wack Memorial Library. It holds many lessons and is also provided in the "Works" section at the end of this book. Wack had developed an image that represented his integrated thinking about scenarios, and he drew it in a few iterations. His original hand drawings are still held in Oxford, and he eventually arrived at a version that appeared in his manuscript; "The Gentle Art of Re-Perceiving."

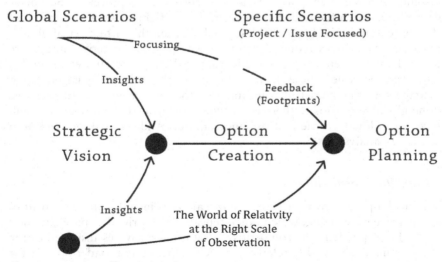

*Chart 6.1* Option Generation

## Organizational Nervous System

This version of the diagram framed his thinking and his presentations to the Operating Companies, and it was included in the final HBR articles. However, the final articles included only a few sentences dedicated to the elements other than scenarios. He described the diagram, which he decided to call the organizational nervous system, at length in his presentations to the operating companies and the transcription by van der Heijden captures it all. The key points are summarized here; However, the full document is a tremendous resource worth reading in full.

Some additional context for those presentations is important to consider. Wack had been travelling all around the world. He had been studying Michael Porter, Peter Drucker and Henry Mintzberg, among others. Wack was aware of the developments in American business schools and the emerging focus on strategic management that would dominate the 1980s into the early 1990s. MBA programs in the US were starting to focus on a finance approach to strategy, and Wack saw that for scenarios to have a chance, they needed to be integrated with other strategic processes.

### Global and Focused Scenarios

Wack advocated for a multi-phased approach to producing scenarios—clearly demonstrated in the tiered scenario work after 1975. His famous cherry tree metaphor captures it nicely—you find the blossoms on the smaller branches. By this he meant that global scenarios are the trunk, and focused scenarios are the branches, on which the blossoms form—the insights. Another metaphor—a camera lens—is also powerful. Scenarios gain power when focused. But to begin with a tight focus means you lose the context and miss key variables. Wack learned that a first set of global, macro scenarios was required before it was possible to move onto more focused micro scenarios that really captured the uncertainties around a more specific issue. These micro scenarios enabled deeper engagement of managers' mental models: "You cannot do focused scenarios until you have done global scenarios. Otherwise, I would bet you that the manager will have a too low-level view of the uncertainties. And you will go back into sensitivity analysis."

### Competitive Positioning

A critical input to any thorough scenario analysis includes an assessment of competitive positioning, which Wack repeatedly described as pure common sense. He explained that competitive positioning provides insight into the decision makers' world of relativity, which helps create broader options for thinking: "Suppose two powders, a black powder, coal, and a white powder, flour. And suppose I mix them well at our scale of observation it is a grey powder. But suppose little insects the size of the grain of flour, from their scale of observation they would see black rocks and white rocks. Unless you go at the scale where you can see black rocks and white rocks competitive positioning is meaningless." Insight can only be achieved if generalities and vagueness are avoided and an appropriate scale of observation is used.

## Option Planning

Scenarios must lead to options and the set of options requires design: "In any situation, there is always more than just one possibility." Again, emphasizing that scenarios are not the outcome, Wack realized that unless scenarios led to novel options, the process was sterile: "In most cases strategies have no options, and in the very few cases where there are often put forward as a way of convincing managers to agree to a previously decided and preferred strategy." Unwillingness to generate and entertain a variety of real options is a serious pitfall for would-be scenario planners and their sponsors—the exercise must be taken seriously and project participants must be open-minded to a set of thoughtful alternatives, no matter how uncomfortable they may seem at first.

## Strategic Vision

Drawing from his experiences and interviews with Japanese companies in the 1960s, Wack clarified that strategic vision captures the kind of company you want to be: "It is a system for dominance ... You want to dominate one segment of your habitat, one segment of the market. If you don't want that then you don't need a strategic vision." All this Wack learned in Japan by studying its top-performing companies. Wack used Sony as an example— Sony decided to be excellent in three technologies at once: color, solid-state, and magnetic tape recording. Sony realized that other companies would be equal or better in one of those technologies, but none would be as good in all three simultaneously. Strategic vision "is expressed as a commitment to excellence in a few key capabilities, more than two but less than ten." These elements are combined and coalesce into a unified vision of the ideal company.

Strategic vision serves another important purpose. Wack emphasized that plans cannot be set in stone—they need to be flexible. But it is impossible to change plans every six months and maintain any progress toward goals or competitive positioning. Strategic vision is the one element of permanence in any strategy system. It defines the areas of excellence and describes the company you want to be. It does not deal with how to do. But it is situated at a high enough level that it does not need frequent revisiting. To be sure, with major market changes companies can re-invent themselves, and this means recreating the strategic vision. Usually, a strategic vision is held for some time.

## Footprints

Wack mentioned something else in his presentations to the Operating Companies called "footprints." It is more enigmatic and seems to have been lost in the general practice of scenarios—yet it connects scenarios to decisions in very concrete ways. And it is one very specific way to link scenarios with decision making and strategy. After describing the idea of bio-feedback devices (a loop back to Willis Harman) and the idea that feedback changes entirely on the perception of uncertainty, Wack made a series of connections leading to "footprints" as a critically valuable device for assessing strategic options. He began with the simple example of driving a car—the novice driver is very tense and holds the wheel quite tightly. Eventually, the driver loosens up and learns to move around in the seat and consider a variety of error signals (rear view mirror, the feel of the car under specific speeds, etc.). So the idea of feedback is critical to "Footprints" and is the very premise on which it is built. Wack stated:

> If you accept this, there is a software which prints this, and prints it in a nice way, and gives you a dot zone of impact of various possible shocks and uncertainties, which takes the shape which we will call a footprint. Now the footprint is in terms of feedback what the colour was for the bio feedback of your temperature. These are three real cases of business units of a company like GE. In the dot you see the traditional estimate, the single line and then you see the footprint and you see how much more rich the information in a footprint is.

It is difficult to imagine without an example. Further, there are very few documents or reports that give the idea of "footprints" any further clarification. However, there is one document—directly from Shell—kept in the Pierre Wack Memorial Library that gives further clarification to the concept of "footprints." The document is titled "Footprints: Purpose and Practice" and is labelled "Confidential, Group Planning, March 1984." It provides the example we need:

> The Footprint Approach is becoming more widely recognised within the Shell Group. It is essentially a *process*, aimed at facilitating management discussion and broad-brush quantification of strategic options. The process has acquired the "Footprint" label from the diagram used to portray its output. This report attempts to expound some of the basic ideas behind the technique, and to give guidance on the concepts and practicalities. It represents the current perceptions of the state-of-the-art, and will be subject to revision as greater experience of the technique is obtained.
>
> The process itself is iterative, involving senior management commitment to participate in considering options, expressing perceptions, receiving feedback and recycling towards, a decision.

The report begins by explaining the footprint diagram, its use, and its meaning. The next section (3) describes the footprints approach as a whole and is followed by a section (4) covering certain peculiar aspects. Section 5 outlines the stages in a typical footprints analysis and Section 6 contains a summary. The report goes on to describe several hypothetical examples of "footprint" analysis, none of which are real; however, they do suggest the utility of the process. Imagine a simple two axis matrix on which areas of uncertainties could be plotted according to the X and Y variables. Variable definition is obviously the most important part of the activity and could include such elements as risk vs. benefit, capital expenditures vs. profit, among many other possibilities. Perceptions or other data related to uncertainty on the selected variables can be plotted on these axes and a range of uncertainty can be easily seen. Drawing an oval to capture the range of variation results in an image that looks like footprint. Wack was quite clear that what is most interesting is when the footprint moves, and logically the movement would be due to scenario conditions.

While the report is dated two years after Wack left Group Planning, the ideas must have stuck—at least to some degree. The report is attributed to M.J. Atack and J.M.V. Hugo (neither known to be affiliated with Group Planning for long). It is impossible to say whether or not "footprint" analysis gained any traction within Shell as no other report containing this sort of analysis was found, and the scenario packages publicly distributed after Wack's time do not make reference to the idea. Yet, such a method of plotting a range of views for strategic options remains a potentially fruitful means for connecting scenarios and strategy.

## Frustration at the Shell Centre

When Wack concluded his presentations to eight of the operating companies around the world in 1982, he set a meeting with Arie de Geus. It was not clear the topic of the meeting, but the two were joined by van der Heijden—trying to learn, capture, and record as much as he could from Wack. The three sat down and de Geus asked what Wack had in mind for the meeting, at which time he indicated he had concluded his reflection and was ready to retire. It was to be expected as Wack had reached the mandatory retirement age of 60. According to van der Heijden, de Geus was really upset—he was expecting a bit more from Wack than a series of presentations. A report, book, document or some other form of guidance for sustaining scenario work after he left would surely be appropriate. After all, Shell had made a considerable investment in Wack and his teams over the years. "That was the last we saw of Pierre. He didn't come back, he went his own way and we never saw him there again." However, the CMD responded very positively to Schwartz as he took over the scenario leadership and Wack had ensured that Group Planning was in capable hands.

## Harry Oppenheimer and Next Steps

In 1982, before he left Shell, Wack was starting to explore a variety of opportunities. Anglo American had an office in London run by a subsidiary called Charter Consolidated. One of Anglo's Belgian economists, Luc Smets heard about the work Pierre was doing at Shell. At the time Anglo was the largest mining company in the world, and a few key insiders were asking themselves why they weren't using the technique as many of their commodity price forecasts had failed dramatically. Wack made a presentation to the group in London which included Luc Smets, Allan Newey and Michael O'Conner. As usual, the presentation was enthralling and the wheels started turning to bring scenarios to Anglo American. Word travelled fast up the chain and Chairman Harry Oppenheimer was interested in the progress Shell had made. He wanted to learn more to pass along to his successor, Gavin Relly who was about to take over the role. A meeting was set in Johannesburg. All the players assembled again in South Africa including Wack, Newland, Smets, Newey, O'Conner and Clem Sunter. The conversation quickly turned to the volatility of South Africa as a nation.

## Chapter 6 Sources (in order of use)

Kleiner, A. (1996). *The age of heretics: Heroes, outlaws, and the forerunners of corporate change.* New York: Doubleday.

Kleiner, A. (2008). *The age of heretics: A history of the radical thinkers who reinvented corporate management* (Vol. 164). New York: John Wiley & Sons.

Kleiner, Art, Pierre A. Wack interview in Curemonte. (n.d.). 53 pp. The annotated transcript of an interview between Art Kleiner and Pierre Wack regarding the development of Shell's scenario planning. Retrieved from the Art Kleiner Archive, University of Oxford.

Gurdjieff, G.I. (1960). *Meetings with remarkable men.* New York: Penguin Group.

Gurdjieff, G.I. (1964). *Beelzebub's tales to his grandson: All and everything.* New York: Penguin Group.

Gurdjieff, G.I. (1976). *Views from the real world: Early talks in Moscow, Essentuki, Tiflis, Berlin, London, Paris, New York and Chicago.* New York: Dutton.

Gurdjieff, G.I. (1950). *Beelzebub's tales to his grandson* (Vol. 1). Alexandria, Egypt: Library of Alexandria.

Kleiner, Art, James C. Davidson telephone interview: Spring 1993. (n.d.). 21 pp. The annotated transcript of a telephone interview between Art Kleiner and James Davidson regarding the development of Shell's Group Planning Department. Retrieved from the Art Kleiner Archive, University of Oxford.

Royal Dutch/Shell Oil. (1978, June). *Scenarios for the next five years, 1978–1983 (June 1978).* Unpublished internal document. Copy in possession of the Pierre Wack Memorial Library, University of Oxford.

Excerpt from personal communications with Ted Newland. Author held interviews and discussions in 2014–16.

Royal Dutch/Shell Oil. (1979, April). *Scenarios to 1985 (April 1979).* Unpublished internal document. Copy in possession of the Pierre Wack Memorial Library, University of Oxford.

Excerpt from personal communications with Michael Jefferson. Author held interviews and discussions in 2014–16.

Royal Dutch/Shell Oil. (1979, October). *Scenarios for the long term (October 1979)*. Unpublished internal document. Copy in possession of the Pierre Wack Memorial Library, University of Oxford.

Excerpt from personal communications with Cheryl Aldons. Author held interviews and discussions in 2014–16.

Royal Dutch/Shell Oil. (1980, September). *Links from the medium to long term scenarios, 1980/85 to 1990 (September 1980)*. Unpublished internal document. Copy in possession of the Pierre Wack Memorial Library, University of Oxford.

Excerpt from personal communications with Napier Collyns. Author held interviews and discussions in 2014–16.

Excerpt from personal communications with Kees van der Heijden. Author held interviews and discussions in 2014–16.

Excerpt from personal communications with Peter Schwartz. Author held interviews and discussions in 2014–16.

Wack, E. (n.d.). *Quelques dates et événements de la vie d'un "homme remarquable": Pierre Wack* [draft; 12 pages with note by Eve Wack]. Document retrieved from the Pierre Wack Memorial Library, University of Oxford.

Wack, E. (1998). *Pierreve: 1977–1997*. Curemonte, France, Unpublished manuscript.

Excerpt from personal communications with Eve Wack. Author held interviews and discussions in 2014–16.

Bandler, R., & Grinder, J. (1982). *Reframing: NLP and the transformation of meaning*. Moab, UT: Real People Press.

Presentation by Pierre Wack to the manufacturing function in Shell, transcribed by Kees van der Heijden, Shell Int'l Petroleum Co., Amsterdam, Holland, 1983, Unpublished manuscript.

Wack, P. (1985a). Scenarios: Shooting the rapids. *Harvard Business Review*, *63*(6), 139–150.

Wack, P. (1985b). Scenarios: Uncharted waters ahead. *Harvard Business Review*, *63*(5), 73–89.

Wack, P. (1985c). *Scenarios: The gentle art of re-perceiving*. Harvard Business School, Unpublished manuscript.

Wack, P. (1984). *Scenarios: The gentle art of re-perceiving*. Harvard Business School Working Paper 9–785–042, December 1984.

Excerpt from personal communications with Ged Davis. Author held interviews and discussions in 2014–16.

Porter, M. E. (1980). *Competitive strategy*. New York: Free Press.

Porter, M. E. (1985). *Competitive advantage*. New York: Free Press.

Drucker, P. F. (1980). *Managinginturbulenttimes*. New York: Butterworth-Heinemann.

Drucker, P. F. (1968). *The age of discontinuity: Guidelines to our changing society*. New York: Harper & Row.

Drucker, P. F. (1977). *An introductory view of management: Instructor's manual*. New York: Harper and Row.

Drucker, P. F. (1971). What we can learn from Japanese management. *Harvard Business Review*, *49*(2), 110.

Drucker, P. F. (1959). Long-range planning-challenge to management science. *Management Science*, *5*(3), 238–249.

Mintzberg, H. (1980). *The structuring of organizations*. Englewood Cliffs, NJ: Prentice Hall.

Mintzberg, H. (1990). The design school: Reconsidering the basic premises of strategic management. *Strategic Management Journal, 11*(3), 171–195.

Mintzberg, H. (1994). *The rise and fall of strategic planning.* London: Prentice-Hall.

Davidson, J. (1998, February 10). [Letter to Eve Wack]. Copy in possession of Eve Wack.

Mintzberg, H., & Lampel, J. (1999). Reflecting on the strategy process. *Sloan Management Review, 40*(3), 21–32.

Royal Dutch/ Shell Oil. (1982, January). *Footprints: Purpose and practice.* Unpublished internal document. Copy in possession of the Pierre Wack Memorial Library, University of Oxford.

Excerpt from personal communications with Clem Sunter. Author held interviews and discussions in 2014–16.

Kleiner, Art, Pierre A. Wack interview in Curemonte. (n.d.). 53 pp. The annotated transcript of an interview between Art Kleiner and Pierre Wack regarding the development of Shell's scenario planning. Retrieved from the Art Kleiner Archive, University of Oxford.

Wack, E. (n.d.). *Quelques dates et événements de la vie d'un "homme remarquable":* Pierre Wack [draft; 12 pages with note by Eve Wack]. Document retrieved from the Pierre Wack Memorial Library, University of Oxford.

Burt, G. (2010). Revisiting and extending our understanding of Pierre Wack's the gentle art of re-perceiving. *Technological Forecasting and Social Change, 77*(9), 1476–1484.

# Part III

# The Post-Shell Years

When Wack retired from Shell in 1982, he had gained a reputation as the world's foremost scenario planning expert. Word had gotten out about Shell's success with anticipating two oil shocks during the 1970s and Shell's competitive position had improved among the "Seven Sister" oil companies. This was in large part due to their ability to act faster than their rivals based on things they had "seen." Naturally, leaders in other oil companies, as well as some in completely different industries started to wonder if the approach could help them, too.

Part three of this book describes Wack's scenario work in three other instances after Shell and provides details on these projects and the outcomes. In addition, it covers the late part of Wack's life, his illness and the more personal story of his last years. These events are described through the use of materials in the Pierre Wack Memorial Library, interviews with people he worked with during this time and many of his wife Eve's reflections and recollections of those years.

Chapter 7 accounts for Wack's two years as a Visiting Professor at Harvard University, followed by his deeply insightful work on diamonds with De Beers, work on gold with Anglo American, and the new application of scenarios to the national agenda and the end of apartheid through Old Mutual and Nedcor in South Africa. This chapter also describes the production of his manuscript "The Gentle Art of Re-Perceiving," which was eventually split into two articles that won the 1985 McKinsey Award in the *Harvard Business Review*. Finally, the death of his wife Yuko Iwanade and reunion with Eve Baudoin are recounted.

Chapter 8 documents Wack's rekindled love with Eve Baudoin and diagnosis with myeloma. These were his twilight years—he had become the guru, with many visitors attempting to learn what they could from this mysteriously remarkable man. The chapter is a more personal account of his travels with Baudoin, his struggles with sickness and remission, and eventually his death in 1997.

# 7    Diamonds, Gold and the Dark Side of the Moon

*Kruger National Park is hailed by many as one of the most beautiful places in the world. All of the "big five" game animals (African elephant, black rhinoceros, Cape buffalo, African lion and African leopard) can be found there. As the jeep rolled slowly along the trail, Pierre, Nathalie, her fiancé, and JP were simply in awe. The vast expanses of the savannah were like nothing they had ever seen before. As the jeep pulled up and over a hill, suddenly a herd of African elephants came into view. The driver pulled the vehicle to a stop and everyone was silent—taking in the incredible sight. A particularly large elephant, possibly the matriarch took notice and fixed a gaze on the new visitors. Moments later the large elephant began moving toward the jeep. Then faster, and even faster. Pierre, Nathalie, Michael and JP looked at each other with slight smiles. As the large creature drew closer and closer with increasing speed the smiles quickly faded. Nathalie took her place under the back seat of the jeep and the ranger stepped up on top of it. With two tons of elephant rapidly approaching in a threatening manner, the group did not know what to do—it all happened so fast! The ranger held out a bamboo cane and the elephant stopped a few feet short of the jeep, turned and ran away. On their ride back to the lodge, the ranger confided that the giveaway had been the elephant's ears. They were flapping and not pinned straight back which usually indicates a real charge rather than a fake one.*

Wack and Newland retired from Shell on the same day. It was October 26, 1982. Wack was 60 years old—the mandatory general retirement age. There was a nice party at the Shell Centre for both of them and every Managing Director was in attendance. "It was the end of an Epoch," Wack said. His assistant Aldons commented: "He was very much a loner really, he really liked his own company and doing things that interested him. Pierre didn't get that close to people—but it was easy to have been fond of him. He wasn't a sort of a team person in that sense, but I think there was the feeling he would be very hard to replace." While Newland had arranged to continue working for Shell as a contractor, Wack, Yuko and a young JP packed their bags for Boston—Wack had arranged a Senior Lecturer position at Harvard. Before they left London, Aldons came by for dinner:

> I went to their flat for dinner once just before Pierre went to Harvard—I thought Yuko would be a very demure Japanese lady and they were packing up—they were going to be moving to Boston. She was very casually dressed and packing stuff everywhere. She was very much on a kind of level with him and he said something and she smacked him on the shoulder and told him off! They had a very kind of easy relationship. JP must have been about 3 at the time and he was dragging my hand bag across the floor. He was walking across the top of a coffee table and furniture. They were both very proud of him but certainly not overprotective and I was watching him in case he fell. They were both very . . . not parents who bothered over him at all.

## A Meeting—By Chance

In the August of 1982—just after Wack retired from Shell—Eve Baudoin was back in Paris. And with a sudden and overwhelming feeling, she thought:

> "If you take this road, Pierre will be there." I go up the Champs Elysees, I turn right, a small white car stops before me. Pierre descends. Double miracle: I can park. Pierre hesitates before recognizing me. Even if he had changed, I know who he is. I have the advantage to have been expecting to see him. On the sidewalk, he tells me that he has a son one year old. He still travels as much as before. He takes my telephone number and promised to call. He never called. It is time that I begin to live without the myth of Pierre.

## Harvard University

Wack had made plans with the help of a very long time friend, Bruce Scott, for a two-year Senior Lecturer position at Harvard University. They were to co-teach a course called "Country Analysis and Scenario Planning." According to Scott, "Pierre very much enjoyed the teaching, and the contact with some 110 very bright students." Scott recalled how he met Wack back in Paris 20 years earlier:

> I met Pierre when he was Chief Economist of Shell in Paris in 1964. John MacArthur (who became the Dean of Harvard) and I, had a school sponsored research project to go find out how the national planning process worked in France, not the whole thing, but the part that aimed to influence sector by sector, company by company. And the Planning Commissioner, Pierre Marseills was a super smart mathematical economist and virtual cabinet member. So Pierre also knew him. John and I spent this time living in Lausanne and we would take the train into

Paris to spend the week and we did that for almost two years. We knew the people in the ministry of finance, the planning commission and a dozen of the big companies. Shell was one of them.

As something of a funny side note, Scott recalled that Shell's headquarters in Paris were right near the Champs Elysees and the Arc de Triomphe—within walking distance. When they would finish with work for the day, Scott and MacArthur would walk about four blocks to a Wimpy's hamburger stand to have a hamburger: "And Pierre thought that was very, very curious."

The first year at Harvard, Wack supervised a student group to develop scenarios for Japan, and the second year the focus was the gold industry, which furthered his opportunities in Anglo American. Wack also went to Harvard with the idea of writing what turned out to be two papers on scenario planning. They were eventually published by the *Harvard Business Review* in 1985 and have become the most cited works on scenario planning to date. Scott helped to make the arrangements for Wack to visit. At the time, Scott was able to negotiate anything he asked for. But at the same time Scott was also somewhat ostracized from any real role in the school from 1982 onward. There had been a change in the Dean and according to Scott,

It was like switching from Jimmy Carter to Ronald Reagan. And I mean that. The school changed its philosophy. Ronald Reagan was interested in the lives of rich people and so was our Dean, including the big shift from European style stakeholder capitalism to shareholder capitalism where all you're interested in is enriching the people that are already rich. And that was the change that we made.

Wack did not enjoy the political aspects of his time at Harvard. He found it stuffy and confining—not a place where ideas could be freely exchanged. Rather, it was a firmly established bureaucracy. True to his life's theme, he did not like to feel trapped and the situation at Harvard was more of an intellectual trap than anything else. The way he made connections was through his scenario presentations. It was a mechanism for finding more remarkable people who may have something interesting to offer:

Practically every year I made presentations. I did it at MIT, at the Sloan School and at Harvard. The only thing we asked was to have a list of the people who attended. And we would not give any charts but it was a full presentation and it was very helpful because I got very good elements in return. When I was at Harvard, and I went to the Sloan School, the Dean of Harvard asked me to come in his office. He said, "You know you are on the faculty of Harvard, you are not supposed to talk to the Sloan School." I found this very strange—I said, "I'm not really on the faculty of Harvard and I need input also in exchange."—I found this very narrow minded.

## Competitive Positioning

Wack continued to work out his reflections on scenarios at Shell for most of 1983 into 1984 and he received help from Bruce Scott and a young Norman Duncan in getting his story down on paper. Scott recalled: "His office was right across the hall from mine for about two years. I was trying to help him to write his work so that it was in a way that reached a broader audience. Not changing what he was doing or saying." Wack was also keeping in touch with his friends at Anglo, and Newland had been working with a select group on Anglo's global scenarios.

Throughout the next 18 months, Wack met many interesting people and had several conversations with other Harvard professors, including Michael Porter, who no doubt helped shape Wack's thinking about competitive positioning. Porter did not see significant utility of scenarios beyond what he called "industry scenarios." Porter clarified his view that scenarios are really only useful in exploring industry dynamics and how they might change in his second work *Competitive Advantage*. Wack had been paying attention to the importance of competitive analysis for a few years, as he recognized it as a critical part of his organizational nervous system that he presented to the Operating Companies before he left Shell. Conversations with Porter gave him an even deeper understanding of competitive advantage and positioning, building on earlier ideas.

Wack met others—both academic and corporate as the gravitas he had built at Shell had spread. Harvard—being focused on the contributions of corporate and other wealthy donors—was eager to put Wack in front of potential clients. Eve remembered that he learned to be protective at Harvard. He suspected that some who came to see him wanted to know the things he knew in order to further their own careers. It was part of the environment. Wack also met with many Americans who tried the scenario technique in their own practice:

> When I was at Harvard I saw a number of people who told me "we also tried scenarios and our management, contrary to yours is just not good enough to cope with scenarios." And I told them not at all. "Look, all management teams with great experience in dealing with uncertainty who face those mechanical scenarios which just focus on an outcome, they cannot do anything with it. Despite the fact that at least every month they take major decisions which are extremely risky where they can appreciate uncertainty. Why? Because once they can really understand it [through scenarios], it's not focusing just on black and white."

There is a major insight to be observed from this exchange related to the cultural implications of scenarios. The failed cases these Americans were describing probably did not invest the five or six years working to gain support from the top as Wack and the others did at Shell. Further, they were attempting to work their scenarios out on a much shorter timeline. The US had changed dramatically from the days of Herman Kahn and in the early 1980s . . . After the vast economic development and high productivity of the 1970s and 1980s, reintroducing the technique was tough with the efficiency-focused Americans. According to Newland, there was an attempt at doing some scenarios for the US government under Wack's leadership while he was at Harvard, but "this proved countercultural." The dominant way of thinking in the US had shifted toward efficiency and Wack's approach to scenarios favored going to the lengths required to achieve deep insights. This included investing significant time in the process. The tension between efficiency and investing time is a dilemma to this day for scenario planners.

There is not much accounting for Yuko and JP during this time, though they all lived in Cambridge together and JP was only two years old. We do know they took a family vacation to Mexico in early 1984. Presumably, Yuko was busy being a mother and she did work at a shop selling Japanese food in Boston. Wack's less intense schedule allowed him the time to enjoy fatherhood and attend to his family more closely than in the Shell days. The Wacks spent time with the Scotts at their place in Wilmot, New Hampshire. Scott recalled: "They visited us not long after we bought our place in the summer of 1983. Having heard us describe our struggle with squirrels getting at the bird seed in the feeder, they brought us as a house gift a squirrel proof feeder!" The Wacks visited the Scotts again during winter, this time bringing Clem Sunter with them. Clem was able to try cross country skis for the first time, which he recalled felt like breakneck speed even on a mild slope.

## The Gentle Art of Re-Perceiving

There are several versions of Wack's paper "The Gentle Art of Re-Perceiving," the final one dated December 1984. This is the finished version of Wack's efforts at Harvard and represents his most comprehensive reflection on scenarios. He was largely helped by Bruce Scott, Norman Duncan and Peggy Evans in producing this work. The paper is generally an account of the early scenarios at Shell and what Group Planning learned in working with their scenarios throughout the 1970s. The paper captures Wack's use of metaphors and generally colorful language. With permission from the Harvard Business School, Eve and Jean-Pierre Wack, the December 1984 version of Wack's paper is included at the end of this book. It remains the most insightful and substantive written product attributed to Wack.

The paper was judged too lengthy, and the editors at the *Harvard Business Review* went to work on the manuscript. Wack wanted nothing to do with the process so he asked Collyns to help. As the Head of Shell's Public Relations in the US, he was very interested. Yet, even with Collyns assistance HBR editors removed most of Wack's colorful language, metaphors and quotes from lesser known sources. Although, they did allow for one of Wack's more famous examples to explain an important essence of scenarios:

> As any adult knows, a magician cannot produce a rabbit unless it is already in (or very near) his hat. In the same way, surprises in the business environment almost never emerge without warning. To understand the warnings, managers must be able to look at available evidence in alternative ways. Otherwise, they can be badly misled by apparently valid facts if that is all they see, or they do not interpret them in different ways.

Ultimately, the paper was split in two, and published in the *Harvard Business Review* in 1985 as "Scenarios: Uncharted Waters Ahead," and "Scenarios: Shooting the Rapids." It is somewhat well known that Wack did not approve of the final product, although the work won the McKinsey Prize in 1985.

Wack, of course, had many options for other scenario work and things continued to develop around his meeting with Harry Oppenheimer back in late 1982 and the courses he taught at Harvard. According to Peter Schwartz, "Pierre was not intellectually ready to retire—he loved doing the work. The finances were not the major driver here. He loved working on scenarios and wanted to continue doing interesting things after Shell—he had become the foremost authority on scenario planning." And when Harvard turned out to be a disappointment, it is no surprise he would quickly have access to other opportunities. When the paper was finished, the Wacks packed up their life and moved back to the Lennox Gardens apartment in London in December of 1984. Soon after their arrival in London, Yuko was diagnosed with cancer. She began thinking of returning to Japan for treatment.

## Post-Shell Scenario Work

Wack was first connected to Anglo American in London and made a presentation there to a group of their senior managers in late 1982. Newland also had ties to Anglo American in London through his own network of remarkable people:

> It was through Lord Rothschild (head of Shell's Research Division—and also a great spy man during the war) and he intimately knew Oppenheimer in South Africa. Oppenheimer was interested in doing some planning work like Shell, and he asked Lord Rothschild whom to contact. And he said—I don't know how he found out about us, but he said there were two people in Shell one was Ted Newland and the other was Pierre Wack who were doing this sort of planning work. Lord Rothschild to my great surprise turned around and said don't take Pierre Wack, take Ted Newland. That's how I got into that. Suddenly

I was given a contract which lasted for 10 years basically Anglo American—how do we affect change. And what they were talking about was business opportunity.

Wack took a trip to the Anglo American headquarters in Johannesburg in 1983 as their interest in scenarios was growing. Schwartz recalled: "Clem Sunter hired him to do scenarios on the future of diamonds. He was incredibly interested in this. He loved what he was doing—loved the travel and getting out and talking to interesting people," which is no surprise. Wack was able to keep developing his network of remarkable people—a necessary activity given the confining feeling at Harvard. Sunter also recalled bringing Wack into Anglo American:

> Because many of our commodity price forecasts were incorrect in the 1970's, we said "Why not give Pierre a hearing." He came out to South Africa and gave a presentation for the Executive Committee of Anglo and he really blew the whole executive team away—because he was Pierre, and his mannerisms—the way he spoke—and everything else. And I at the time was the secretary for the Executive Committee and the Chairman, Gavin Relly asked if I would mind looking after the scenario planning function. So I said fine—really having no knowledge of what it meant.

Among the tribes of Northern Natal in South Africa, a common greeting is "*Sawu bona*," which in English is equivalent to saying, "hello." The phrase "*Sawu bona*" can be literally translated as "I see you." It is no wonder Wack was very comfortable in South Africa.

## De Beers

Back in 1927, Ernest Oppenheimer was elected Chairman of the Board for a diamond mining company named De Beers. In the 1930s De Beers began its famous US marketing campaign in an attempt to stop the sharp decline in diamond sales. Equating diamonds with love and coining the phrase "A Diamond is Forever" led to an overwhelming turnaround in the US diamond market. In the 1960s, after having totally conquered the US market, company leaders set their sights on Japan. In 1959, no diamonds could be imported into Japan according to the post-war trade laws. De Beers launched a very strategic campaign and planted the idea of romantic marriage in the minds of young Japanese women: "By 1981, almost 60 percent of Japanese brides wore diamonds, up from 5 percent in 1967." By 1983, when Wack met Sunter, the Japanese market had significantly opened up. At the time, Anglo American owned a 45 percent stake in De Beers and it seemed like a good trial project for Wack and his scenarios.

## Diamond Scenarios

It was some time in 1984 that Wack officially started working on diamond scenarios for De Beers and AAC with Gill Devlin. Devlin remembered one of Wack's sayings: "wonder is knowledge." The Pierre Wack Memorial library contains many documents and files related to diamonds and De Beers from 1983 until 1989. The final and confidential report containing four diamond scenarios was produced in 1986, though it is clear Wack maintained an interest in the diamond industry for several more years, collecting articles and other information on the topic. We also know that Wack began working on gold scenarios for AAC as a case study for his students at Harvard, which evolved into more consulting work. The introduction and scenario summaries for the Diamond scenarios are provided here.

### Diamond Scenarios—1986 to 1993

We present four scenarios of CSO (Central Selling Organization) sales from 1986 to 1993. The scenarios propose figures both for the volume that would be "econometrically indicated" and for the volume that we might actually sell. All amounts shown include a measure of inflation, but the figures should be seen as illustrative of scenarios and not as forecasts.

### Pre-determined elements:

We have assumed for these scenarios that for the years 1986, 1987 and 1988 we will actually sell $2.3bn, $2.5bn and 2.8bn respectively (a real growth of 0.1bn p.a.) whatever is indicated econometrically.

During this period all contracts with the major outside producers will remain in force.

By 1990 one way or another the following present problems will be resolved:

> the US trade deficit brought within bounds
> the US budget deficit significantly reduced

There will in the early '90s be a need (which may not be satisfied) for a renewal of infrastructure (roads, phones, etc.) in the U.S.A. and Europe.

### "Hard Landing"—1986 to 1989

In this scenario AAC's "Oil Collapse" is in play, when the shock of the oil price precedes the benefits, so that consumer expenditure falls sharply before recovering. Then the oil prices fall far enough to "bring banking/energy sector financial problems for which the policy response has to be an acceleration in US money growth. This triggers a dollar collapse bringing a Recovery Turns Sour scenario." In the rest of the OECD money policy is loosened but there is insufficient policy stimulus to prevent a sharp slowdown in world growth. OECD growth is tempered by weak US (and OPEC) demand and a sharp turnaround in the US net export position following from the weaker dollar and low US demand growth.

### "Soft Landing"—1986 to 1989

AAC's "Oil Drift" is in play. Inflation is held in check and modest but constant growth is sustained with the US deficits being brought within reasonable bounds at a gradual rate.

### "Industrial Renaissance"—1990 to 1993

During the previous period USA and USSR have reached agreement which allows them to limit their defense spending. In the USA the defeat of the military lobby allows the Executive to resist the welfare lobby. By 1990 significant growth has returned to the USA and ROECD economies, and work has begun on the renewal of transport and communication systems. Government policies throughout the Triad favour privatization and liberal economies. Trading co-operation is effective with Japan and the rest of the Triad.

### "Protracted Recovery"—1990 to 1993

No arms agreement has been reached by 1990 and defence expenditure plays a significant part of all OECD budgets. Although the US budget deficit has been brought within reasonable bounds, confidence has not returned to the economies in enough measure to cause any real growth. No real trade co-operation emerges among the members of the Triad and policies verge towards protectionism.

The scenario book goes on to chart the CSO sales along with the excesses or shortfalls of actual sales for each of the four scenarios. There is no documented reaction to these scenarios, although Scott was clear that Wack had so impressed the AAC leadership that they asked him to look more closely at their gold operations.

## The Anglo American Gold Scenarios

In 1983, Wack began working on scenarios for AAC's gold market. Scott recalled (as they were working together at Harvard at the time): "Pierre had a very successful experience with the guys from Anglo on their gold. Actually it was quite similar to his work in oil—he told them 'Look there have been some fundamental changes in the relationships in your industry and you haven't taken that into account. He said, 'You're drilling holes that you are gonna wish you didn't have.' "

Just like the work on diamonds, the files in the Pierre Wack Memorial Library cite documents between 1982 and 1991 related to the dynamics of the gold industry, indicating a long interest in the topic. However, the most comprehensive set of scenarios specific to gold were produced in April 1985 in a report titled "Gold: Scenarios for the short-term and for the nineties." The document is a confidential, internal, AAC report and lists Pierre Wack as the primary author, with C. L. Sunter, R.M. Weinberg and M. F. O'Conner as the AAC support team. Because these scenarios represent significant post-Shell scenario work authored by Wack, the basics are included here:

1   *Introduction*

Pierre Wack stressed that the short-term could be defined as two years, because the critical element was investors' behavior and this was their time horizon, (plus or minus one year). In the short-term, the price would be determined entirely by factors *outside* the gold industry.

For the longer-term, and for capital investment whose horizon was in the 1990s, fundamental factors *within* the gold industry became more important, and the level of "industrial" demand critical

The gold market was a complex system because:

(i) There were different logics operating in various parts of the system; for instance, in investor behavior, jewelry, Soviet sales, the oil price, etc.

(ii) The system exhibited the phenomena of evolution: It did not return to its previous state.

The application of econometric techniques gave unreliable results in such a situation. At the moment, there were greater changes in the perceived attractiveness of gold to holders than there were variations of physical supply, or of demand in the 'industrial' sector. The success of any short-term study depended critically on its capacity to provide light on the behavior of investors.

To explore this "terra incognita", PW had devised an analytical system based on nine motivations for investors to hold gold. These were Treasure, Pessimist, Inflation, Anonymity, Threat to the Dollar, Savings, Political Threat, Portfolio and Speculation.

In order to illustrate the use of his analysis, PW gave these contrasting examples in recent years: 1979, 1981, and 1983–84. In the last period there were two phenomena: that of disinvestment, and the insidious erosion in the price of gold tending to diminish the size of the investment "cake". A notable feature was the shortening of the time horizons of the remaining holders, leading to a situation where the only people who would buy were other investors at lower prices.

2   *Two Archetype Scenarios for the Short-term*
    *Scenario 1:* The key element here was the threat to the dollar. In this
    scenario the prices of gold might rise way above $450. However, if
    such a rise came about, it would be short-lived and fall back, per-
    haps to a lower level than seen so far this year.
    *Scenario 2:* This scenario was essentially a continuation of the hostile
    conditions for gold experienced over the past two years. In consid-
    ering the likelihood of such a scenario, PW stressed the possibility
    of such 'shocks' as:

    *(i)*   a further drop in the oil price
    *(ii)*  the introduction of general import taxes by the US
    *(iii)* A new détente leading to a reduction in Western defense
            expenditure,

    any of which would prolong the attractiveness of the US dollar. In this
    scenario, the price of gold would suffer continuing erosion.
    The main conclusion, under either scenario, was that *there would not
    be a sustainable high price for gold in the short-term.*

3   *Longer-term Factors*
    Before presenting his longer-term scenarios, PW noted some key factors:

    (i)   A potential increase in new mine production in the Western
          world outside South Africa, as a result of the high level of
          exploration under way at the moment, and the relative lack of
          other opportunities for mining companies.
    (ii)  The threat of increase Russian gold production in the 1990s
          due to privatization of that sector of the economy, plus sales
          from stock, to meet foreign exchange needs of revenue from
          energy exports or arms sales declines. Similarly, there would be
          increased production in China.
    (iii) The totally conflicting objectives of the mining and jewellery
          industries, the former being to maximize offtake and the latter
          to maximize margins. PW likened the situation to "fighting a
          battle with an ally who was secretly one's enemy".

    In a detailed analysis of the jewellery trade, PW highlighted the follow-
        ing feature:
    Jewellery shops were not gold shops: they sold watches, sliver, etc. as
        well. Their margins were very high. Turnover was extremely low.
        Stock management was 30 years out of date.
    Marketing was poor: Much worse than that of a small supermarket.
        Very few jewellers offered real credit. Gold jewellery was compet-
        ing for the same middle-class market as videos, photography, hi-fi,
        holidays abroad, etc., which were marketed with low mark-ups,
        much imagination and on modern credit terms, often with the sup-
        port of the upstream producers.

When gold went up in price, jewellers maintained their margins; when it dipped their prices did not reflect this. PW showed how the price of gold, expressed in terms of hours of work needed to earn an ounce, had fallen substantially this century. However, jewellers took an elitist view, and did not address themselves sufficiently to the now-affluent middle classes.

4    *Two Scenarios for the Nineties—"Plan' or 'Be Planned"*
1    *The "Be Planned" Scenario.* A scenario of drift, where gold producers stayed "white-anted" but the jewellers downstream.
Three downside forces could reduce gold to a mere commodity status, where the number of investors would be severely limited and mainly speculative:

(i) Increased output of newly-mined gold from Western countries
(ii) Increased sales from Russia
(iii) If in the short-term there was another significant increase in the price of gold, albeit of short duration, when it declined there would be an even greater proportion than at present of short-term holders and speculators.

2    *The "Plan" Scenario.* PW considered that it was possible to influence the whole market system beneficially, including the investment component. This could be achieved by:

*(i)* Vigorous marketing of gold in the jewellery sector, employing demonstration "gold shops" to change the "logic" of jewellers. Such measures as the introduction of credit, hedging, etc., could proceed in parallel with this.
*(ii)* Taking advantage of the rise in discretionary income which could be expected in the next wave of economic development.
*(iii)* Using the improvement in "industrial" demand to create a better climate for investment demand.

*The key point was to increase "real" demand in the gold system, (i.e., in the "industrial" sector), faster than newly-mined supply.*
Gold would then establish itself at a price level considerably above the marginal cost of production: $450 would be a reasonable equilibrium for the 1990s.

This report for AAC marks the second set of scenarios that Wack had primary responsibility for developing after Shell. The document timeline indicates he spent at least three years working on the gold scenarios. As they were close friends with offices across the hall from each other at Harvard, Wack confided in Scott about the project:

With field reports that the demand for gold hoarding was declining, his scenarios cautions Anglo that high-priced gold would not return (it had been $800 in 1980), and indeed that even $400 gold probably would not last. He told me that his conclusions were unwelcome, especially by the head of production, who refused to come to a key meeting when they were to be presented and discussed. This was a repeat of the earlier experience at Shell, where the head of transport and trade did not like the scenarios, and thus refused to hear or consider them. In both cases it would eventually cost these men their jobs! In dollars of that period the price of gold is now perhaps $220 (or $290 in current terms), a price that Anglo manager would have considered inconceivable. Pierre had a capacity for seeing trends and relationships that others could not (or would not) see, and correctly anticipating their implications

## Options for the Long Term—Downstream Gold

Another document produced for AAC on July 4, 1986, covered the details of long term gold planning and was published almost a year after the original gold scenarios. The full document is 37 pages in length and is essentially a transcript of a presentation given by Wack first to the Executive team on Monday, May 26, 1986, and then to the Gold Division of AAC on Tuesday, May 27, 1986. The document is remarkable in that it is a verbatim transcription of a presentation by Wack himself. As a result, the document reads as a question and answer session, which yields many insights about how Wack interacted with his audiences. It also clarifies a tight link to his previous work on diamonds. He introduced the presentation:

> I always tried to find good reasons to change my mind [about gold]. I didn't find many. The last year has confirmed two fundamental points of the gold scenarios. That jewellery was really the main driving force in the medium term in the supply and demand relationship for gold and for the price of gold. The figures which will be published in a few weeks' time by Consolidated Gold Fields will show a consumption in jewellery of about 1 100 tons last year. I believe this is underestimated. I come from the oil industry where statistics are reasonably reliable. For some time I have had a feeling of unease concerning the figures for jewellery. I approached Krementz, which is the largest US manufacturer, (Krementz junior happened to be a former student of mine at Harvard), and we had a rather open conversation. Then I came back to Intergold New York, and I told them of my uneasiness, and they were quite happy to show me a study which also concluded there was a very serious underestimation, indeed, an embarrassingly serious one. So I would guess that in the coming years you are going to have an abnormally high increase, which will probably be higher than reality.

Wack went on to describe all of the various jewellery shops he had visited throughout the world, how some were effectively laid out and others were not, from Germany to Japan, including details about the cost breakdown of the US wedding ring, the U.K. gold chain, and the best practices in mark-ups across several distribution channels. He analyzed the value chain, the marketing mix, the capital cost of inventory, inventory size and stock trading systems. In particular, his comments about image are worth printing here to give the flavor of his presentation:

> Image is absolutely fundamental because there are three peculiarities in the act of purchasing a piece of jewellery which are worth noting. First, the customers are not at ease: it is not a normal type of buying situation. They know they need advice, but they do not know whether they are being conned.
>
> Secondly, because discounts are so widely advertised, (you can buy your jewellery with a 50 percent reduction, etc.), they know that margins in jewellery are extremely high and are suspicious. And thirdly buying a piece of jewellery is very different from buying a pack of cigarettes—it is highly ego-intensive.
>
> The point I want to make is this: if you want to go for demonstration shops, you must tell them you have the best price value, and you must prove it, you must say why: "because we have lower costs than the others." Just to say that you are low priced is not good enough, you must give tangible evidence of this.

His presentation also covers the training of jewellery sales staff, and the promotion of using credit to purchase jewellery. At the time, 65 percent of jewellery purchases were made with cash and only seven percent with credit cards. It is, of course, uncertain if his recommendation had any part of the industry change, but five years later, the figures had shifted to 45 percent cash and 25 percent credit card purchases. The report is a rare and delightful record of Wack in a professional setting answering direct questions about his scenario work for a client audience.

## Newland, South Africa and the Dark Side of the Moon

While Wack was working on diamonds and gold for AAC, Newland was working for AAC in London and South Africa focused first on some global scenarios and then on a more specific project:

> When they hired me at Anglo, we started with a few visits and very quickly it became clear that apartheid was the dark side of the moon. We didn't know what the scenario was. And I connected up with a remarkable man. Pierre wasn't involved at that stage. He was working with De Beers doing the diamond thing, which was different—completely different. I met a man called Clem Sunter—he was very much an up and coming man there and he led the effort in South Africa. We did global scenarios for Anglo, but we avoided obviously the dark side of the moon. Oppenheimer was

there and he said—there is nothing more deadly in a presentation when you finish and the Chief Executive gets up and says "Well, that was very interesting, thank you very much." If they say "interesting" it always means they are not the slightest bit interested.

## Clem Sunter

Clem Sunter had been asked to oversee the scenario planning function for AAC overall and he was convinced scenarios had utility beyond just AAC's operations. He had seen the benefits first hand while working with Wack on the gold scenarios. Newland had been assigned to work on global scenarios for AAC, the conversation that Oppenheimer had begun a few years ago about the instability of South Africa and the potential results of ending apartheid had major implications for the whole of South Africa. Sunter recalled:

> Ted started developing global scenarios looking at the remainder of the 80's and into the 90's. This was generally a success, but then we decided why not actually use this to look at the future of South Africa? So we set up a team in Johannesburg that included Pierre as he was just finishing up the gold scenarios. The two main insiders were Michael O'Dowd and Bobby Godwsal. Also Edward Parquier—a nuclear physicist. We all developed these two scenarios for South Africa—the high road and the low road, the first leading to a political settlement and the second to confrontation and Civil War—very simple stuff. We did the predetermined elements, the key uncertainties facing South Africa at the time and then we wrote these scenarios. I was then asked as the person who looked after the function to make a presentation to the employees inside Anglo and that was in late 85 / early 86 and the response was so incredible from them.

The reaction inside AAC was telling. Word spread quickly as Wack had also recorded a series of video presentations in his legendary style detailing the High Road and Low Road scenarios. The presentations were in VHS format and saved by Wack's wife Eve. These are some of the last preserved presentations by Wack and are deeply educational for anyone interested in using scenarios. The various efforts were starting to converge and Sunter felt compelled to do more given all of the excitement that was building. He went on:

> Everybody was feeling the weight of South Africa possibly becoming isolated that I actually went to the chairman Gavin Relly asking if I could give a presentation in public in June or July 1986. I gave a presentation in Durban as a fairly large Indaba (a word for an important meeting with roots in some of the native African tribes) and it really was like detonating a bomb. Over 30 groups were represented there. The following day

my secretary got all these requests to give the presentation to their specific groups. So I brought in a couple of other people from AAC and the three of us over a period of 6 months talked to about 25,000 people including the cabinet—de Klerk and he asked me to talk to the government department. We called it "The World in South Africa in the 1990's," so we started with the global scenarios to give a context to the South African scenarios and it was just the best example of scenario planning I think you'll find because it changed the conversation of an entire nation.

In January 1986, Wack's role on the project wound down, though he would be called back later for additional scenario work in South Africa. Sunter took the lead and went on tour giving numerous public presentations to further promote the conversations the scenarios were provoking. He made presentations to the African National Congress, and to F. W. de Klerk. It was the first time scenarios were being used to address issues at a national level.

## The Good Life

In 1987, Wack started looking for a large house in the south of France. He visited 84 and found something unique in a small town called Curemonte in the Dordogne valley. He bought the Chateau de la Johannie, which was built in 1370. He planned to retire there in a few years. His good friend Collyns described Wack's excitement about the purchase:

> I happened to be living in Philadelphia and Pierre came to see me and he said, "I've brought some photographs." So I thought he was going to show me a photograph of his son or something like that. But he showed me a photograph of stones, or "Pierres," that's the French word for stone. And I looked at these stones, and there was just something magical about them. They were extraordinary colors, shining and reflecting. And Pierre just got ecstatic about these stones. Well, the next time I went to the Chateau with Don [Michael] I went to his wife, and she said, "Look, would you like to see the bedroom?" Well, I'd never ever seen the bedroom before. And I walked in the bedroom, and there behind this enormous fireplace there were these stones. And it was just astonishing to see these stones, which were as if they were alive. And I really knew then why Pierre wanted to buy that chateau.

Yuko did not care for the isolation of Curemonte, and so Wack also purchased an apartment in La Rochelle. She would spend time there and occasionally visit the Chateau, as well as many of Wack's friends and colleagues. One of the first to visit was longtime friend Bruce Scott, who recalled the nature of the building:

The chateau was under architecture restrictions. You couldn't do things that would change the character of the castle. And he had a hard time with that because he was a big enthusiast for anything that came from India and he wanted to be putting Indian stuff into that and changing some of the inside fixtures to be more suitable for his Indian stuff. They just said no and that was hard for him to accept.

## Singapore Airlines

In 1987, the Chairman of Singapore Airlines, J. Y. Pillay heard Wack give a speech on a trip to Singapore. Pillay was Indian and appreciated Wack's references to the Ganges and other metaphors. In 1988 he invited Wack to help him with scenarios for the growing airline. Wack got the project up and running and was known to appreciate a cocktail the airline served called an Orange Campari. During this time, Yuko had become increasingly ill and wanted to return to Japan to be with her family. She was quickly admitted to a hospital in Tokyo where she had chosen to be treated. Wack rented an apartment in Tokyo and visited as often as he could. Unable to manage both Yuko's illness and his work with Singapore Airlines, he asked Napier Collyns to take on the project. Collyns shared the work with Hardin Tibbs and Barbara Heinzen.

Wack relocated to his apartment in Tokyo where Jean-Pierre started pre-school. Wack focused on raising Jean-Pierre, supported by JP's uncle and grandmother, who took him to and from school on her bicycle. JP lived for a few years with his grandmother until his mother made a decision for him to attend school in England. Yuko would remain in Tokyo. On February 25, 1989, Yuko passed away in Tokyo, and Wack made the heart-wrenching trip to Salisbury in England to inform JP.

## Old Mutual and Nedcor

In 1990, Wack was contacted again by longtime friend Bruce Scott at Harvard. The pair went to South Africa in April to meet with executives from Old Mutual and Nedcor. Clem Sunter was also involved as his work with the national scenarios in South Africa had won significant recognition. An insider—Bob Tucker—was to lead the project with Wack and Scott as the two main external resources. Scott remembered:

> We worked together over the next six months in what has proven to be the most exciting professional adventure of my life. Eventually the team consisted of about 18 whites and four blacks, including the president's brother, the head of their office of the budget, a woman who had been Nelson Mandela's doctor while he was in prison and was a close friend and an assortment of executives.

Wack and Scott began by interviewing some 40 executives from both companies and the task was to create a few alternative scenarios for the elimination of apartheid and its impact on financial services firms. They presented a few early scenarios to which one of the senior executives responded, "This suggests that we are on the Titanic. If that is the case, there is not much point thinking about the implications for financial services or for the firm. What do we care if we are the fattest rats on the ship when it goes down?" From that point the focus of the project shifted from the two companies to South Africa and all South Africans. Scott further reminisced:

> The scenario team held most of its meetings at a game farm called Aloe Ridge, a simple but very attractive place about 20 miles outside of Johannesburg. They had hippos and water buffalo, but no cats, no rhino and no elephants.

In October 1990, Wack invited his son, daughter, and future son-in-law to visit South Africa and enjoy the nature reserves. They went to Kruger National Park among other spots and as this chapter describes at its opening, had a very exciting experience with a charging elephant.

The scenarios were necessarily part political, part economic and part social, but at first, did not include the issue of race:

> Oddly enough, both Bob Tucker and Pierre were uncomfortable with my notion that we needed to talk about the black-white issue and they were still more uncomfortable with my notion that South Africans might have something to learn from American experience with desegregation. It took three discussions, and the lobbying of two black women on the team, even to get this on the agenda.

However, from that point, apartheid was a key storyline which enabled conversations that could not previously be held. Once the scenario set was complete, the team went on to make a series of presentations over the course of about a week. First, the team presented to the government, the ANC and the Zulus. A week later the team presented to the full cabinet, followed by questions and answers, and then two days later presented to Nelson Mandela and eight of the ANC executive team. The team made a video of their presentation, with each section being led and presented by a different team member.

Scott commented that Wack was somewhat uncomfortable with the idea of scenarios for a country rather than a firm, but the presentations continued throughout 1991 to many groups of about 100 people. On conclusion of the work, Wack returned to France having no doubt paved the way for additional later scenario work in South Africa by Adam Kahane. In a final assessment of the project, Scott said:

The South African scenario exercise was a great experience, like Pierre's early oil scenarios at Shell-London or the gold scenarios for Anglo. I wish there could have been a real follow up. Pierre said to me at the time that the SA scenarios had too much detail—like a photo. They needed to be simpler, more like a Picasso painting, with just a few key lines. Surely he was right on this . . . There have not been many Picassos, and there will not be many like Pierre!

## The River and the Rock

On April 21, 1991, Eve Baudoin returned to Paris after visiting her grandfather in the south of France to a voice on her answering service she had been anticipating for 14 years. "Hello, this is Pierre Wack . . ."

## Chapter 7 Sources (in order of use)

Gertenbach, W. D. (1983). Landscapes of the Kruger national park. *Koedoe, 26*(1), 9–121.

Braack, L. E. (2006). *Kruger national park*. Chatswood, NSW: New Holland Press.

Durrheim, D. N., & Leggat, P. A. (1999). Risk to tourists posed by wild mammals in South Africa. *Journal of Travel Medicine, 6*(3), 172–179.

Selous, F. C. (1881). *A hunter's wanderings in Africa: Being a narrative of nine years spent amongst the game of the far interior of South Africa, containing accounts of explorations beyond the Zambesi, on the River Chobe, and in the Matabele and Mashuna countries, with full notes upon the natural history and present distribution of all the large mammalia*. London: R. Bentley & Son.

Excerpt from personal communications with Jean-Pierre Wack. Author held interviews and discussions in 2014–16.

Excerpt from personal communications with Cheryl Aldons. Author held interviews and discussions in 2014–16.

Excerpt from personal communications with Fiona Youlton. Author held interviews and discussions in 2014–16.

Excerpt from personal communications with Eve Wack. Author held interviews and discussions in 2014–16.

Scott, B. (1998, March 15). [Letter to Eve Wack]. Copy in possession of Eve Wack.

Excerpt from personal communications with Bruce Scott. Author held interviews and discussions in 2014–16.

Wack, P. (1985a). Scenarios: Shooting the rapids. *Harvard Business Review, 63*(6), 139–150.

Wack, P. (1985b). Scenarios: Uncharted waters ahead. *Harvard Business Review, 63*(5), 73–89.

Wack, P. (1985c). *Scenarios: The gentle art of re-perceiving*. Harvard Business School, Unpublished manuscript.

Wack, P. (1984). *Scenarios: The gentle art of re-perceiving*. Harvard Business School Working Paper 9–785–042, December 1984.

Kleiner, Art, Pierre A. Wack interview in Curemonte. (n.d.). 53 pp. The annotated transcript of an interview between Art Kleiner and Pierre Wack regarding the development of Shell's scenario planning. Retrieved from the Art Kleiner Archive, University of Oxford.

Porter, M. E. (1980). *Competitive strategy: Techniques for analyzing industries and competitors with a new introduction.* Florence, MA: The Free Press.

Porter, M. E. (1985). *Competitive advantage: Creating and sustaining superior performance. 1985.* New York: Free Press.

Porter, M. E. (1998). *Cluster and the new economics of competition.* Florence, MA: The Free Press.

Porter, M. E. (2008). *Competitive strategy: Techniques for analyzing industries and competitors.* New York: Simon and Schuster.

Excerpt from personal communications with Ted Newland. Author held interviews and discussions in 2014–16.

Wack, P. (1984). *Scenarios: The gentle art of re-perceiving.* Harvard Business School Working Paper 9–785–042, December 1984.

Excerpt from personal communications with Clem Sunter. Author held interviews and discussions in 2014–16.

Sunter, C. (1987). *The world and South Africa in the 1990s.* Cape Town: Human & Rousseau.

Sunter, C. (1992). *The new century: Quest for the high road.* Cape Town: Human & Rousseau.

Sunter, C. (1996). *The high road: Where are we now?* Cape Town: Human & Rousseau.

Excerpt from personal communications with Peter Schwartz. Author held interviews and discussions in 2014–16.

Excerpt from personal communications with Ged Davis. Author held interviews and discussions in 2014–16.

Wade, D. (1994). *Long and medium term global scenarios: 1971–1992.* Taped interview with Ted Newland, Cybard, France, Unpublished manuscript, May 1994.

Lessem, R., & Nussbaum, B. (1996). *Sawubona Africa: Embracing four worlds in South African management.* Cape Town: ZebraPress.

Senge, P. M. (2014). *The fifth discipline fieldbook: Strategies and tools for building a learning organization.* Danvers, MA: Crown Business Press.

van Jaarsveld, G. J. (1988). Goeiemore, good morning, kgotso, dumela, sawubona: Opening routines and misunderstandings. *South African Journal of Linguistics,* 6(1), 93–108.

Carstens, P. (2001). *In the company of diamonds: De Beers, Kleinzee, and the control of a town.* Columbus, OH: Ohio University Press.

Kanfer, S. (1995). *The last empire: De Beers, diamonds, and the world.* London: Palgrave Macmillan.

Kretschmer, T. (2003). *De Beers and beyond: The history of the international diamond cartel.* New York: New York University.

Imai, M. (2006). Market discipline and deposit insurance reform in Japan. *Journal of Banking & Finance,* 30(12), 3433–3452.

Anglo American Corporation. (n.d.). *Diamond scenarios—1986 to 1993.* Unpublished internal document. Copy in possession of the Pierre Wack Memorial Library, University of Oxford.

Excerpt from personal communications with Bruce Scott. Author held interviews and discussions in 2014–16.

Anglo American Corporation. (1985, April). *Gold: Scenarios for the short-term and for the nineties.* Unpublished internal document. Copy in possession of the Pierre Wack Memorial Library, University of Oxford.

Anglo American Corporation. (1986, July). *Options for the long term: Downstream gold.* Unpublished internal document. Copy in possession of the Pierre Wack Memorial Library, University of Oxford.

Excerpt from personal communications with Ted Newland. Author held interviews and discussions in 2014–16.

Excerpt from personal communications with Clem Sunter. Author held interviews and discussions in 2014–16.

Excerpt from personal communications with Eve Wack. Author held interviews and discussions in 2014–16.

Excerpt from personal communications with Napier Collyns. Author held interviews and discussions in 2014–16.

Gaullieur, E. (1884). *Histoire de la Réformation à Bordeaux et dans le ressort du Parlement de Guyenne* (Vol. 1). Houston, TX: Champion Publishing.

Çelik, Z. (2008). *Empire, architecture, and the city: French-Ottoman encounters, 1830–1914.* Seattle: University of Washington Press.

Prieur, L., & Delage, F. (1947). Fouilles effectuées au «chateau des cars»: Commune de Saint-Merd-les-Oussines (Corrèze). *Gallia, 5*(1), 47–79.

Tulasne-Moeneclaey, A. (1997). *Châteaux de Corrèze.* Les guides art et tourisme.

Wack, E. (n.d.). *Quelques dates et événements de la vie d'un "homme remarquable": Pierre Wack* [draft; 12 pages with note by Eve Wack]. Document retrieved from the Pierre Wack Memorial Library, University of Oxford. Napier interview about Singapore Airlines.

Excerpt from personal communications with Jean-Pierre Wack. Author held interviews and discussions in 2014–16.

Scott, B. (1998, March 15). [Letter to Eve Wack]. Copy in possession of Eve Wack.

Excerpt from personal communications with Ged Davis. Author held interviews and discussions in 2014–16.

Excerpt from personal communications with Clem Sunter. Author held interviews and discussions in 2014–16.

Schwartz, P., & Ogilvy, J. A. (1998). Scenarios for global investment strategy for the new century. In L. Fahey & R. Randall (Eds.), *Learning from the future: Competitive foresight scenarios,* pp. 175–186. New York: John Wiley & Sons.

Schwartz, P., & Ogilvy, J. A. (1998). Plotting your scenarios. In L. Fahey & R. Randall (Eds.), *Learning from the future: Competitive foresight scenarios,* pp. 57–80. New York: John Wiley & Sons, Inc.

Wack, E. (n.d.). *Quelques dates et événements de la vie d'un "homme remarquable": Pierre Wack* [draft; 12 pages with note by Eve Wack]. Document retrieved from the Pierre Wack Memorial Library, University of Oxford.

Duncan, N. E., & Wack, P. (1994). Scenarios designed to improve decision making. *Planning Review, 22*(4), 18–46.

de Geus, A. P. (1992). Modelling to predict or to learn? *European Journal of Operational Research, 59*(1), 1–5.

Tucker, B., & Scott, B. R. (Eds.) (1992). *South Africa: Prospects for successful transition.* Cape Town: Juta & Company.

Wilson, I. (1992). Teaching decision makers to learn from scenarios: A blueprint for implementation. *Planning Review, 20*(3), 18–22.

# 8   Calm Waters and Tidal Waves

Eve Baudoin had not seen Wack in 14 years, except for the chance encounter in Paris in 1982. She had moved on by necessity, but never really. In the early days after he broke it off, Wack simply quit responding to her, which was unbearable for her:

> Pierre was not a simple man and I was not adult enough to make it easier. I didn't know myself well enough, I was confused by my emotions and I went from a state of total destruction to that of rebellion. I only knew one thing: I loved Pierre. He was an obsession. Like a mantra I pronounced his name 10 times a day. In my sleep I had nightmares. I could stand many things, but not to be abandoned without an explanation.

Faced with no other option, she had to move on. She pursued her own path, in many ways inspired by her time with Wack. He had given her the taste of travel—and always avoiding the tourist traps, she took the difficult roads, following local customs, using local transport, engaging with the local people wherever she went. She went to India many times "looking for Pierre's secret," and Cairo became another favorite spot. She continued on her own pilgrimage, making trips to India that would be dramatically unsafe by todays' standards. Eventually, she met an art dealer from Cairo who was very much the opposite of Wack—highly emotional, extraverted. They travelled extensively together and in March, 1978, they married, but it only lasted a few months. He supported her and encouraged her to study at L'Ecole du Louvre, after which she became a teacher in a school for antique dealers. Paintings were her specialty.

There were always reminders of Wack in the strangest of places. She went to see an old classmate whom she was surprised to find owned an Afghan named Javote. The dog had a striking resemblance to Indra, so Baudoin took many pictures of herself with Javote, sensing that she would one day be able to show them to Wack.

In the summer, she had two months' vacation and her children would spend the time with their paternal grandmother in Ireland. She went back to India four more times in search of her own guru, again following a path ignited by Wack, albeit her own. Her experiences were diverse, including being pickpocketed, staying with a group of disciples and serving a guru, breaking large stones to help Indian men construct a wall, shaving her head, sleep and food deprivation, through it all asking herself, "will I ever see Pierre again? An interior voice said 'yes.'"

Eve married again a few years later. She was 40 years old and they travelled extensively throughout Turkey where she became fascinated by the culture:

> In this country, which has the charm of Asia without its hardness, I met a man with whom I fell in love. He sang beautifully. He introduced me to Turkish culture. I learned its language. I had a house in his village, in Cappadocia, which offers the most mysterious landscapes. I read the Koran in two different versions, got interested in Mevlana and went to see the dances of the dervishes.

Baudoin lived her own life. She took care of her children, learned to love, and became quite successful in her own career. She found ways to blend her interests in art and travel and spent her holidays in Italy or Turkey—both of which she came to love deeply. Her thoughts of Wack had diminished—but they were always there in the background of her life, never dissolved.

## The Meeting

And then he called one day in 1991. "Hello . . . this is Pierre Wack," she heard on her answering service. They were to meet at his apartment on Campagne Rue Premiere. She went to his apartment not quite knowing what to expect. Wack had grown a beard, but the look in his eyes—his regard—was the same, maybe with a few more wrinkles. He offered her an orange Campari, which she accepted. He said he learned to make it when he worked for Singapore Airlines while Yuko was ill. He told her of Yuko's passing and she gave a few parts of her own life. She provided only pieces—it would come in time. He took her to a Thai restaurant and after, invited her up for a nightcap: "Pierre had the capacity as with the strawberries of our first encounters to erase the time that has passed and make me forget his absences." The next day he left for Curemonte.

Three weeks passed and she decided to write him a letter; "I expressed myself clearly, I told the truth, I was hurt." He called her and invited her to join him in Curemonte. Baudoin accepted and recalled her first impressions of La Johannie:

> On arrival at his place, La Johannie, I was very impressed by the house. It resembled him—a high fort, square and austere, a large winding staircase which seemed to climb forever. The steps made like a sun, an

inviting dining room, boxes in every corner. A living room decorated in no particular style, one could see that Pierre did not like guests: The lack of comfort of that large room could only discourage visitors and make the unwanted stay away. There were also some beautiful gothic and Renaissance chimneys. Lots of confusion and dust. There were some lovely things, mostly oriental and strangely displayed any old way.

He opened a bottle of champagne and told her she wrote well. He was impressed by her letter. They talked for hours, trying to account for some of the years that had passed. They asked each other questions, "and because Pierre did not like to ask, it's in the tone of his voice that I understood the situation." It was clear that they quickly developed an unspoken language, a connection beyond words. They spent two days together in Curemonte when she had to return to Paris for work:

> He took me to the train station at Brive. On the platform, he sat next to me on a bench, waited for the train, and waved goodbye with his hand. A great privilege, I found out later. Pierre never attended the departure of others and never turned around to make a sign when he left.

### High Tide

Their romance was immediately reignited and they began travelling together to furnish the castle. They went to Spain to buy large wooden doors—they bought lamps and other decorations. And then it was time for Eve to meet Jean-Pierre: "I was moved by this very Japanese child of Pierre and Yuko. But he who was only nine years old was troubled to see that a woman was sleeping in his father's bedroom." Wack took his son into the village each day choosing very nice places for lunch and dinner. Eve felt ignored. It would take time.

One evening Eve decided to make a meal. Being quite a talented cook, the dinner caused a sensation and Jean-Pierre no longer wanted to go out; "This was the moment Pierre came to trust me. If passed through his son's stomach, why not?" Baudoin continued with her work each morning, organizing files for her school, and in the afternoons they would go on drives through the southern French countryside, always taking the side roads. They listened to Wack's music (Peter Gabriel's music for *The Last Temptation of Christ* was one of his favorites at the time, as well as Olivier Messian and Indian flute) always with incense burning. "His car—at the time it was a Renault, was absolutely filthy. Papers everywhere, dust—a complete mess. He was so particular about some things . . . always knew where his keys were and his mind was so clear and structured. But his office, his car . . . papers everywhere."

In July of 1991, Wack's daughter Nathalie was to marry a man named Michael Kilpatrick. They held the wedding in Curemonte and while

Baudoin helped with some of the organizing, she was not among the invited. Soon after, Baudoin returned to Paris for the start of classes and Wack was on a trip to Pakistan. When he returned, they were together in Paris for a few days when he left for England to visit Jean-Pierre. A few weeks later Wack called Baudoin from a phone booth in La Rochelle—he was having terrible back pain. His good friends Michel and Lilian Cantin would not allow him to be alone in his apartment at La Rochelle, so they brought him to their place. Cantin was a work colleague of Wack's at La Libre Entreprise back in the 1960s. The next day Baudoin received another call; "I have lost a quarter of my blood. They will start chemotherapy."

## Myeloma

Wack was diagnosed with myeloma, or bone marrow cancer. Baudoin rushed to the hospital in La Rochelle and tried to figure out what to do next. She was taken in by the Cantins, who became good friends. Her father was a doctor at a hospital in Chartres where he recommended she bring him; however, there was no bed available. But he advised her that if they came to the emergency entrance, "they cannot refuse you." She did not feel it was appropriate for her to make such a decision on Wack's behalf, so they stayed in La Rochelle:

> He made fun of everything, the I.V.'s, as well as other therapies. But I was still uncertain about this very secret man. He also made plans. "I promised to take Jean-Pierre to California in April." He insisted on being able to give a conference at the OECD a few days hence in Paris. Sometimes I doubted my intuition. How can it be that such a rational man whose job it was always to be able to analyze a situation and not to be able to recognize the seriousness of his condition? Where was his analytical mind?

## Eve the Healer

Like a magic druid with special powers, Baudoin was able to convince him to move to the Hospital Saint Louis in Paris. Before they could go, he was given very strong sedatives and was almost unresponsive when they left La Rochelle. On arrival in Paris, he was assigned the skilled and very empathetic Doctor Mariette, who officially informed Wack of his condition and explained the gravity of the situation. Wack, ever the optimist, kept his spirits up and maintained a positive outlook. He needed several tranquilizers during this time, and asked Baudoin often to replay the events of past weeks. She detected some anxiety in him as he became aware that he needed things repeated. Many visitors came, some French, many English. Baudoin remembered:

Just like Indra, I saw myself curled up around his legs, waiting for him to be alone. As soon as the visitors left, he opened himself up. He was in pain, he wanted some soup, Japanese products and fresh pineapple.

She took great care of him and attended to his needs at every moment. Wack had severe nausea from the therapy and morphine, yet he blamed it on the food. Bad lentils, he said with his head over the toilet. He kept his optimistic outlook amidst painful examinations. Even though his vertebrae were crumbling and he would lose eight centimeters in height, he always answered that he was doing very well. According to Eve, "He always refused to acknowledge what was bothering him and treated with disdain all annoyances, including the most serious events in his life. This had been his strength."

Wack was finally allowed to leave the Hospital Saint Louis in late 1991. They stayed at his apartment on Rue Campagne Premiere in Paris. She tried to tempt him with healthy meals, but the morphine caused constant nausea. There were few visitors during this time, but slowly and steadily, Baudoin saw him improving. Eventually, there was no more need for morphine; his mood improved and so did his interest in life and food:

Certainly we slept in the same bed, but in order not to bruise him with my elbows, I placed a cushion between us. During the day I came, I went, did house chores, told him of my school, brought him what I called "bubbles" of outside air, life. He continued to recover.

Her energy and care continued to support his improvement and healing, and as he grew stronger, he started to assert more and more of his will and preferences. As a man always free and good at taking care of himself, now he needed help. This was not a familiar experience for Wack, and he displayed parts of his personality she had not seen before:

Pierre asked me to get a television set and I discover with this another of his characteristics. His motto could have been, "why do it simply when it can be done with complication?" First, I went to FNAC [the best shop at the time for technology, records, books, etc. . . . ], looked around, saw a Grundig, which corresponded in every way to what Pierre wanted. I opened a file "TV" and brought it to him. That was an error. He dived into this file and started a proper study. He sent me to at least five other stores, so that I could bring him all of their documentation. In the final analysis, he told me to buy the Grundig at FNAC's. Everything had to be done on subway or bus because Pierre was horrified by the thought that one might take a taxi. Sometimes, I cheated.

During the Christmas break in 1992, Wack was feeling well enough to travel. He and Baudoin went to La Rochelle where they spent time with the

Cantins and enjoyed the holiday, though he still needed support and assistance from time to time. On the return to Paris, Wack was finished with the trays, beds and easy chairs. He could come to the table to eat and went out on the subway or bus to buy books. With some deliberation, he asked Eve if they should make a more permanent move to Curemonte. It was the first time he used the term "we" with her.

Of course, she agreed and things were soon settled. Three days each week she commuted by train at six a.m. to Paris to manage her school, and back to La Johannie about midnight. The other days she invested in cleaning and bringing order to the castle. This lasted about three months when Wack asked her about closing her school. She needed only minor encouragement and then she was able to end the long days of commuting. She had saved enough to support her three sons and was ready to be fully with Wack at La Johannie. She finally felt comfortable to bring the sheets she had saved for 15 years.

Each month, they went to Paris for Wack's treatment—what they called a "magic potion." His tastes were always specific and sometimes challenging. Eve recalled; "Honey came from Paris, jams from Brive, peaches from a far-away farm, but near a greenhouse where I profited from buying some plants . . ." And when in Paris they would go to the cinema and dine at carefully selected restaurants:

> In Curemonte Pierre was like the guru and I was the moon. I felt I was his reflection. The majority of the furniture was French and he had imported the fabrics, curtains, woodwork, and other decorative elements from Spain, India, Pakistan and other countries. But I had to study every corner to find the right place where to put each object in the best light . . . We created our life decoration. And I hung up and brought down. I climbed and descended: There are seventy-three steps in La Johannie from the cellar to the roof.

## Visitors

During this time, Wack and Baudoin had many visitors. Baudoin meticulously noted who visited, when they came and the meals she served them. She never wanted to serve a guest the same thing twice. The most frequent visitors of this time period were Napier and Pat Collyns, Don Michael, Michel and Lilian Cantin, and, of course, Ted and Elena Newland. Most stayed only for two days, but why always only two days? Wack's mind was always seeking new ideas and he often referred to his "appetite" or being "hungry" (see Figure 8.1).

Jean-Pierre also came to visit frequently and he was always impressed with Baudoin's talents. She built a base for the mattress in his bedroom, constructed tables and shelves for his things in his room—he could feel the

From  Pierre Wack to GBN.
At the attention of Napier Collyns

Curemonte, April 26th

Dear Napier,

I am now back in Curemonte after a lengthy time in Chartres for intensive kinetherapie. My main illness is apparently stabilised but I have now to fight the side effects of the chemotherapy I had for these last five years and a half. Most of them have contained "cortisone" which after a while attacks the muscles and I must catch up with gymnastic. They cut the cortisone by two and I hope to recover within a few month.

Otherwise I feel well and my appetite for interesting things has not diminished. So when you mentioned interesting papers you had I would be more than pleased to read them.

I cannot reach Ted Newland, but I hope your April gathering went well. We hope also to see you after your family reunion in Provence.

Best wishes to Pat. Et toute mon amitié.

*Figure 8.1* Wack's Letter on April 26

important changes there. Wack himself watched her work and was equally impressed with her skill. He reflected: "There are three brains in man: the one in the head, the one in the heart, the one in the hands." While he had no skills in working with his hands, Baudoin continued to refine the castle and after clearing out the cellar, she took it upon herself to manage the "garden." Up to that point it was simply a mass of vegetation that Wack mowed twice each year. She went after it with vigor—but was afraid of the vipers: " 'Don't be afraid, there aren't any vipers on this side of the hill,' he told me. Not logical, but surprisingly true. How did he know? A mystery."

Art Kleiner came to visit and interviewed Wack for three days, resulting in his chapter titled "Mystics" in his book *The Age of Heretics*. Wack was positive, and looked forward to refining the work with Kleiner a little further (see Figure 8.2).

Baudoin threw herself into creating a masterpiece of a garden. She arranged everything in her mind according to lunar and solar symbols and then making

To Napier COLLYNS GBN fax 1.5105478510
from Pierre WACK fax 33.56840741

Curemonte, May 15th 1994

Dear Napier,

Art Kleiner has send me the chapter of his new book. Quite interesting but it certainly deserve a further conversation. I invited him anytime in August. Congratulation for your April Forum.

At the phone last time (six weeks ago) you said you would send me some papers of interest. Nothing has arrived and I remain quite hungry. When will you come to Curemonte ?

Warm regards,

*Pierre Wack*

Pierre Wack

sheet 1/1

*Figure 8.2* Wack's Letter on May 15

sure certain colors of flowers would appear in certain places at certain times of the year. She also knew that Wack liked to view the garden from their terrace. With this in mind she set out to make a drawing of her plan:

> One day I took some copying paper. On the first page I designed the layout of the garden. On the other four copies, I used crayons to note the colors that the garden would have in the four different seasons. I had many compliments. I had not forgotten the lesson about the purchase of the TV set.

They travelled to all kinds of nurseries, sometimes even to England for plants. There was always an eye to bring a little of Asia to La Johannie whenever possible, so Wack sought bamboos and other Japanese plants: "We had to deal with Pierre Wack. He never thought like a common mortal." They planted a grove of black bamboos which were a favorite of Wack's. And indeed, the roots eventually became a problem that required concrete enclosure. It was a time of remarkable happiness for both:

> Pierre's gentleness, his encouragements concerning me were sincere. But he approved only of what pleased him. I knew, and Jean-Pierre knew it before me, that to obtain something one had to start with the sentence

"you know, come to think of it . . . I think it might be a good idea . . . what do you think about . . . ?" Pierre would then ask for time to think about it, sometimes three days for decisions he judged to be important, like the one about replacing some shingles on the roof, or to add a bathroom, or still to make an opening in the wall for a new window.

Wack loved solitude and would frequently disappear all day into his office emerging only for meals. This was another instance of his coded language—"do not disturb", it said. Baudoin described his office as having a sacred atmosphere. She immediately and intuitively took off her shoes when entering. There was a temple door, a totem, Indian pillars and an alcove with a small photo of his Indian Master—Svamiji Prajnanpad. A shrine, as so many disciples tend to create would have been too emotional. He also hung Japanese scrolls on the wall, and according to Japanese custom, changed them with seasons or meanings. Two of his favorites were the Japanese deity Fudo Myoo, and a classic Japanese scroll depicting a smiling monk hugging a sleeping tiger. During these times when Wack sought isolation, Baudoin focused on her garden project. She buried herself in her new hobby and became completely absorbed.

One year, during a local fair in Curemonte, Wack purchased a kitten "whose grandfather had been a wild animal in Bengal." He named him Tao. The cat appeared almost as a leopard and spent his days on Wack's lap, purring, or sleeping on his sofa or desk. Eve was jealous. As the kitten grew he could not be contained and used to stroll throughout the garden. Wack followed the feline everywhere and crushed the flowers in the garden without much hesitation. Eve planted more flowers. Eventually, they had to get rid of Tao because of Jean-Pierre's allergies. It was fine with Baudoin.

## GBN Scenario Planning Master Class

In 1987, two key former Shell Group Planning members relocated to California to create a company called Global Business Network (GBN). The founders were Wack's successor Peter Schwartz, old friend Napier Collyns, and three others who were not affiliated with Shell (Jay Ogilvy, Stewart Brand, and Lawrence Wilkinson). Arie de Geus, Kees van der Heijden and Bo Ekman were strong supporters. The company focused on delivering a profitable service from the concept of remarkable people. Early on, corporate members would pay an annual fee to be connected a network of truly diverse thinkers, attend workshops and seminars, and, of course, the emerging scenario planning training sessions. By 1993, GBN had a profitable part of their business from running scenario planning training events, and Collyns had been working to recruit Wack as a guest.

It is interesting to observe Wack's comments about writing in this facsimile to Collyns. Point number three in his note in Figure 8.3 states: "I would be glad to see Harriet provided she is aware that I have no intention of

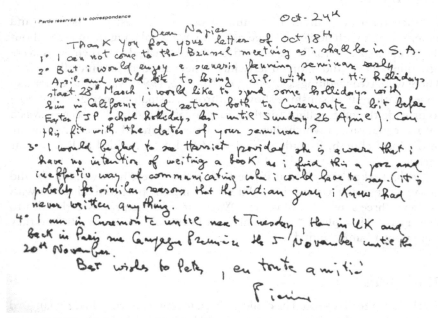

*Figure 8.3* Wack's Letter on October 24

writing a book as I find this a poor and ineffective way of communicating what I could have to say. (It is probably for similar reasons that the Indian guru I knew had never written anything)."

In April of 1993, Wack and Baudoin made the trip to California for a week. Wack had not given any formal presentations or speeches in some time, but true to form, it was almost word-perfect. Of course, he used all of his metaphors and told the stories of the early days in Shell and a rather lengthy summary of the work on Gold for Anglo, which he called one of his favorites. A transcript of his presentation is kept at the Pierre Wack Memorial Library in Oxford.

**Collyns reminisced on the visit to GBN:**

He had already been quite sick—I was very concerned about him. He brought his wife and he brought his young son, and I really tried to protect him. I didn't want him to see anybody and there was this big crowd of people. I brought him down to our office and I put him in a private room. He always had this habit before he spoke of going almost into a kind of trance . . . And he spoke for nearly four hours, I think, non-stop. And he hadn't given any kind of speech for several years and it was the last speech he ever gave.

## Calm Waters

On their return to Curemonte, Baudoin became interested in Ikebana and experimented with flower arrangements for Wack, placing them throughout the castle and eventually in his office when he asked. As their lives were becoming more and more intertwined, they decided to officially marry. There were two weddings. The first, on May 22, 1993, was in the Cistercian abbey, with a ray of sunshine showing through a small stained glass window to provide the perfect light for their long-awaited union. The second was a formal ceremony in which they were married by the Mayor of Curemonte in the local church. It made official what had been decided at least a year earlier.

Eve had taken care of Jean-Pierre as though he were her own, but she did not want to make assumptions. After checking the potential adoption with her own three sons, and, of course, Wack himself, she proposed the idea to Jean-Pierre. He replied: "This is the most beautiful Christmas gift." So they were now a family united.

## Those Years

Wack was in remission and he could go back to a more normal life. He laughed a lot. He laughed at English TV shows—"Absolutely Fabulous"—and he also laughed at more seemingly important things. One day Eve was robbed of a substantial amount of money—she was upset—yet Wack broke out laughing: "He was incapable of making someone feel guilty, not me, nor Jean-Pierre at other times. What a sense of responsibility, what freedom he knew how to give." During these years as the garden was still young, they would drive around the south of France looking for wildflowers. She would spot them and call for him to pull over. Equipped with her cutters, she ventured out into the fields and cut the flowers that had caught her eye. During these drives, Wack told her about his childhood, the stories of escaping the German army, Gurdjieff, and all other aspects of his past. They sorted out old photographs and he told her about Chantal, made her follow the road he had taken so long ago to escape the authorities. Eve recalled: "I realized also that to be Alsatian at age 18 during the forties explained a lot of the contradictions." She even went so far as to call him a misanthrope—avoiding human society at times:

> During our first years in Curemonte, we received the visit of many friends—almost all of these people in Pierre's profession. But if he was very glad to have them discover the cultural riches of the region, share memories of his work, on a certain morning he no longer spoke to his guests and shut himself up in his office right after breakfast. It was time for the guests to depart. The pressure became unsustainable. "Friends are like fish, after two days they smell," he used to say. I liked his capacity to impose his will.

Another similar story captures the same stance. Wack's niece and nephew suddenly arrived one day unannounced as Eve was preparing a dinner. Wack was giving a car tour of the nearby area to some friends and when he arrived back at La Johannie, he told them: "One does not come without calling. You will find a restaurant further down in the village." As they were leaving a thunderstorm erupted and Wack turned to Eve, saying: "I should have given them my tent."

## The Question

Wack was known for getting right to the heart of the matter. He queried people in many ways and by this time had made an art out of getting to the core of a person—to understand their mental model. It was what he came to master at his interviews in Shell and other companies:

> Professionally, he asked unexpected questions just to observe the reaction. He told me that his pet question was: "If I were a magician and I had the powers to make your wish, one wish only, come true, what would it be?" He never gave me the answer to this question for himself, but I imagine the face of the economist who before the interview with Pierre had been memorizing all kinds of figures.

He picked up an early version of this question from Ted Lipinski at the Institute for the Future in California in 1976. Obviously, it was a favorite of his and he used it throughout his life. Wack subjected people in his life to all kinds of tests and challenges. It was efficient and rewarding for some who intuitively understood him, but unbearable for those who did not. For example, one of Eve's sons struggled with drugs and dropped out of school. With Wack's approval, Eve invited him to Curemonte. They arranged for a place he could stay in town and come to La Johannie for work each day. They jointly decided that discipline was needed:

> Pierre never invited Adrian to a single meal during the three months he spent in Curemonte. Though Adrian, after having put his house in order, after washing up every morning came at 9 am to work in the garden. He went home for lunch and returned at 2 pm until evening. He did a terrific job. He planted the Japanese garden near the terrace, dug out the dry river and replaced stones. "Your arrangement is perfect," Pierre said to him—Adrian knew that this was the most beautiful of compliments, because a stone arrangement, like a Japanese flower arrangement, reflects the interior life. Wack later called Adrian the man who displaced mountains.

Wack loved to seduce. Above all, he was a good listener, he asked questions, he made women dream, he was interested. There are varying accounts of Wack's physical attractiveness, but the majority seem to indicate it was his mind that women responded to most. That, and the fact that he engaged with people in a genuine and real way. Of course, only when he wanted to. Nonetheless, he enjoyed an audience, or even an individual, paying close attention to him in return. Baudoin increasingly managed the workings of La Johannie and the visitors who came, as well as the logistics of the garden and family members. As her role increased, Wack could dedicate more time to reflection and meditation:

> Pierre dreaded those who asked him questions regarding the origin of this manner of thinking. This interest seemed to him often not very sincere or, of an emotional character. He discouraged the curious as one repels a voyeur. He did not have to explain his philosophy to understand it, one only had to watch him live. He was free of all contingencies, he thought beyond the ideas he received. All decisions that were to be taken awoke his spirit of adventure, the one to consider all roads possible, even the most unexpected ones. He had the art of perception. Doing him justice, in his professional environment he was considered a visionary, some even thought him a genius.

Of course, Wack was happy to have had success with his work. He could not help but be proud of the function he served within Shell and other companies. He had an ego like each of us. But he managed it the best he could, and he always thought back to Gurdjieff and Svamiji to "stop" the flattery where and when he could. He did not seek recognition. He made it clear: "There is no worse slave than the one who is slave to the opinion of others."

It is true that Wack could be dismissive. Anything he found to be mean or undignified, he declined any interest in. Some called this arrogance, others called it egotism. But according to Eve, he was always concerned with others. But to be sure, he did not do well when facing mental narrowness—he did not have room in his mind to take account for such a thing. Much the same for trite conversation or gossip. He simply had no interest in trivial things.

## Beyim

In Turkish, the word "Beyim" indicates "my lord, my master" and this is how Eve introduced Wack while they travelled around Uchisar, Turkey in 1992. The Turkish language had a demeanor that was familiar to Eve and fully suited the way she felt about Wack. In Turkey, Eve was more knowledgeable than Wack, which surprised him, though he delighted in every experience. They wound up with a stalled rental car and took refuge with a family Eve was able to negotiate on the spot: "Pierre was happy with this unexpected experience, glad to discover people with such warmth and certain customs, where in addition, and not to be disdained, the cooking was very good." Once their car was repaired, Wack took the wheel and insisted on the back roads all the way to Antalya—a 12-hour drive on the main roads but it took them two days. He spent and additional two days in bed after, but said the landscapes were worth it.

## India

A few months later the Wacks took a trip to India to celebrate their marriage. Wack studied, planned and re-planned the itinerary for two weeks, changing his mind four times on the route, airline and overall schedule. He enlisted the help of former assistant Fiona Youlton to help with the planning as she had done this sort of thing so many times for him before. Everything was first class, of course. Wack wanted to show Eve the best possible experience of India—so different from both of their early travels on a shoestring. Eve recalled:

> Tolerant and rigid, curious and discreet, introvert and open to all experiences—what fascinated me with Pierre is that he was everything and the opposite, every morning I asked myself with which of these men I was going to wake up with. I, who am Gemini, love diversity and loathe routine. With Pierre I was being gratified. Being always faithful to himself, he offered me daily a new facet of his character.

The couple travelled to India as planned but the itinerary took some adjustment. First the plane departing Paris was delayed 24 hours. Therefore, the agency Wack had arranged in Bombay was not there. From this point forward the trip, given that the drivers, hotel reservations and other bookings were delayed or automatically cancelled, became an adventure of improvisation. It also happened to be that they finally arrived in India on Diwali—the Indian equivalent of Christmas. The pair were somehow adjusted to a suite of five rooms in a former palace of a Maharajah. They sat on suitcases on trains and took wooden third class benches where they had previously booked first class tickets. Eve took a small girl on her knees as they squeezed in with a variety of families.

As they changed trains Wack gave her a fresh coconut off the road offered by the children and they shopped for antiques among the rural villages. They purchased wall hangings, fabrics and other gems from the heart of India. They visited a series of temples and a group of musicians invited them to listen to their rehearsal: "The music is beautiful, played only for us at sunset with the ochre-red desert for a background. One evening the moon is so low in the sky, and so big as to be unrealistic. I don't dare to ask the chauffeur to stop to take a photograph. The sound of my voice might break the spell."

They visited the Pakistani border which had only recently been opened and found a rural village. The men were dressed in orange, no hotel, no restaurant, no merchants. Wack said: "Just like Channa," as it reminded him of his guru's home. The tour of India was complete and it was time to return to France.

## Tidal Wave

In November, 1995, Wack had a serious relapse. Like a tidal wave, it all came crashing down. The pair had tickets booked for a trip to Egypt which needed to be cancelled. This was the start of a long, dark time. The pain was suddenly much worse and Wack had difficulty sleeping. When he felt up to it, Wack and Eve took short trips north to Relais, a famous and very nice getaway about an hour drive north of Curemonte. After these short excursions, Wack had to give up driving and walking became difficult. From this point, in mid-November, 1995, he did not leave La Johannie:

> He spent hours on the terrace looking at the garden—he seemed to get nourishment from that. On the bottom of the terrace, the flowers were all yellow, orange and red, with a touch of blue which enhanced the colors of the sun. I had the impression he sucked energy from nature . . . He recuperated from his fatigue in the contemplation of the black bamboos which border the dry river of his Japanese garden. They had become tall and very beautiful. Did he still have the temptation to throw a pebble against one of the trunks? I don't think so. I told him, "I am not too contemplative," to which he replied "too bad for you." I have still so much to learn from him.

If only we knew what question he had asked so many years ago at that temple in Japan. But it is clearly none of our business.

## Scenarios and the Art of Strategic Conversation

In September 1995, Kees van der Heijden visited Wack in Curemonte, France, after the first publication of his book *Scenarios: The Art of Strategic Conversation*. Wack was ill, and it was a difficult time. Wack agreed to provide an endorsement for the book on the condition that Kees visited him to talk about the book in more detail. Van der Heijden wrote a letter to Collyns detailing his reflections on what he learned in his conversations with Wack. First, there were many positive comments and he was pleased that the book was published: "Then he went on to say: 'But you have of course, missed the main point.'" Van der Heijden's comments in his letter to Collyns reflect with elegance some of the most important insights that Wack left behind:

> In Pierre's view the main purpose of scenario thinking is to come to a point where one sees the world as no one has seen it before and the

potential for a new strategy is born. Scenarios can do that for you, but it is not a trivial matter. It certainly is not, in Pierre's opinion, a mechanistic process in which one works through a predetermined set of steps during one or two workshops. Instead it is a process of long-lasting commitment to deep thinking about the situation, a willingness to find out what the world already knows, and a willingness to engage with what Pierre called "remarkable people," not necessarily experts but people who enjoy looking at the situation in multiple and unexpected ways.

Van der Heijden said that it was his attempt to complete his assignment as Wack's understudy from so long ago. He still had many questions, but Wack's health did not allow for long conversations. The two spent a few hours over three days and would talk when Wack felt up to it. Van der Heijden went on to revise some 40 percent of his book based on those conversations when the second edition was published in 2005.

## Undertow

Baudoin contemplated the possibility that Wack wanted to pass away at home in Curemonte, but she felt sure he would have talked with her about this. It was just after Christmas in 1996 that Wack himself realized the complete seriousness of his condition, and then Eve "closed the house, shut the suitcases, helped him down the stairs, and in less than one hour we were off. There were 550 km to Paris . . ."

From this point Wack's health varied wildly. Back and forth from Curemonte to Saint Louis they drove a half a dozen times. Once, when his health seemed better, they rented a place in Fontainebleau to be close to one of Eve's newborn grandsons. She felt considerable guilt about leaving him to see the baby but it had been clear from 1995 that Wack's time was limited. She struggled for the next year, in and out of the hospital, seeking her own solace where and when she could, yet attending to Wack the absolute best way she could manage. She continued to cook his favorite foods for him—pork with ginger, Japanese style, curry and all of his other preferences. She brought Indian decorations for his hospital room and good wine he had stored away in the cellar of La Johannie.

Thus began the worst of it, and Wack sometimes faded in and out of consciousness. They had times of intensely lucid conversation and times when Wack became incoherent. Eve sometimes fell asleep in the easy chair, always by his side, exhausted. Their plan involved one more treatment before heading back to Curemonte but Doctor Mariette advised against it. So they made arrangements to stay at Eve's father's clinic in Chartres:

Pierre wanted next to his bed the photograph with me and Javote, the Afghan dog, an image from the past, in black and white, which he had framed above his bedside table in La Johannie the last few months. Pierre asked me after our marriage that I grow back my hair and I think that in his head, Eve and Indra were one.

In mid-November of 1996 they were back at the Hospital Saint Louis under emergency conditions—Wack had an extremely high fever. While they treated him as best they could, Wack began to lose his eyesight to cataracts and he had trouble recognizing his daughter Nathalie and son Jean-Pierre. He could detect their voices, though and as he struggled for coherency, he came to the realization he needed to stop the treatments. He told Eve he sometimes could not even recognize his own voice—it had changed so much, and when the doctors indicated this could go on for weeks or months, maybe even years, he determined it was not feasible any longer:

> I related to him the doctor's words, but the tone of my voice, my emo-
> tion told him how shocked I was. His serenity calmed me down. Pierre
> once again helped me even in such a difficult moment. He gave me
> his last words of advice and recommendations for "afterwards." Yes,
> I could have a mass in Curemonte. His cousin Amelie was to take care
> of the protestant ceremony. His ashes would go under the bamboo in
> the Japanese garden, decorated with a funerary statue, Chantel's gift
> and a "tori," a bird house for the spiritual "bird" . . . the house, which
> I should continue to embellish, always in our image. 'Never sell La
> Johannie' he trusted me. I became the guardian priestess of the temple.
> I put my head on his shoulder, he caressed my hair.

They returned to her father's clinic in Chartres as he was able to make nice arrangements for them, including a small separate room for Eve. There were visits from his daughter Nathalie and Jean-Pierre, but they were difficult due to Wack's semi-consciousness. He continued to struggle with breathing and his words became more and more nonsensical. On Sunday, December 21, 1997, Eve decided to move him back to the hospital as his condition was worsening. On the morning of December 22, she went into his room and saw him breathing badly. He died in her arms just then. He had time to hear her say that she loved him: "His face became gray, then for a few seconds lit up. It was Monday December 22, 1997. The time was 10:15 am." It was the shortest day of the year.

Not long after, she notified Wack's closest colleagues by fax, specifically Napier and Pat Collyns, Don Michael and Peter Schwartz and all Pierre's friends:

> "At the hour of the funeral, the bells were ringing in Curemonte; in
> Chartres, at the temple, there were Indian flutes, sunflowers, and many
> friends as well to share my pain."

—Eve Wack

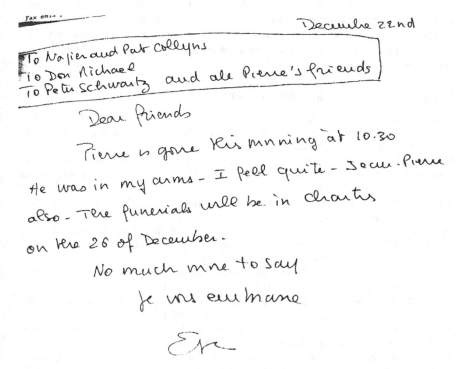

*Figure 8.4* Eve's Fax on December 22

## Last of the Magi

Some did not see that there was anything magical about Wack, and that it had no part in what he was able to achieve with scenario planning. Van der Heijden was very clear: "There is nothing mysterious I saw about Pierre and scenarios. Even if there is truth in it, then still, it is not very clear what anybody else can do with it. These things didn't come out of clouds in the sky—you have to focus on the logic of the process. It is focused and deep, analytical thinking."

Others expressed a different view—perhaps taken in by Wack's own interests in diverse cultures and belief systems. It is tempting to recount the stories of similar people who achieved remarkable things. In one of his speeches given about Wack, Collyns recalled that when Isaac Newton died, a very wealthy economist named Keynes bought Newton's papers at auction in 1936—almost 200 years after his death—but only the non-scientific papers that portrayed Newton as a kind of magician: "Keynes wrote a paper years later in which he called Newton the last of the magi. And somehow I feel that Pierre was in that same tradition, that he combined this sort of magical side with this deeply rigorous, analytical, structural, systems way of looking."

The term "magi" is an old one that has carried many meanings through-out history. From references to Zoroastrian priests, to the Mediterranean use meaning "magician," and further to the English use referencing the "Magi" who visited Jesus from the East in the Gospel of Matthew. Today we simply call them "wise men."

## Chapter 8 Sources (in order of use)

Wack, E. (n.d.). *Quelques dates et événements de la vie d'un "homme remarquable":* Pierre Wack [draft; 12 pages with note by Eve Wack]. Document retrieved from the Pierre Wack Memorial Library, University of Oxford.

Wack, E. (1998). *Pierreve: 1977–1997.* Curemonte, France, Unpublished manuscript.

Excerpt from personal communications with Eve Wack. Author held interviews and discussions in 2014–16.

Excerpt from personal communications with Jean-Pierre Wack. Author held interviews and discussions in 2014–16.

Wack, E. (n.d.). *Quelques dates et événements de la vie d'un "homme remarquable":* Pierre Wack [draft; 12 pages with note by Eve Wack], Document retrieved from the Pierre Wack Memorial Library, University of Oxford.

Wack, P. (1997, April 26). [Letter to Napier Collyns]. Copy in possession of the Pierre Wack Memorial Library, University of Oxford.

Wack, P. (1994, May 15). [Letter to Napier Collyns]. Copy in possession of the Pierre Wack Memorial Library, University of Oxford.

Wack, P. (1994, October 24). [Letter to Napier Collyns]. Copy in possession of the Pierre Wack Memorial Library, University of Oxford.

Excerpt from personal communications with Napier Collyns. Author held interviews and discussions in 2014–16.

Transcript of tapes 1, 2 and 3 from GBN Scenario Planning Seminar 19 April 1993 [transcription by Peggi Oakley, 2 copies]. Document retrieved from the Pierre Wack Memorial Library, University of Oxford.

Transcript of tapes 4 and 5 from GBN Scenario Planning Seminar 19 April 1993 [transcription by Peggi Oakley, 2 copies]. Document retrieved from the Pierre Wack Memorial Library, University of Oxford.

Transcript of 'Wack @ Curemonte' from Tape 1/Side A to Tape 5/Side A [94 pages, 2 copies]. Document retrieved from the Pierre Wack Memorial Library, University of Oxford.

Wack, P. (1994). *Speech & interviews* [37 pages, 2 copies]. Document retrieved from the Pierre Wack Memorial Library, University of Oxford.

Royal Dutch/Shell Oil. (1977, January). *The seven questions: Typed document with the name "Pierre Wack".* Unpublished internal document. Copy in possession of the Pierre Wack Memorial Library, University of Oxford.

Kleiner, Art, Pierre A. Wack interview in Curemonte. (n.d.). 53 pp. The annotated transcript of an interview between Art Kleiner and Pierre Wack regarding the development of Shell's scenario planning. Retrieved from the Art Kleiner Archive, University of Oxford.

Şahin, İ. (2011). The Turkic word 'bay' in Onomastical names: An etymological approach. *Central Asiatic Journal, 55*(1), 72–90.

Karahan, F. (2007). *Language attitudes of Turkish students towards the English language and its use in Turkish context.* Cankaya University Journal of Arts and Sciences, 1(7).

Heyd, U. (1954). *Language reform in modern Turkey* (No. 5). Jerusalem: Israel Oriental Society.

Vidyarthi, L. P., & Rai, B. K. (1977). *The tribal culture of India.* New Delhi: Concept Publishing Company.

Sopher, D. E. (1980). The geographical patterning of culture in India. In D. E. Sopher (Ed.), *An exploration of India: Geographical perspectives on society and culture,* pp. 371–389. Ithaca, NY: Cornell University Press.

Ling, T. (1974). *The Buddha, Buddhist civilization in India and Ceylon.* New York: Penguin Books.

Excerpt from personal communications with Fiona Youlton. Author held interviews and discussions in 2014–16.

Excerpt from personal communications with Kees van der Heijden. Author held interviews and discussions in 2014–16.

Van der Heijden, K. (1996). *Scenarios: The art of strategic conversation.* New York: John Wiley & Sons.

Van der Heijden, K. (2011). *Scenarios: The art of strategic conversation.* New York: John Wiley & Sons.

Excerpt from personal communications with Jean-Pierre Wack. Author held interviews and discussions in 2014–16.

Van der Heijden, K. (2005). E-mail to Napier Collyns. Copy in possession of Napier Collyns.

Wack, E. (1997). Facsimile to Napier Collyns, Ted Newland and Peter Schwartz. Document retrieved from the Pierre Wack Memorial Library, University of Oxford.

Wack, E. (n.d.). *Quelques dates et événements de la vie d'un "homme remarquable":* Pierre Wack [draft; 12 pages with note by Eve Wack]. Document retrieved from the Pierre Wack Memorial Library, University of Oxford.

No author, a series of documents relating to the GBN Scenario Planning Seminar, April 18–23. (1993). 14 pp. Annotated throughout. Box No. 3:1, Folder No. 1. Retrieved from the Art Kleiner Archive, University of Oxford.

Kleiner, Art, Consequential Heresies: How "thinking the unthinkable/changed Royal Dutch/Shell", Currency. (1989). 23 pp. Box No. 3:2, Folder No. 2. Retrieved from the Art Kleiner Archive, University of Oxford.

de Geus, A. P. (1992). Modelling to predict or to learn? *European Journal of Operational Research,* 59(1), 1–5.

Wack, E. (1997, December 22). [Letter to Napier and Pat Collyns, Don Michael, Peter Schwartz, and all of Pierre's friends]. Copy in possession of the Pierre Wack Memorial Library, University of Oxford.

Rivers, W. H. R. (1924). *Medicine, magic, and religion.* New York: Harcourt, Brace.

Flint, V. I. (1991). *The rise of magic in early medieval Europe.* Princeton, NJ: Princeton University Press.

Yamauchi, E. (1991). Persia and the Bible. *Theological Studies,* 52(1), 176.

Molnar, M. R. (1999). *The star of Bethlehem: The legacy of the Magi.* New Brunswick, NJ: Rutgers University Press.

# Part IV

# Reflections and Legacy

Having recorded the story of Wack, there remain only two objectives. First, to consider how people reacted to the news of his death and capture their reflections about how they knew him in life. Second, to make an attempt to synthesize what his story means for the discipline of scenario planning. Wack would be pleased to know how popular scenarios are today. The term is now fully embedded in the language of even daily conversation. The method has evolved, and while the purpose here is not to critique current approaches to scenario planning, in the context of Wack's story, it is interesting to consider how he practiced the discipline he so loved.

Chapter 9 is a set of reflections, stories, recollections and comments from a variety of people who knew Wack—some from work colleagues at Shell and other companies, and some from lifelong friends. These excerpts from all the available materials are meant to provide a few glimpses into how deeply Wack affected those around him.

Chapter 10 is a suggestion for approaching scenario planning in a most Wackian way. Truly, the chapter may be a little "Wacky." It is a set of principles and tools that Wack was known to believe in and use. Today, there are many different scenario planning methods, and several texts introduce the various 10, eight, or six steps involved in the process. This chapter is intended for anyone looking for a deeper approach to scenarios, driven more by intuition than by steps. Of course, these are also my own interpretations of what I have observed over the course of this project. The intent was to provide something for other scenario planners to ponder based on the remarkable life of the discipline's most mystical pioneer.

# 9  Reflections

After Wack died, Eve wrote to many of his colleagues and asked them to share any memories of him. She had many responses, some of which have been woven into this story—the anecdote of an interview conducted from a yoga posture on the floor, for example. Others are best positioned in this chapter and simply called reflections. Many of Wack's colleagues were eager to tell stories of their interactions with him, and some wrote tributes that were published in newspapers or journals. And even after 20 years, responses to the question of what they remember most about him were still as vivid as the day they occurred.

> Pierre taught us far more than a new methodology. He taught us a new way to think about—and plan for—the future. He showed us the need for the "gentle art of reperceiving," of redrawing our 'mental maps' of the future. Because of him, we are better thinkers, better planners, better executives.
>
> —Ian Wilson, from *The Futurist*

> What everybody felt was the magnetism that surrounded him, and I used to watch amazed as he held spellbound people in our company, whom I had striven for years to influence. Apart from magnetism and charm, which were natural to him, he had also for the purpose a number of tricks of rhetoric. One I remember in particular: he used to crystallise the attention of his audience with the quotation—*Wonder is Knowledge.* Pronounced gravely and distinctly with his slight foreign accent, it introduced to us the notion on an almost philosophical level. He ascribed the quotation variously to Plato and to Aristotle, and was always rather furtive on the matter when I questioned him. I must suppose the dictum to have been his own. For I never found it in the classics. Certainly, it was firmly at the centre of his methods and of his beliefs.
>
> —Gil Devlin

At one stage Pierre had to endure the most politically incorrect co-ordinator I ever met. Tom Hart often referred to Pierre as "The Frog" and would stand outside his office shouting "where is The Frog?" and Pierre would appear smiling although what he really thought, I shudder to think. As a memento, when I left Group Planning for Public Affairs, Tom presented me with a small china frog which sits on my desk to this day as a reminder of my years with Pierre who truly was quite unforgettable. There is no doubt that Pierre made Group Planning of seminal importance in the development of Shell and its response to the turbulent times through which we passed.

—Keith R. Williams

Pierre believed, correctly, that current forecasting methods were flawed. At his first presentation, he started off with the statement *"those who forecast the future are telling lies, even when they believe they are telling the truth."* The effect of this statement on the audience was electric and he had us all eating out of his hand for the rest of the presentation. Pierre was in fact one of the best public speakers I have ever heard. He brought a whole new approach to business strategic thinking. His approach was to use common sense and intellectual rigor in identifying the risks and opportunities that could exist for the product, whether the product be gold, diamonds, South Africa, oil, toys, airlines or anything else. His aim was to identify as many *"predetermined elements"* as possible in order to reduce uncertainty to a minimum. In this context his memorable phrase was that *"we must reduce the cone of uncertainty."* It was in essence a simple concept, but simple concepts usually need clever men to identify them.

—Keith Ives

One of the things that impressed me the most about Pierre was the way he would listen to you and your question and respond from where you were coming from. He drove with my family over a long weekend out into Devon; it was my three daughters, ex-wife, Pierre and me. He couldn't have been more sensitive to my daughters' needs and was able to communicate with them in a way that lifted them up, and at the same time he never talked down to them. Working with him for those two years was one of the greatest experiences of my life. He opened my eyes to meditation, to deep intellectual curiosity and to the joys of red wines. I loved him very much.

—Ray Thomasson

His love of travel was legendary. He never went straight to a place and back home again. We would spend ages trying to find out the best route for visiting the most places en route to his main destination and on the return. He was often gone from the office for several weeks. But of course, he did his best thinking in out-of-the-way places. The most irritating things about these arrangements was that he frequently changed his mind about where to go, of which airline to use. And then he sometimes went back to the original plan, but I became used to it. However, it did teach me how to organize very complicated itineraries!

—Fiona Youlton

For those who knew of him, Pierre was a legendary figure. Not only for the brilliance of his work but also for his engaging eccentricities. There are many stories (some apocryphal, others not) about his sometimes bizarre behavior. While at Shell, Pierre would disappear for a few days from time to time. Ted told us that, after one such episode, Pierre returned to say that he had been to visit a particular tree near Exeter, in the county of Devon. The tree was supposed to have a special spiritual significance. Pierre would also absent himself for longer periods. It is said that he more than once joined Hindu pilgrims on their annual procession from Varanasi to a shrine in the foothills of the Himalayas. I accepted this as fact. Pierre always spoke of India with great feeling.

—Allan Newey

When at the Harvard Business School, Pierre invited me to sit in on one of his lectures. It was as brilliant as ever, but the audience was somehow cool and the questions were far from profound. Afterwards, a post-doctoral student asked to have a word with me. It appeared that she and many of her colleagues could not understand why Pierre's methods were so successful at Shell; they had analysed his talks and, although very interesting, they could not point to a specific factor which made them outstanding. After some two hours of discussion, I suddenly realized the problem. Pierre's talks gave a verbal presentation of a picture, but the picture was impressionistic. Just as one can't make sense of a Monet by looking at the brushstrokes through a magnifying glass, so one can't appreciate Pierre's talks by analysing his sentences or paragraphs. One needs to stand back and look at the whole, just as with a Monet or Sisley. I realized then that Pierre was not just a thinker but also a brilliant painter who used words instead of paint. And that made him such a good communicator.

—Bruce Scott

In getting the scenarios accepted throughout the organisation and especially the CMD and the OpCos the genius was Pierre Wack. Without him it would not have been accomplished because his presentations were so extraordinarily insightful and intellectually impeccable. Everything could be debated and he could answer questions on the spot. He gained a rapport with the organization and people wanted to listen to what he had to say.

—Ted Newland

Pierre was so unique. He had a remarkable capacity to bring together a deep insight into the mind of the people he was trying to reach in terms of what was happening in the world in a highly synthetic way. This led him to incredibly useful conclusions. It is a very rare combination in a single individual—there has not been anybody better at it.

—Peter Schwartz

He would invariably surprise. One day, probably in 1989, Pierre rang me at the office and suggested lunch. We would go to an Indian restaurant that he had discovered. I anticipated a vice-regal meal at one of London's many fashionable Indian gourmet establishments. I was wrong. We took the Underground to Tottenham Court Road (which is certainly not fashionable). In a dingy side-street nearby Pierre led me down some stairs to an unmarked basement and thence into a crowded cellar. This was the restaurant. We were easily the oldest customers. I was the only person wearing a suit. Everyone else seemed to be a student (or worse!). Pierre thought it wonderful. How he knew of the place I never found out. We ate a mysterious vegetable curry; in fact that was all there was to eat. The plates were dirty but the food was delicious. Pierre knew that I would like it. But he also enjoyed the look on my face when I saw where he was taking me. He was very pleased with himself. This was of course typical of Pierre. He was simply unimpressed by conventional hierarchies of fashion, power and wealth. As far as I ever witnessed, he treated all people with the same kindness and consideration, at least until he found a reason to dislike them. He was intolerant of arrogance, narrow-minded stupidity and the abuse of power. He was a humane man.

—Allan Newey

Pierre's life was being Pierre. He had nothing to prove to anyone. Equally he was insensitive to reproaches. Listening to unflattering comments, he breathed in and exhaled imperceptibly, passed his hand over his ears. So there, it was over, the affront did not hurt any longer, he had overcome.

—Eve Wack

These excerpts are small windows into an extraordinary person. They give the impression of a man as human as any of us, with tendencies, peculiarities and a generally exciting outlook on life. They also suggest a man who was extremely passionate about his work—almost as though he could not help it. Scenarios were something he simply needed to do as part of his seeing, his freedom and his acceptance.

## Chapter 9 Sources (in order of use)

Wack, E. (n.d.). *Quelques dates et événements de la vie d'un "homme remarquable": Pierre Wack* [draft; 12 pages with note by Eve Wack]. Document retrieved from the Pierre Wack Memorial Library, University of Oxford.

Wilson, I. (1998). *Pierre Wack: A tribute-obituary*. Futurist; Apr 1998, Vol. 32 Issue 3, p. 43.

Roussopoulos, G. A. (1998, September 18). [Letter to Eve Wack]. Copy in possession of Eve Wack.

Devlin, G. (1998, June 11). [Letter to Eve Wack]. Copy in possession of Eve Wack.

Williams, K. R. (1998, February 11). [Letter to Eve Wack]. Copy in possession of Eve Wack.

Ives, K. (1998, February 18). [Letter to Eve Wack]. Copy in possession of Eve Wack.

Thomasson, M. R. (1998, February 27). [Letter to Eve Wack]. Copy in possession of Eve Wack.

Youlton, F. (1998, June 24). [Letter to Eve Wack]. Copy in possession of Eve Wack.

Youlton, F. (1998, February 7). [Letter to Eve Wack]. Copy in possession of Eve Wack.

Newey, A. (1998, March 5). [Letter to Eve and Jean-Pierre Wack]. Copy in possession of Eve Wack.

Scott, B. (1998, March 15). [Letter to Eve Wack]. Copy in possession of Eve Wack.

Wade, D. (1994). *Long and medium term global scenarios: 1971–1992*. Taped interview with Ted Newland, Cybard, France, Unpublished manuscript.

Excerpt from personal communications with Peter Schwartz. Author held interviews and discussions in 2014–16.

Newey, A. (1998, March 5). [Letter to Eve and Jean-Pierre Wack]. Copy in possession of Eve Wack.

Excerpt from personal communications with Eve Wack. Author held interviews and discussions in 2014–16.

# 10 What Can Be Learned from This Remarkable Life?

After exploring the life and major contributions of Wack, it feels appropriate to consider how anyone interested in scenarios can benefit from his story. While much of that will be left to the reader, there are a few points that are worth particular observation in this concluding chapter. In some ways, Wack's approach to scenarios was dramatically different than how the discipline is commonly practiced today. Debates about the inductive or deductive method, pros and cons of the 2x2 matrix approach, how scenarios may fit with back-casting, three-day workshops versus 12-month scenario engagements, etc., are moot points. Though some may disagree, any scenario planning—regardless of the finer points of how it is practiced—is better than no scenario planning. However, to achieve truly deep knowledge and profound insights, to embed scenario thinking throughout the organization, to influence decision making with strategic options, and to change the culture of the entire organization and its view of the future the way Wack was able to achieve, well, all this is incredibly rare.

## Key Elements of Wack's Scenario Approach

This book has been a summary of Wack's life and the things he was able to accomplish personally and professionally. For anyone who studies this material deeply, or has an intention of developing a knowledge of scenario planning, there are elements of his approach to scenarios that are critically distinctive. Wack kept a small notebook he titled "Pieces of Wisdom", in which he wrote down quotes of things he found interesting or provocative. For the most part, the quotes were from other peoples' work rather than his own ideas and it may be a coincidence that the title uses his initials. The quotes are in his own handwriting which is difficult to decipher. While he never fully articulated a scenarios process, there are pieces of the puzzle embedded in the phrases and quotes he found interesting, and more importantly throughout his whole life. A vast collection of sources over the last 20 years has informed these critical elements in a view of what might be learned from considering his story.

*Team*

While some former team members have criticized Wack for taking all the credit, he was clear from the start just how important his team was. He required free thinkers—people willing to take risks, and even commented at one point that "the whole thing rests on your team." It is true that when he arrived in London in 1971, he was worried about the quality of the players on his team and indeed he made adjustments. He hired people he respected and some who challenged him, as in the case of Jefferson, among others. He acknowledged that scenarios needed a figurehead and, given his presentation skills and rapport with the CMD, agreed that he was best suited for the role.

Wack avoided consensus. Consensus meant one of two things: either everyone genuinely agreed, in which case it was likely a situation of groupthink, or people were not expressing their true views. Both were scenario planning killers. At his presentation for the GBN seminar in 1992, Wack reflected on the details of the team, and how important they were:

> When you have a team, try to have the highest variety of expertise, of background, of nationality. In our team, we never had during my time less than ten nationalities, and I regret very much that it has sharply decreased since we left. And we tried to have people with roots at least in two civilizations if not more. We also tried to have the right mix in different psychological type. First, bright young people, because creativity is linked with young people and they are really up to date in the latest thinking.

The second category was seasoned, senior people who had been all over the world in various functions for Shell. And the third category was mid-career people who would come to Group Planning to expand their horizon: "They bring their business expertise and make the two other categories much more productive and they bring their credibility to their parent function." The composition of the team is clearly important, though today it is not common to find a team dedicated to strategy or scenarios.

*Isolation and Inspiration*

The "in the green" sessions were obviously a critical aspect of the insights achieved at Shell. Most people today say it is difficult to leave the office even for a day. When they do, it is usually for a conference or some form of required training, and devices are always attached, always on, distracting people from deeply engaging. Wack's off-site meetings were in remote locations—the south of France or a College in Oxford. There were no cell phones, no cell service, and in some cases no telephones or television. These were truly dedicated sessions, which our global society simply no longer has the capacity—or willingness—to handle. The sessions were also deliberately planned in inspiring locations. Scenic landscapes and unexpected choirs, chanting, museums or remote vineyards gave inspiration to what was undoubtedly hard, hard work. The benefits were well worth the investment.

## Tension

Wack was not afraid of making people uncomfortable in the process of building scenarios. It was necessary in order to have breakthroughs, moments that felt like a sudden flash of insight—Aha! It was also a sign that the process was getting through to the mental models of the team members, and, therefore, much more likely the scenarios would do the same for the CMD and the decision makers who would use them. Newland recalled the importance of deliberately creating tension:

> The process of creating scenarios cannot be accomplished unless one undergoes a period of intense suffering. By this, I mean at least a week "in the green." This must be entered into without any predetermined ideas of what needs to be done. In other words, enter into it with the highest degree of chaos. The number of people involved can be as few as four "remarkable people" but ten or twelve would be the maximum otherwise there is a tendency to be sidetracked too often.

Off-site workshops are somewhat common today, but their tone and direction is substantively different. Great care is usually taken to ensure that no participant is too upset or offended and that everyone is included and feels their voice is heard. The substance and tone of Wack's "in the green" meetings was one of intentional discomfort, chaos and planned argumentation and disagreement. Members were required to be comfortable with conflict, but always in a spirit of freedom. People needed to feel free to say what was on their minds, and all understood that the intention was to challenge each other to achieve insight. But it was also really deep thinking aimed at making sense of an uncertain environment from multiple perspectives.

## Meditation

You can call it flow, concentration, focus or nonsense. For Wack, meditation was a key part of his personal thought process—whether he used it to further test his ideas, seek a moment of calm, or just generally reflect. He was hesitant to say much about it during his time at Shell for fear that some might think a far-away Indian guru or a Japanese monk was influencing the operations at a global oil company. After he left Shell he became more open about his mental discipline, but he was not flattered by those who tried to imitate him.

Wack was known to meditate every morning, in his office before anyone else had arrived at the Shell Centre in London. He was also very clear that he did not want people to blindly copy his own practices. When asked directly, he said: "I think this is a very personal element. You must find what suits you. Yes, I certainly would recommend mental discipline to anyone, but you must find the one which suits you."

## Testing Ideas

The people closest to Wack indicated that he constantly tested and rehearsed his thinking, his presentations and his work. He tried out ideas and refined them over many informal, mini-presentations with people he trusted. Schwartz recalled a particularly memorable instance of this:

> I remember when we had finished one round of oil-focused scenarios and it was the late 1970's and the second oil shock was just about to take off. The Iranian revolution was happening and so on, so it was a tense environment. And I remember he showed me his draft of the scenario book that he had been working through. It wasn't yet in good English and it wasn't yet polished. But what he really led me through was how he had thought about it, from beginning to end, what the right questions were, what the management really needed to understand and how to link that to the logic of the scenarios. It was a deep revelation of how the leader of such a team addresses that overall set of question and how to frame the process, to produce a result like he could produce. He was also testing his ideas but what I also saw was a mind at work—I could see him having realization of "oh, this isn't quite right" or "this needs to be framed differently" and so not only was he revealing the description of what he had done, but also in the process as he re-engaged with the material to tell me. This is one of the ways he worked—he would tell his tale a number of times and over the course of telling it, it would get refined in a very profound way. That was amazing—I can still see the pages in front of me as he was going through the draft.

For Wack, testing his ideas was a way to help him refine what he truly wanted to say, as well as a totally discreet way of teaching. He used these rehearsals for the benefit of himself and others, and they were an important tool for honing the presentations for which he became so famous. This is how he became so well known for coming right to the essence of what he wanted to say—he practiced relentlessly. The more common practice today is no practice.

## Predetermined Elements

Wack identified the importance of predetermined elements early on. They are found through building the wide-angle first generation or global scenarios. Predetermined elements are the results of actions that have already been taken, but their consequences are not yet known. There is a degree of predictability with predetermined elements, and pushing hard to identify them was of particular importance to Wack. They were not just events in the pipeline, they were more subtle than that. The less obvious predetermined elements were the target and once isolated, the true uncertainties emerged with more clarity.

He developed his legendary stories of the Ganges and the Nile to illustrate the point and he knew that if the scenario team could identify subtle and hidden predetermined elements, they had already achieved a degree of insight that gave them an advantage.

### Remarkable People

It is easy to see why a network of remarkable people was so important to Wack. At Shell, he was an insider, and even though he was eccentric, he had an oil mental model, and an economist's mental model. He was using his network of remarkable people to ensure his own biases didn't rule the scenario work for which he was responsible. Quite literally, when he invited people to visit Shell, they were performing the function of an external consultant. They said things he couldn't say, and had a license no internal person could. It seems that a true balance of internal and external function dedicated to the scenario process is essential for effective results.

When Wack left Shell and worked with Anglo American, Clem Sunter was given internal responsibility and Wack took the role of external consultant (along with Newland and others, at various times). The major insight here is that to maximize the effectiveness of scenarios, there must be an internal responsibility for it. Otherwise, the work becomes subject to a consultant and a contract which can jeopardize insight.

### Presentations

Wack was a mesmerizing presenter. And this set of skills was essential for the evolution of scenarios in Shell. Newland highlighted the important combination of scenario creation and scenario presentation as dual role archetypes necessary for success. Wack's interest in stories from different cultures and how he wove them into his scenario presentations was a part of his mystique. For example, the Japanese characters for "Crisis" are "ki" and "ki," and they are commonly interpreted as "danger" and "opportunity." He would use such ideas to demonstrate the ways in which other cultures generally thought about things, particularly when they were different from the traditional Anglo-Dutch culture of Shell. His heavy French accent was another device. Allan Newey recalled: "Ted used to claim that Pierre had arrived at Shell speaking English perfectly, but had re-acquired a Gallic accent when he realized that it made his pronouncements sound more authoritative. Pierre merely smiled, inscrutably." To be sure, Wack's presentations were performances, but not just performances. They were well-rehearsed, and he was deeply immersed in the relevant facts so that he could answer questions on the spot.

## Mental Models

Mental models became perhaps the most lasting and central feature of Wack's scenario approach when he realized that the early scenario attempts failed because they had no connection to managers' deepest concerns. He knew he needed to find a way to make the link. After visiting the Institute for the Future in California in 1976, where he found a set of interesting and provocative questions by Ted Lipinski and Roy Amara, Wack began interviewing managers as the first step of scenario work. He spent the rest of his career refining and developing his interview craft, determined to be able to see inside the minds he was trying to change. Understanding the mental models gave him valuable knowledge about how people framed their experiences, and their decision making tendencies.

## Decisions

Finally, Wack concluded that if scenarios did not link to present day decisions, only half of the exercise was complete. Schwartz' recollection, as his mentee, captures this elegantly:

> Pierre's most important legacy and greatest impact from my point of view was to define the objective as not getting the future right, but making better decisions today. His view was that the task has two dimensions; first, understanding the outside world, and the other is the mind of the decision maker. You must devote as much energy to each to have an impact. This is associated with his mystical sense—he had to get at the minds.

Studying peoples' mental models through interviewing reveals the things foremost on their minds. It is equally important to identify the critical decisions right at the start of any scenario effort.

## An Important Note on the Use of Probabilities

In 1991, a discussion arose among then modern scenario planners about the role of probabilities assigned to scenarios or events within them. It was a conversation started by several GBN members including Ted Newland, Jaap Leemhuis, Ged Davis, Alain Wouters and Charles Hampden Turner. The conversation took place online through a community called the WELL, and after being provided the various threads and exchanges, Wack composed a rare, detailed response:

This issue of scenario probabilities teaches, in a very subtle way, something that is absolutely critical: the sense of excellence in scenarios. It looks very attractive to use probabilities in scenarios, both from the perspective of the client—which scenario will really occur?—and from the perspective of the scenario writer, who can communicate more of the information he already has. But I have a strong feeling that it will be poisonous and will contaminate the logic of scenarios.

These are strong words: let me explain. First, I do not know of any successful case of scenarios using probabilities, not one, and I think there are good reasons for this. Probabilities are more of a nuisance than a help in the non-trivial process of communicating scenarios to management. By focusing on the outcome instead of developing an understanding of the forces leading to an outcome, they will have a superficial and mechanical impact, and will not change management mind-sets in depth. More important, in the development of the scenario, the use of probabilities seems to direct the attention and efforts of the scenario designer in the wrong direction.

Wack goes on to describe a case and recommend the reading of "The Future World Price of Gold." He described the process by which many reputable and expert analysts assessed the future price of gold based on the various dynamics they deemed important. Their analyses included interviews with mining executives, finance people, gold dealers, bankers and Russian leaders—all of whom were asked about the fundamental drivers of gold price. The expectations, forecasts and predictions were wildly wrong and "They saw only a one-percent likelihood that the price of gold would be lower than $600 in 1986." In fact, the low price was $368. He went on to make the point:

The sense of excellence—and there is a sense of excellence in this study—in developing probabilities is definitely not the one you need in developing scenarios. A good scenario, in my opinion, seems to emerge, naturally and miraculously, from an intensely-experienced polarity: on one side, obviously, a good analysis of the unfolding business environment (this is a big subject in itself, with exploratory scenarios, predetermined elements, etc.). On the other side, a clear knowledge of the existing mind-set of managers, which covers their view of the unfolding business environment, which is usually a mix of very rich understanding and some dubious extrapolation, some myopia and selective inattention to certain aspects. The existing concerns of managers also matter, including those that they should have but do not yet realize.

What matters finally is the existing view of what makes, and especially what will make, a company successful in this unfolding business environment. This side of the polarity is the most underdeveloped in most scenario exercises, and in my opinion there is much more to be gained by understanding and making explicit this polarity than by explicitly assigning dubious probabilities.

Others agreed to disagree with Wack on this point, mostly outlining the advantages of statistical modelling and advanced algorithms given a specified set of variables. It should be clear that Wack's opposition to probabilities is grounded in his ambition to evade the confinement of statistical models and a deep belief that the human mind is a still unexplained and as yet unexplainable phenomenon.

## Opportunities

In light of his contributions, there are aspects of scenario planning that Wack clearly thought about, but did not fully develop over his career. There are two opportunities for significant development in scenario planning that come directly from Wack's unfinished work. They focus on generating management options, and "footprints," both of which Wack described in his final presentations to the Operating Companies in 1982. These aspects of the process remain generally undeveloped. Most scenario planners today position the scenarios as the product of the work. However, these two underutilized tools can support the connection between scenarios and decision making—Wack's own ultimate intent.

### Generating Management Options

Options are the subtext of decisions. Wack was clear that scenarios need to connect to today's decisions in order to be useful. One step further, decisions must have genuine options under consideration. Working through scenarios can reveal options that might not have been previously considered. However, decisions with multiple corresponding options should be identified at the start of any scenario exercise. This makes perfect sense. Without decisions and options, there is simply no uncertainty.

Wack further stressed that the nature of the options is extremely important. Drawing from his own experiences, he described instances in which options were put forward as "straw men," meaning they were not truly entertainable. He described a leader who had already chosen the course of action, and added options that were not genuine. In other words, he was just walking through the exercise. This was obviously time wasted, and as expected, did not result in any real insight. The message is clear—identify real decisions and their related options early on in the scenario work, and remain open to new options that may emerge from the hard work of developing the scenarios.

### Footprints

Footprints appear more complicated than they are—the idea is to assess options within and across the scenarios and display that assessment visually. Footprints refer to a way of assessing decisions and options. Imagine a simple set of options. For each option, the risk and potential benefit could be approximated by a ranking from 1–10. Option 1 could have a ranking of 8 on risk, and 10 on potential benefit. Asking a team of decision makers to complete an exercise like this, individually, for a set of multiple options results in multiple data points that can be plotted. The outcome is a scatterplot, in which each data point represents an individual's assessment of the option. The process must be replicated in two ways: first, for each scenario (because the dynamics of each scenario would be different, and therefore the rankings would change), and second, for each option.

The example below (Figure 10.1) shows four scenarios (Wearable Tech, Rotary Phone, Smartphone, and Cans and String) with the plotting results for a generic "Option 1." The plotting area is what Wack called the "footprint" and it shifts position under the different scenario dynamics.

Wack discussed this process in his presentations to the Operating Companies at Shell in 1982, but there are no examples of its use in Shell's scenario

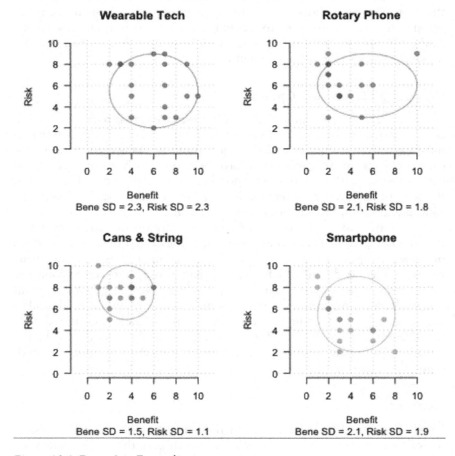

*Figure 10.1* Footprints Example

planning. Further, Wack did not use the approach in his work with De Beers or Anglo American when he left Shell. It is easy to see how a process like this can connect scenarios to decisions, and seeing the footprint move in the different scenarios provides unique information for decision makers. Yet, it does not appear to be a tool commonly used with scenarios, and it remains an opportunity to evolve scenario methods in new direction. The example here used risk and benefit as the main parameters; however, almost any variables could be used. Cost, timeline, financial return, capital expenditures, cost of energy, cost of labor, product price, etc. would all be useful assessment dimensions depending on the context and decisions.

These two opportunities provide a way to develop scenario planning in a way that directly connects scenarios to decisions, making them even more valuable to leaders facing tough choices. It is not clear why these practices did not receive much attention in Shell's scenario books or Wack's scenario work after Shell. They are left for others to define and clarify.

## After All These Years

Perhaps the most significant thing that can be taken away from Wack's story presents itself in a commonly asked question: After all these years why are we still talking about Wack and about Shell as the main examples of scenario planning success? The answer is simple: No organization has invested the time, energy, resources, patience and commitment in scenarios comparable to Shell. Anglo American has taken scenario work very seriously but is still a distant second to Shell. We live in a world of great impatience and lack of commitment. Decision makers want answers and recommendations quickly, as if insight can be achieved through a rote process which simply needs to be executed more efficiently. But experience has taught again and again that insight and innovation do not work that way. Wack was given tremendous support, resources and freedom to deliver his scenarios and insights where and when he was ready. He was protected and supported by several Managing Directors during his career. Today, the strategy and planning functions have generally been dissolved. Even the legendary Shell Scenario team now consists of four people when it was once 52. The task of planning has been absorbed by the CFO in most organizations, meaning that it has become a budgeting exercise for which things like insight are not often a central feature. Specifically, with regard to scenario planning, leaders increasingly use consultants. This practice has product-ized scenario planning into a workshop format, and for better or worse, most scenario processes are delivered in a one or two-day format.

The antidote is equally simple. If serious insights about the future are expected to come from scenario planning, it must become a dedicated function inside the organization. And it requires support and patience to develop the function—insights will not come overnight. It took six years from the time Davidson took over Group Planning for successes to emerge.

Fortunately, there is enough history of scenario planning and variation in method that there is no need to start from scratch as Wack and his teams did. There are many books and other resources that provide scenario processes, steps and frameworks. Wack never believed in any set of steps that could simply be followed—he was always clear what hard work it was. His articles in the *Harvard Business Review* and his works provided at the end of this book are tremendously instructive, and they slowly reveal secrets to those who patiently and deeply study them again and again.

Wack certainly laid the foundation for the discipline called scenario planning—and he was particular in calling it a discipline. He was obviously a very thoughtful man and the approach to planning he developed with his talented teams over the years can only be called pioneering. He was a complicated person who grew up under unique circumstances, and his main ambitions in life were to "see things as they are", to "be free" and to "seek to accept" the things with which he was confronted.

## Chapter 10 Sources

The sources used in previous chapters, as well as the sources I have encountered in my study of scenario planning over the last 20 years were used in writing this chapter.

# Afterword

The interview with Ted Newland took place on September 18, 2015, at his home in Chelsea, London. Laura M. Coons and I were greeted by his wife Elena and brought up a few flights of stairs to the top floor. We sat in a sparsely but comfortably furnished room looking out over the view of Chelsea. We spent almost three hours talking with Wack's closest colleague of over 25 years, and his scenario planning counterpart who said their relationship "was ordained in heaven—we intuitively understood each other." Newland had been battling stomach cancer for a few years, and he was tired. At the end of the interview, when the recorder and notebooks were put away and we were about to leave, Newland said something else that stopped us in our tracks.

He said he was the last person to visit Wack in Curemonte. Wack was very sick and spent most of the time in bed. Wack asked Newland something like, "Ted, what does it all mean?" He was sensing that he would soon move to another world. Newland's response was: "Pierre, you have been searching for the face of God your entire life, and I have watched you see it in yourself, on your own face, changing over some 25 years, and you are about to see the truest one, the real one."

Newland turned quiet and it was time for us to leave, but I will never forget the scene of him sitting in a comfortable chair with a slight smile on his face in remembering his old friend, looking out over the rooftops of Chelsea.

Ted Newland died in London on May 9, 2016.

# Works

There are two main documents that best represent Wack's original works. They are a transcription of his final presentation at Shell, and his original manuscript titled "The Gentle Art of Re-perceiving."

These are provided with permission as the most substantive contributions Wack made by his own voice or hand. Their lessons reveal themselves again and again each time they are considered. They are as relevant today as they were when he spoke the words or wrote them down.

## Work A—Wack's Final Presentation to the Manufacturing Function at Shell—1982

In 1982, as Wack was approaching retirement, he was asked to document what he had learned about scenario planning over his career there. Wack spent 1981 and 1982 travelling around the world, visiting all kinds of people and places. He particularly visited a variety of business schools, wondering how to integrate scenarios with the larger and increasingly popular domain of strategy and strategic planning at the time. Before his retirement, he made a series of presentations throughout Shell, intending to disseminate what he had come to know about scenarios and significant opportunities for development and advancement. Wack's understudy, Kees van der Heijden, attended most of these presentations and was sure to attend the last one, which he recorded and later transcribed.

Presentation by Pierre Wack to the Manufacturing Function in Shell, 1982. Transcribed by Kees van der Heijden

This is one presentation out of a series of eight that Pierre did around the Shell Group (Including to the Managing Directors), following a two-year study he had undertaken around the world on the current state of Strategic Planning, in and outside the Group. In this presentation he considers what he has learned and the repercussions for planning in Shell. This was the last presentation in the series, delivered shortly before Pierre's retirement from the Group.

## Introduction

It is not easy to plan under uncertainty. For instance I couldn't take you now to any seminar that exists ready-made, either in the States or in Europe, where you will hear how to plan under uncertainty. It just does not exist. The knowledge exists but is scattered. It is scattered among a dozen large companies, half a dozen business schools and half a dozen strategy consultants. It is not put together, it is not structured.

Financial planning is very important, I have nothing against it. But there is an over-emphasis in most of our plans on the financial dimension. What I mean by this: In many cases when I read plans I got the impression, the strong impression, that these were merely 'hoped-for financial results,' merely financial projections without strong strategic specification of how you will get there. I believe that I will make clear later in the morning what I mean by strategic justification of financial results. In many cases I had the feeling: "I just do not believe you." Now this is not the kind of diplomatic remark to make. But let me say this, strong emphasis on finance without strategic justification does not lead to a good sound strategic dialogue. This also is a very common characteristic. In most cases our strategies are single-line strategies. Now this is more dangerous than single-line forecasts. In most cases our strategies have no options, and in the very few cases where there are options in fact they are straw men, not real options. The purpose is merely to . . . I have been on the side of the fence in Shell Francaise, and I know how easy it is, deep down in the hierarchy, to close definitively some options, to make some choices, and afterwards there is no way these surface as options. Again this is not the way towards a sound strategic dialogue. This is a very striking feature of our management culture, the fascination with the optimum. Maybe we have not really invented linear programming, but we are certainly the company who have done the most with it. During the long time when we were lifted by the enormous wave of growth we did very well with the optimum. But would you not agree now that in the present business environment in most cases what was the optimum at the time of conception is far away from the optimum when the project comes to fruition? The notion of optimum now is very short-lived, and in many cases when a project is based on the optimum this optimum is non-existent at the time of fruition. Now while most people are prepared to admit this still there is no real substitute for the concept of optimum, and there still is deep nostalgia for this concept of optimum. This is another feature, very widespread. Competitor analysis still is way underdeveloped. There is striking progress made, also in the Shell world, but still underdeveloped. And for very good reasons. During the last 25 years we hardly needed it. Was not the rule of the game to be the first at doing the right thing? And then to be on the crest of the wave and then we could extend . . . And we did very well. Now it is very obvious that in declining or stagnant markets really competitive positioning, something that other industries know already, becomes for us absolutely vital. This is also a very striking feature of our management culture. I discussed the package with Peter Drucker for 3 days, and when I showed him this he was very surprised, and at the same time stressing that this is a dangerous point. In a time of discontinuity you learn from mistakes. If you refuse to learn from your mistakes it is really the whole learning system that fails. And it is very strange in a company where E&P plays such a role. In exploration you know that you learn from mistakes. Still we have great reluctance to do so. Now, if there is an accident there are two objectives, either you find out who is responsible—I am not interested in this—or you can find out why the accident happened. This is the object I am interested in. Let me just show you as an example you can have, really, a kind of strategic audit, which is completely impersonal.

Would you not agree with me that Japanese managers are really more sensitive than Shell managers are? And I know the case of a Japanese company in Europe, where the Japanese manager transplanted his management culture. Japanese companies deliberately use self-criticism. So every two weeks he had a meeting where he asked at the end for self-criticism. While the French managers are not used to self-criticism, but he insisted. And after a few weeks he got through and now it works very well. Look, the communication specialists know what the Japanese company has experienced intuitively, the dynamics of information is based on bad information, not on good information. And it is by using bad information that you can really make information circulate. If you go to Japan you have always the impression that things are going badly, that we are on the verge of catastrophe. This is very useful. Let me suggest . . . of possible reasons for regret. This can be developed further, it is just an example.

Either something went wrong because a certain development was not known at all, it was a complete dice throw, it was not in the scenario. Or it was not internalised, it was not understood. Quite frankly in my own county low growth was never accepted. It was something that could not happen. Or it was not considered, it was not taken as a real option, not acted on. From my personal analysis the two reasons by far are 2 and 3, and especially 3, "not considered." And finally another strand in our management culture is a very high sensitivity to what I would call Gresham's law. Economists have very few laws and when they have one they are very powerful. So in every economics textbook you can read about Gresham's law. It works in all human societies. And it states that if you have two moneys, two currencies, the bad currency will displace the good one very quickly. For instance if you have coins with a bit of silver in them and other coins the silver coins will be displaced as soon as the other coins are in circulation. Something very similar happens in Shell. If there are two ways of doing planning: a procedural one, a form-filling one, a mechanical one, and one that needs thinking I bet you that the form-filling one will displace the thinking one. The thinking part in planning is a very fragile component unless it is protected and nurtured it runs the risk of disappearing.

A few other considerations as background. If you look back at Shell history it looks like a very robust tree that has gone through all types of weather. Well, as you know, we enter a period in the eighties which will be the period of highest vulnerability of the Shell history—after that, in the nineties, it will be better—because we will rely on a very limited number of countries for substantial amounts of cash surpluses. And at the same time we enter really new markets, terra incognita. You know, we have no experience in declining markets. We have still very limited experience of metals, of coal. And at the same time we enter mega-projects where we commit enormous amounts of money usually on an irreversible element. This combination of the limited number of cash countries and this irreversible element is a very great fragility for the eighties. And last week you have heard the scenarios and you will agree with me that we are facing the greatest possible change in our company, we are facing a major adaptation. So for this reason I would come to the conclusion that we have to change gears in our approach to planning. If we continue to do what we did in the past that will just not be good enough. Let me try now to make space in your glass, in your cup, for positive reason, which is more important after all. What I have to say I could condense in a few sentences, in less than 2 minutes. But then that would be an intellectual input. I find this rather important, it must be an existential experience. Therefore I am going to apply a Socratic approach. You know, where you start from a few basic observations and then you raise questions. First basic observation. If you look at plans in general, both inside and outside Shell, broadly speaking you will find two categories of plans. The great majority is in the white area and you will have a very few in the yellow area. Let's first deal with the white one.

Formal plans. Well in every well-organised decentralised multi-national organisation like Shell you will need formal plans. But formal plans don't make a difference. I know the case of a large operating company who for three years answered all the questions of the Group by a software, by a model. People were impressed by the huge consistency, but there was no thinking whatsoever. We have already looked at financial projections, a nice hoped-for financial results, without strategic justification. Extrapolative mode. Let me say very strongly, in a time of change a plan which is merely "let's do more of the same" but let's try harder. This could very well be a pseudo-strategy in a time of change. The real purpose of planning is to make innovation and change. If it is merely doing more of the same then you don't need planning. Mainstream strategy. This also a key point. You will see that a concept, the concept of rent, the concept of above-average returns, will play a key role in what will come afterwards. Let me make an assertion, it is impossible to make above-average returns if you have just a mainstream strategy in your industry. If you do, in a given situation, just what is normally expected from any reasonable company? You must do something different. No way can you expect above-average returns just on a mainstream strategy. And then you have the corporate rain dance, you know, at a certain time at a particular pace on the calendar, at the end of the dry season, start the corporate rain dance. It has no impact whatsoever on the weather but everything that come afterwards is nicely linked to and explained by this rain dance. And some people enjoy it very much. Quite some planning is of this kind, formal plans extrapolative mode corporate mainstream rain dance strategies.

And then you have a very few plans which really are remarkable. By remarkable I mean this. A remarkable plan ex-post is very easy to analyse. It is such an exceptional success. It is a success where like a lever the result is out of proportion with inputs. I will give you a few examples. I collect remarkable plans. You always find that there is an element of surprise, of effective surprise. And an element of creativity. It is really the power of creative foresight. Which manifests, which is exercised in two dimensions. First, it is a combination of decisions. One decision alone is never a strategy—it is a coup. It is the combination, a congruence of decisions, on the one hand that makes the difference. And then, in the other dimension of time it is an expression of—this beautiful expression of Peter Drucker ¬the futurity of present decision. Playing with the shape of cause and effect in time, of different decisions . . . There is always some unique insight, by which I mean: at the time it is unique, at the time it is not conventional. Afterwards it will become conventional, but when it is taken it is always unique. Usually you have an element of riding a wave. It is very difficult to have a remarkable plan without riding a wave. Let me give you an example. I choose on purpose an example you certainly know but maybe not in enough detail to see the brilliance of this foresight. I have chosen the example of Sloane when he took over General Motors. At this time the market was 60 % occupied by Ford. With two models, the model T and a small production of the Lincoln model for the upper part of the market. General Motors at this time when Sloane took it over was a mix of 8 companies, 6 of them were practically bankrupt and only two, Buick and Cadillac, were breaking even. Now Sloane tells how strongly he was put under pressure by all the managers of General Motors to invent a GM model capable of competing with the Ford model T, and they all had ideas of what it could be. We know that he refused to go this way. What I am describing to you is not the problem of a form-filling exercise. It took 6 weeks while he did something else. It is not number crunching, it is really thinking. He perceived, he analysed, he saw in the car market something different from the common view at this time. At this time the common view was still let's produce the cheapest possible car. He saw that with rising income people would become more sophisticated and they would buy a car not like commodity but like a nice car, a car with which they could identify. He carefully segmented the market in 6 segments. He defined the upper segment, he carefully positioned there one GM model. He refused to position any GM model in the lowest segment which was occupied by the model T. He got the insight that people would keep the car not to the end of its technical life but they would buy a new car after two years, you know, and he would use the second lowest segment to compete with the model T. Brilliant. And within 4 years the whole situation was resolved. Now it is not in this audience that I will . . . We would not be Shell if we would not also have a number of remarkable plans. And in other audiences I use the Brunei case, because it is a beautiful case in a part of the world where we have not so many successes. Well you know it in detail. I find this a very remarkable case. And in downstream I use the case of the domestic heating market in France when I was there. (I don't need to go there because I know it.)

Let me put another observation. If you look at remarkable plans, and I have a whole collection, I have some 80, most remarkable plans are the product of an individual. It is really a single brain who usually is much better fitted to produce superior plan. The degree of sophistication which can go inside a brain is much higher than the degree of sophistication in inter-personal relationships. Intuition is part of the right part of the brain capable of coping with a much higher degree of complexity than what you can do with the left part of the brain which has to explain. When we have to explain to convince others it gets much more difficult. So my second question becomes: Is it possible in a large company like Shell where we need to convince others, is it possible to institutionalise this creative foresight which is usually the product of an individual. Most "remarkable plans" are the product of Individuals (genius) strategies. Bureaucratisation is the worst enemy of remarkable planning and this will colour the whole rest of the package. I am glad to be exactly on the same line as the company for which I have a high level of respect in terms of planning, General Electric. Gentlemen, this is the wisest and deepest definition that I know of strategic planning. Strategic planning is a discipline. While later in the morning you will hear a few techniques, the techniques are not the most important part. Remember, when you have learned to play a musical instrument or if you have trained for a sport there are always some elements of technique; but the key element of the discipline is a standard of excellence. Same thing for strategic planning. Take this as an assertion at this stage, although I would like to develop it further this morning. I strongly believe that it is possible, provided we really gain—let's say modestly—"gain excellence" in 5 capabilities, not one, five.

Each is important, but the combination of the 5 is much more important than each single one. Scenarios, yes, but use of scenarios as well as development. Competitive positioning, this is something very important. This is starting from the realisation you always do well compared to relative competitors. Or you do poorly compared to other competitors. It is a world of relativity. Remember that sometimes in a mountain peak there are several routes, you have a north route and a south route. This is another route to climb the same mountain as scenarios. Not as important but nearly as important. You can go quite a way here. From these two elements you get insights for developing a strategic vision. This is one type of company they you want TO BE. This is upstream of what you want to do. A new investment is doing, entering a new market is doing, divesting is doing, what you want to be is upstream of this. Option planning, by this I mean realising that in any situation there is more than just one possibility. To bring all these possibilities honestly on the table, in a non-advocative mode, but in a neutral mode. And finally sequential consensus building. Again very important. If you just focus your attention on designing a strategy and going afterwards towards implementing I bet you that the strategy will be implemented very differently from the one you have designed. You must build in at each stage of the development of your strategy the consensus and commitment of those who will be implementing. At each stage, and not afterwards. Otherwise the strategy gets implemented at a very low key and get different from the one you had in mind. I would like to go into each of these topics in more detail. Before I start I would like to go on a little hill to make some observations. To make basically 3 remarks.

We confuse sometimes in Shell language two things that are very different. We use planning for reporting and for strategic planning. I would like to separate these very clearly. You need to report on anything, the Centre needs to know what happens, rightly or wrongly. But you don't need to plan everything, you only need to plan, gentlemen, when the speed of change in the business environment is faster than your own speed of reaction. Look, when you leave the office by car, or in your case by bicycle, you don't need to plan. If you see a traffic jam just change your itinerary. You don't need to plan. But the first cars that reflect the present price of gasoline just came out this year, 3 and a half years after the price event, because they were crash produced. And the real one which are really going to reflect the situation will take two more years, because it takes between 3 and 5 years to retool. Now the point I want to make. For a number of reasons the speed of change in our business environment has increased and you realise it. And our own speed of reaction for a variety of reasons has decreased. As a result the space where you need to plan, not report but plan, has increased. And, gentlemen, in this space either you plan or you will be planned for by others. If you add to this the low economic growth now, you realise the penalty for wrong strategy is much more important and you have to live with a result of this for a number of years. It shows that the present situation is completely different from the happy situation in the 50's, the 60's and the early 70's. And you have to take planning slightly more seriously than in the past. The second point I would like to deal with is forecasting. It is very normal for planning to be based on forecasting, very normal. And if it is not based on forecasts it is based on enlightened intuition, which is based on past experience. Now, in the time in which we live this is a very dangerous exercise. Let me show you a few elements. MIT has an energy laboratory to which practically all American companies belong. Because of the anti-trust laws it is a good neutral meeting place, and also the . . . agency which deals with energy. Here are the estimates, made in 1977, for world oil consumption in 1980 and 1985. It was very reasonable, to make these types of estimates. By the way, Shell producer logic was 51. Let me show you another example. This is a serious company, Dresser (?), which has made scenarios for the drilling activity which is its main business. Now I show this for two reasons, first the danger of forecasting but also these are so-called scenarios. These are in our language and in our definition no scenarios. These are mechanical, they use the word scenarios but the reality behind it is very different. Scenarios in our terms meet the condition of a real understanding of the forces that drive the system. In this case it is a mechanical mix of a few things, they have taken different rates of economic growth, different energy policies, natural gas would be regulated or deregulated and so-called scenario 1 is a combination of all the nice things and scenarios 3 all the bad things and scenario 2 is in between. Now look at reality. This is a serious company. They missed a key element. For instance they missed the speculative drilling activity; on top of the normal drilling activity by oil companies you find an enormous speculative activity. You know, dentists, doctors and so on. Because inflation rate was very high interest rates low, the real cost of capital was low, taxation was high. Now when these elements changed this speculative activity completely collapsed. There is one point I would like to put very clearly. Forecasts obviously are still useful. We in Group Planning, despite our work in scenarios, we use forecasts. But forecasts are very similar to a particular mushroom that is very well known in my own country. This is the famous amalyte. It comes in three shapes. These two shapes, just by looking at them you would not touch them, they look poisonous. This one is also very poisonous but does not look like it. It looks very similar to a delicious champignon and if you just eat one you will be seriously sick. If you eat two you die unless you . . . And you eat its brain and its stomach. Forecasts in the present world are exactly like this mushroom. This is the product of a team of forecasters that no single oil company could afford. OECD has a brilliant team of economists, and, as you know, twice a year they make forecasts for the rate of economic growth of the member countries. I have taken the forecasts they have published in December for the next year. The forecast is in red and the reality is in black. Look. Sometimes it works (except for Italy. For Italy it never works). But forecasts fail you just when you need them most. Forecasts fail to announce major shifts, major discontinuities in the business environment, which render our strategies obsolete. If you work with forecasts, gentlemen, you may be satisfied for 3 or 4 years but I bet you the 5th year will be a Russian roulette. The third observation I would like to make. Would you not agree with me that the success or failure factors for a manager in the happy times of the 50's and 60's and the early 70's were largely under his own control. You could be a very successful refinery manager in Berre, devoting 80 % of your attention inside. Now of course it changes from country to country, but I am sure that in most countries you would agree the most important factors of success or failure are now outside. And, look, if you take a poly-technician and take the approach; "give me what will happen and it is my affair to do afterwards, to react" this is really in the present world opting out of one's responsibility. You have to internalise these elements outside your own control. You cannot really say: "well, I was right but the forecast given to me in the book of premises, or by this expert, has been wrong." Otherwise you really opt out of the largest part of your responsibility. Gentlemen, to be or not to be for a manager in the 80's is either you internalise this part of your business environment or not. Now I love making an exercise. I am not showing you how dangerous the uncertainty will be. The purpose for doing so is I want to show elements by which we can regain control in uncertainty.

In this new habitat traditional planning (based on forecasts/past experience) is in an evolutionary cul de sac of increasing uncertainty—a change as from hard skin to internal vertebrae.

Let's put this in perspective. In the new type of habitat, in the new type of business environment in which we are now and which will continue for the 80's really the traditional way of doing planning, by forecast or on intuition, based on past experience, are in an evolutionary quicksand and you must find a way out. It is a little bit like evolution. Evolution normally starts with hard skin. You have an enormous variety of species based on hard skin, because it is the obvious way of doing. But hard skin has limits. For instance there is no species which is more than 30 cm at the surface, and the biggest animal based on hard skin are the large . . . And even if it gets 2 meters . . . is not . . . the evolution. So if you want to go beyond certain limits you have to go for something different. Now, what you need is three things to get out of this bind, you need an approach that gives you an understanding of the forces that drive the system. Look if we ask our chief economist: give us the best guess of European economic growth for 1985 he will give us a number but this figure will be an extra-ordinary impoverishment of the information. It is a distillation where nothing remains, it is impossible to build a remarkable plan on such impoverished information. What you need for a clear foresight-based plan is a clear understanding of the forces that drive the system, and not the substitute for thinking which is the one-line forecast. Secondly, you need an approach that recognises uncertainty, chains of uncertainty, which does not push it under the table, on the contrary, which puts it on the table. Look, in many ways the golden nugget of the scenarios are the uncertain ones. I wish we would have taken the "rabbit in the hat" more seriously, you know, the fact that the second oil shock would have an impact on consumers out of proportion with the first oil shock. It is the uncertain part of the scenarios where you can do very well, compared with competitors. And finally you need an approach which sensitises to novel information. I hope that each time the scenario brought you some novel elements and that has to continue This is what we call scenario planning. But the point I would like to make . . . Look, my impression looking back at what we did: in many ways—and again, don't take what I am saying to apply to your part of the Shell world—in many ways I would say Shell had nerves. But they did not have the nervous system to make it work. And when I heard some manager asking me: "which is the most likely of your scenarios" this is the reaction of the hard skin nervous system which does not know how to do with . . . So it is not good enough to have scenarios, you must have a nervous system to make it work.

This is what we call the nervous system. You start with global scenarios. You then develop specific scenarios, mini-scenario, custom-tailored around either a large project or around a key strategic issue. Let's take Canadianisation for Shell Canada as an example. A key strategic issue. Or our partner in Japan, is a key strategic issue for Shell Sekyu. And you develop feedback. You have another route, competitive positioning. This is the world of relativity. From the inside and from the outside you develop a strategic vision, what type of company you want to be. You have a system for manipulating your options, presented neutrally, non-advocative. But look, the point I would like to make: the purpose of the scenario and the scenario system is not to produce scenarios, the purpose is option creation, is to generate new options that you would not have thought of otherwise. If it does not do this it has not performed its function. Like the purpose of the vertebra is to do movements which you could not do with a hard skin the purpose of scenario planning is to come with options that you would not have found. If it does not perform this the whole system is worthless. Now I would like to go successively in each of these dots and then conclude to take an overview of the whole system.

## Scenarios

Let's start here with scenarios. Gentlemen, I will not tell you anything about scenarios that you do not already know. But maybe because some other company knows that Shell uses scenarios sometimes people ask: what do you mean by scenario planning. Of course by scenarios we mean something very different from what many people usually put under the label scenario. I will use just 10 minutes to refresh your memory. Let me say very clearly what scenarios are not: scenarios are not sensitivity analysis. For instance, if I look at the price of crude at $34 and then I look at the price of crude at $40 this is not scenario planning in our terms. For two reasons. In the real world you cannot move one dimension alone. It is very clear that price of crude at $40 will have consequences on the demand, the demand will be different, it will have consequences for oil revenue in oil-producing countries, it will have consequences for the energy policy of oil-consuming countries. Scenario planning is to look at the world of oil at $34 and the world of oil at $40, but not at one dimension in isolation.

Sensitivity testing is not scenario planning for another reason, sensitivity analysis will never do the trick. One essential element of scenario planning is that it is help to break the most dangerous thing when you look ahead. When you look ahead you have great difficulty to perceive change because we are always conditioned. We have a perceptual world framework and scenario planning means having two or more of these frameworks. And it breaks your condition. It helps you to reperceive the situation. And in many ways it is by reperceiving the situation, by breaking out of your wiring, of your conditioning that you come to a solution of your problem. And sensitivity can never bring you this reperception of a situation. So scenario planning in our sense is not sensitivity. Secondly, a scenario in our sense is also not a Herman Kahn alternative story about the future. In the next hour I could bring you half a dozen Hermann Kahn style scenarios about what could happen. It would need very little input but it would also bring you very little information. Scenarios in our sense of the word would put all the emphasis on understanding how and why a situation develops from where it is in the future. It is what we call producer-logic, consumer logic, the backward sloping supply curve etc. The how and why. Because it is my last presentation let me give you a few key things. Usually you get the scenarios ready-made. Let me introduce you in the kitchen and show you one of the key ingredients, and remember what I tell you. The more uncertain the world is the more attention the planners must bring in identifying the predetermined elements. And it is a painstaking exercise that no planner likes. It is far less interesting than dealing with the more imaginative parts. But unless it is well-done the whole scenarios are weak. I am sure you have heard my story of the Ganges, you know, the heavy monsoon rains in the upper part of the Ganges and then you can anticipate with certainty that something is going to happen lower down. I want to renew my story because the point is too important, and I want to tell you about the Nile. The Nile is an extraordinary river. It is the longest river in the world, but what makes it really extraordinary is this: for the last 3000 km's there is no river coming into it, no rain, and it is practically flat in the desert. And regularly, once a year, it has floods. Now needless to say that the Nile and the flood of the Nile are the topic of conversation in Egypt, but in early times it was much more important than it is now. First the whole taxation system of the old Egyptians was based on the floods. Below 16 grade on the Nilometer there was no taxation. The Pharaoh was a kind of half-God and he had close links with the Nile. Now they built at Abu Simbel between the second and the third cataract a temple which was manned by special priests which were the real ancestors of good planners. They were asked to watch the colour of the Nile. Most historians believe that they really did know the spring of the Nile. Because, you know, it starts from Lake Victoria in the middle of equatorial Africa. In fact the Nile is made up of 3 rivers, the White Nile which starts at Lake Victoria, and which is really white with white sediment, and you see this one is practically . . . And then you have two other rivers, which come from Ethiopia and these are rivers which are fed by monsoon type rains from the mountains in Ethiopia. And the people in Abu Simbel were watching. There can be differences, depending on the three ways that mix together. They then made light signs during the night passing on the size of the floods. What was even more dangerous than low floods . . .

The Nile is not dissimilar to the Rhine in terms of quantity. 19 billion cubic meter. But is can go down to 15 or up to 140. The worst was when you had very high floods, because high floods was the beginning of 7 years of trouble. High floods were destroying irrigation channels and were bringing swamps and pestilence. So high floods were the most dangerous. They were using human bodies to make dikes against high floods. Now these priests in Abu Simbel were simply watching the colour of the Nile and transmitting their signal could estimate the quantity of water coming down. With high floods the Nile was very fast and they had only 3 or 4 days warning. In this way they transformed what would otherwise have been panic into an early example of anticipatory management. This is the basic identifying predetermined element. It has nothing to do with the crystal ball gazing. Identifying future consequences of events that have already happened. It is one key ingredient of scenario planning as we understand it. Then you analyse internal links and dynamics. In many ways real uncertainties come from these internal linkages. Look, uncertainty is not something in the future, in many ways uncertainty starts right now. How do you interpret present signals and a scenario is a way of interpreting the meaning of present day information. Obviously it has to focus on crucial uncertainty, what is at stake. And it has to be internalised. Again, this is so important. Many of you will have heard me before, but for those who have not let me transmit this. It starts with a very obvious observation that future-oriented studies have a very low effectiveness. A vacuum cleaner has an effectiveness between 25 and 30%, and the rest is dispersed in heat and noise. Future-oriented studies usually are way below a vacuum cleaner. Now if it is your profession you try to understand what makes the difference between an effective and a less-effective one, and one key element is the following. I got this very clearly in Japan, I never forgot it this example. It has to do with the basic psychology of decision making. Everyone, you and your neighbour, you have, we have, a mental image of the world in which we have to act. This mental picture is based on past experience and on the information we have digested. If we have a decision to take we confront the alternatives of behaviour with this mental image. And when a man takes good judgment, takes good decisions people say he has good judgment. In fact he has largely a mental map, a mental image, which is a good match with the real world. We call this micro-cosms, as opposed to the macro-cosm, the real world. Now unless the micro-cosm of the manager is really affected by scenarios nothing happens. I remember having been once with one eminent member of this audience in a large European company who were doing an exercise in futures. It was not France. And I happen to know a few of the vice-presidents very well, and they were very good people. And if they would be exposed in real life to only half of the difficulties this operating company was anticipating they would have devoted energy, imagination, resources. While the . . . and the corporate reaction was really very weak. This was because this one was not internalised. Unless scenarios are really internalised and have an impact on you no way can you capture your deep intuition and your gut reaction. It is a key element in scenario work. Let me now go a step further. Gentlemen, scenarios are like cameras, their effectiveness comes from being focused. And we would very much encourage you on this. You know Pernis has been the guinea pig for intensive planning for the rest of the Group. So you know. We would very much encourage most operating companies to develop focused scenarios, specific scenarios, mini-scenarios, custom-tailored around their concerns, their real concerns on either a large project—let's imagine we would have a specific scenario for Berre in France, next to the global scenarios for France. Or a scenario around a key strategic issue, Canadianisation. You will be surprised at the effectiveness of scenarios if you apply them to one of your real concerns. You will see how effective a tool it is. It is much easier to do mini-scenarios, first in terms of time, you will see that the cost-benefit relationship is much more favourable than the global scenarios, much more favourable. It does not take very long, once you have understood your problem. You identify the critical variables, and you look what are the forces behind these. The other part I would like to stress is the power of feedback. You certainly have heard me say in one of my past presentations that we all live in two worlds, the world of facts and the world of perceptions. And both are equally important. Now what the lever of Archimedes is for the world of fact, feedback is for the world of perception. Let me give you two or three examples. If I would ask you: can you raise the temperature of your body by several degrees you will probably say no, only yogi can do so. Now, statistically 40% of this audience can do this within 2 hours. And if you would continue to train before two weeks 80% of this audience could also do it. Provided you have an element that gives you feedback. There is a device that is now very popular on the campus in the US, especially on the west coast. You buy it for $30–35, it is called a bio feedback device and you put it, for instance, around your hand and it changes colour with temperature. Or you put it on your brain and it gives you the type of brainwave you are having. Now I did not bring it here as it did not deserve so much attention. But provided you have a feedback you can increase the temperature of your body. Let me give you another example. When a beginner drives a car he usually is stiff and he holds the steering wheel with both hands in an attempt to stay out of trouble. You need some movement, you need error signals to be capable of reacting to them. And the faster you get the more error signals you need. When you drive a racing car you are told to move around in your seat in order to multiply the number of error signals, which is the only way to stay on track. Feedback is a very powerful tool. What I would describe you now is a very simple device, as simple as the bio-feedback, not worth more than $35, which we borrowed from a strategy consultant that a number of you know, from Braxton. But this small element of feedback changes completely the perception of uncertainty. And what I would advise you is to mix the two, to mix specific scenarios with feedback. Let's first start with the feedback. Suppose you would want to have an estimate of the earnings of a very simple company, or a simple business unit out of a portfolio. It always depends on number of critical variables. Let's take the simplest case, you see volume of activity, the price at which you sell the product and the cost. And normally a single-line plan would have a single-line estimate for each of these variables. But we would all accept that there can be shocks behind each of these variables. And honestly, we would admit that we are not little Gods, that we don't know the future, where there is real uncertainty. Now if you accept this, there is this software which prints this, and prints it in a nice way, and gives you instead of a dot a zone of impact of these possible shocks and uncertainties, which takes this shape which we call a footprint. Now the footprint is in terms of feedback what the colour was for the bio feedback of your temperature. These are three real cases of business units of a company like GE. In the dot you see the traditional estimate, the single line, and then you see the footprint and you see how much more rich the information in a footprint is. Now this is a nice case where it so happens where the dot is just in the middle of the footprint. But this is a real case. So is this. You can also apply this to whole strategies. And if you would look at the single point, at the dot estimate, obviously you would go for strategy B, it seems so obvious. But if you would look at the total footprint and you have a portfolio where you have other elements which then you have a much better way to exercise your judgment. Finally, you may prefer to go with strategy A. Again, much richer information.

Where it becomes really interesting is where you move the footprint. This is where you internalise, where you tame uncertainty. This is the dot estimate and the footprint of an existing manufacturing investment. Suppose you change the footprint, and you see the change. Or suppose you divest a very vulnerable element of your portfolio. Again, you see your footprint changing. And here some elements of the outside, here for instance, what does . . . really mean? Or here an increase in competition. Look, I do not suggest that this software is miraculous, you know. Even if we now have something that is better than what we originally got from Braxton. What I would strongly suggest is, because of the great impact of feedback in the world of perception this is an element which increases enormously the real relationship the manager has with uncertainty. It is much better than a series of figures, which you do not internalise. And it is also a brilliant tool of communication. If you have analysed a project for weeks and weeks you have a deep feeling of uncertainty. And then you have to communicate this uncertainty in 20 minutes. It is very difficult. Now this is a powerful aid for this. Now usually we use the Pernis case. Because there are at least two persons in the audience who do not know this, allow me 5 minutes to show you something that you already very well know. As everyone in Shell knows very well Pernis is a highly complex plant. I'll be describing work that has been done by Jaap Leemhuis and others in Shell Nederland. First you identify the critical variables for each project for each concern you have. And you must really start with this, and you ask the managers to feed in their estimates, their own estimates, not of someone else. You feed this in and the footprint comes out of the software. It is something like this, dots surrounded by footprints. And you introduce them in a frame which is . . . this way . . . On the one side you see the gross margin, and on the other side the volume of production. And you have three levels, the first one cost, then capital charges on new investments and this one . . . The second footprint assumes there is a crisis in the next 5 years, therefore you have two. Where it really becomes important is where you compare things. So you can move the footprint, this is the original footprint and then this is the present configuration plus something new, and you can see the footprint moving. And you can analyse what in the footprint is due to this element. For instance what would be the effect if the price differential between distillates and fuel would be lower than assumed? Let me say two things. You will be pleasantly surprised on what you can get from specific scenarios, custom-tailored around your concern. But the second thing I would like to say very strongly. Be careful, while this is the right way to apply scenarios, to focus scenarios, remember that scenarios are like cameras, they get all their power when you focus them. But you cannot do focused scenarios until you have dome global scenarios. Otherwise I would bet you that the manager concerned will have a too-low-level view of the uncertainties. And you will go back into sensitivity analysis. Where, for instance, if you analyse the uncertainty in demand or on the price you will forget completely on other uncertainties, maybe foreign exchange or cost of construction or something else. You need the global scenario first to expand you mind, to get out of your conditioning. So the two are indispensable, you cannot start with the specific scenarios. You get the benefits of scenarios by the specific scenarios, not the global scenarios, but you need the global scenarios to break your conditioning, otherwise it is too narrow and it is just going back to sensitivity analysis.

## Competitive Positioning

Gentlemen, we have briefly analysed this line, I would now like us to approach this problem through this aspect: Competitive Positioning. Competitive Positioning is a wholly different optic, and for some for whom it is a new domain, you will see it is a very interesting optic. It starts from a few common sense observations.

Very few things are good or bad in absolute terms. In most cases we do well compared to our competitors. Or we do poorly compared to them, the relevant competitors. This is a world of relativity. It is a whole new optic, and in this optic planning can be defined as the management of advantages. It is really this. You need another type of information than the usual financial information to watch competitive positioning. And let me stress something important, profit, gentlemen, profit is a late warning signal. When profit has deteriorated it is sure that the competitive position has deteriorated way before. Now in this optic you don't have to deal with uncertainty, because you start from relativity. It is an enormous advantage. It creates its own difficulty, and the difficulty is the following: you must get out of generalities, of vagueness. And you must find the right scale of observation. The right scale of observation is so important that I would like to use a comparison to put it across.

Suppose two powders, a black powder, coal, and a white powder, flour. And suppose I mix them well at our scale of observation it is a grey powder. But suppose little insects the size of the grain of flour, from their scale of observation they would see black rocks and white rocks. Unless you go at the scale where you can see black rocks and white rocks competitive positioning is meaningless. This is the difficulty. It is not uncertainty, it is finding the right scale of observation. Now, I have a difficulty too, because you will see there are a number of concerns, and concepts alone are like dry bones, you need examples to make them alive. And usually examples take 30 to 40 minutes. And you need at least two examples. And if I do so it completely unbalances the presentation, and you will have the impression just by the time I give to competitive positioning that really Group Planning is pushing for improving our way of dealing with strategy by competitive positioning, which it is not. So for coping with this I will show you a few concepts and I will pick up just one example. We are going to have a one-day seminar just on competitive positioning. But I will not develop it here because otherwise it will put everything out of balance. Let me put across nevertheless a few concepts. This is very important to distinguish pseudo-strategy from real ones.

A strategy should always be a concept for changing the existing competitive advantage. If it is not, you know, it is not a real strategy. And it must be very clear on the cause and effect relationship that will bring the new equilibrium along. Otherwise it is really hoped-for financial results. There are three things that are critical, first the concept of asymmetry. That you really get above-average returns through differences, through advantages, and not by being the same as the others. The concept of barrier, which is very critical. A barrier is a competitive protection, which costs you less to defend than it costs the competitor to overcome. And always in your strategy you think what the competitor will do. You don't think that only Shell will upgrade, you automatically think what the others are doing. Before I show you the toolkits we have for dealing with a few of these problems let me stress immediately the limits of this approach. It is a very powerful approach, but it has important limits that one must be aware of. I remember having read a detective story of Sherlock Holmes where he was with his friend Watson . . . He had to reach a villa on the top of a hill. And they could not distinguish anything so deep was the fog. And Watson suggested: let's just go along the steepest line upwards, and Sherlock Holmes observed very wisely: yes, but what if there are several hills. This is the danger with this relativity, especially on the slopes where you are strong. You can have the impression, the dangerous impression, that everything is perfect, because you are the strongest. So be careful, it is a very powerful tool, but with limits. This having been said let me show you how powerful a tool it is. These are a few elements in the toolkit which we have borrowed from business school professors, strategic consultants and so on. These are a few questions that are useful to address, and these are a few of the tools. I will just pick up one of those tools: analysis of rent, because this one I can really develop in 10 minutes, and I think I can show you a useful insight at the end of the 10 minutes. But don't think that competitive positioning is just this one. Now rent in the jargon of the business school is a sustainable supra-normal return, above-average return. Two things are important. The return must be above average and it must be sustainable. And you analyse rents via a rent map. On the one side you put the competitive advantage and you look always for protected activities, how high the barriers are, and on the other side you analyse the intensity of competition, the intensity of rivalry. Now here are a few elements which make for competitive advantage, for instance if you are sure you can benefit from economies of scale this is such an example of competitive advantage. Providing learning, providing technology and so on. There is nothing very striking, it is just common sense. You will see that most of competitive positioning is pure common sense. But what is very remarkable is this: it is a disciplined approach to thinking. Now then you arrive in this map, you find that most cases fall in this red part. Either you have high return when you have very high competitive advantage and low rivalry, but then you have a dynamic usually in the situation, and don't expect that just because you had historically, or just last year, a situation like this it will stay like this. Usually you have a dynamic that pushes you this way. Let me just show you a quick example, because I choose the one which I can put across the quickest. This is aluminium smelting in Austral-Asia. Where it start by a new situation, it is a near monopoly, Alcoa, the only one. The barrier drops because during the war the United States creates more aluminium plants and at the end of the war there are others, Reynolds, Kaiser and so on. Now you have several forces on the industry. You have environmental concerns, the fact that the power availability and the sites are limited, this is obviously one force that gives an element of barrier compared with the others. You have a demand calls and the fact that bauxite producers may be attracted, and you have a unique situation if you would only add this to demand you would be somewhere in between. But you have these uniform power prices. It is just two situations. The real point I want to show you is the following: As you can analyse positive rents, above average returns, you can also analyse negative rents, below average returns. It is this I would like to show. Now there are a number of analyses made on mature and declining industries. You remember the horizontal bar on the rent map, the intensity of rivalry, these are elements that are particularly strong for mature and declining industries. For instance if you have a rapid decline of course it is an element. If this decline is not believed by everybody, if it is only believed by some as temporary, it is an element. If you have low transport cost, low switching cost, and so on. You see it is not extra-ordinary, it is good common sense. Where it becomes interesting is if you do real cases. Now in red you have the case of the decline of the receiving tubes, which were used for radios and which were really sharply declining when transistors came. It is a decline that was very strong. But because you had practically none, or very few, of the negative elements this decline, this retreat, was very normal, no catastrophe, no cataclysm. On the contrary, on the crude oil crisis, where the decline was far less sharp than the receiving tubes, because you had a number of negative elements we all know what were the results, way below average. I would like to suggest that we take an honest look at the refining situation in Europe and, honestly, we put in each of these elements, and you see that it is quite striking, practically all the negative elements are very active in a situation like refining. So be careful when you hear some people telling you: "yes, but, you know, everybody must live," this is dangerous thinking, it is not justified by rigorous analysis. Normally you would expect way-below average return in a refinery. If you do not expect that, the burden of proof is on you to say why. Normally on the rent map you would come very low. Again here is one element. In your files you have many other tools and let me stress we develop now in Group Planning a unit which is quite strong on Competitive Positioning. And which could give you advice, both where you can get help, both in Business Schools and with strategy consultants on these specific points.

### Option Planning

I would now like to go into Option Planning. I will deal with options in two ways. Here, first, what is merely option manipulation, and option creation I will comment at the end. I could choose E&P as an example of option planning. Here is Central Cormorant, which was done really well on an option planning basis. And I am sure in Manufacturing you also have cases like this. You remember the problem for Central Cormorant, you could not reach the whole reservoir, you had to find some other way to reach, and there were a number of technical solutions. Nine options were analysed in great detail against two completely different fiscal backgrounds. The reason why I do not show this example is that there is one key dimension which is missing here. It is merely technical options against two business environments, but there is no impact of competition, which is obviously a very important dimension. This is the reason why I chose Shell Oil. And there are other reasons. Shell Oil not only is the most complex operating company in the Group—and what can work in Shell Oil can probably also work in less complex operating companies—but for another reason. I think I can say—and I will say afterwards—some nice things about Shell Oil so I can be forgiven one little remark. Shell Oil has always be very strong in competitive positioning. It is the company which has done the best competitive positioning. They have a whole tradition, which is now 7 years old, of what they call Intensive Business Reviews. Which is really by segment—they have 78 segments, here are half of them—which are really analysing their business, and for each of these 78 segments they have an Intensive Business Review. I must say a few years ago this IBR's were very strong single line approach. After the business review was made there was one conclusion, and you couldn't disagree, you couldn't even raise questions, or you were ostracised. It was a strange feeling, nearly, nearly brainwashing. Now this has completely changed, and Shell Oil now has introduced a real honest option planning approach. If this can happen against such a psychological background which was like many American companies, it is very much like American football, you know, where the whole team goes in one direction, this is a normal American reaction, and for John Bookout to have really implemented an honest option planning approach is quite remarkable. And if it can happen in Shell Oil, it can happen everywhere. Now, it is done at two levels. It is done at the business unit level and it is done at corporate level. At business unit level now, always plans and strategy are presented in this way. This is for instance in the ethanol business unit, a case where really the strategy and the options depend on the behaviour of the competitor, Roman House. Either Roman House agrees to a participation and then Shell has this option. Or Roman House does not go with a joint venture with Shell but with another one and then Shell has this option. They can still expand, but this time it is only with the merchant network, the commercial network. You see, each of these options is a valid one. It is a decision tree, nothing new but what is interesting is that it is really developed on a neutral base and the types are very structured, very clearly put forward. This is another case, which is nearer your own experience, where the development depends if you are going to increase your R&D investment activity or not. If you do not you just consolidate your business but you must expect that your market share is going to decline. If you do you have this type of option. Look, it is not the decision tree as such which is interesting, it is well-known. It is the way it is done. Here are a few rules that Shell Oil has developed after this experience which are interesting to look at. And the key one is the last one, do not make choices in advance, develop the options on a neutral, non-advocative basis. Then, once a year, you have the planning exercise which starts by the base-business. Now here I must say the first time it has done base-business was very limited, it was only oil in the ground that was considered base-business. You well know that Shell Oil is a remarkable retailer. It is in terms of market share either the first or the second. But in terms of profitability it is recognised to be the first. Even the retail network was considered as an option. Only the very obvious was taken as given, everything else put under question. And then was tested against scenario, was tested against profitability in terms of finance and was tested against resource management, also a key element-you know, in project economics they once went into many more projects than they could handle. Here again a few definitions. Base case, this is the base case. And every three years they do something much more fundamental, they really try to find out, this is a tentative approach by Shell Oil to do something that we will recommend afterwards as strategic vision. You know, what type of oil company Shell Oil should be. They have really tested here 16 types of possible developments of Shell Oil. And for doing so they have a very remarkable corporate model, very remarkable, a very friendly model. Which really gives in 40 minutes half a dozen diagrams and 20 pages of figures. Nobody looks at the 20 pages of figures, but in Shell Oil-as in Shell management culture—if the 20 pages of figures would not be there people would not take the exercise as serious. This is again a very good feedback, like the footprint for the project it is a clear perception of how your company can be affected. Now, this is a demonstration case. You see one of the graphs, these are some other graphs. The type of situation they tested, the first time they did it was: let's see what happens if Shell Oil would only go for hydrocarbons. Basically EP, only E&P domestic, or outside. They are engaged just now in a new exercise like this and they had expanded their model for E&P from 20 years, as you see, to now 40 years. Because one of the key questions of Shell Oil is the following. As you know, it is basically now a domestic E&P company. But suppose that Alaska would be less promising geologically than expectations then Shell Oil could be in a dangerous situation. It takes some time to move on. Suppose that the prospect domestically is E&P would be limited in terms of quantity, it is very important that Shell Oil knows what to do, and it is this type of issue that they are testing out. You see, it is exactly what type of company you want to be. Let me stress a few things. You can really say that it is a practical system, which really works. A very complex company, and a company where the psychological climate was not in favour of such a neutral non-advocative mode. It has really promoted a much higher level of decision making. And much more flexibility. Shell Oil recognises that the reason why they could really jump very fast and very far is because of their option planning. They knew what options they could drop in order to mobilise the cash-flow necessary. They could explain; it is really a case where it has to do also with consensus building and implementation. They could really persuade the people downstream of the importance of mobilising and getting rid of a few things for the overall benefit, thanks to this remarkable tool. I must say it is now declining in effectiveness. It has been very powerful the first three or four years. Like always a bureaucracy begins to know how to play the system. After a certain number of years you must find new rules otherwise things get stuck.

*Strategic Vision*

Let me try, while you are still here, to approach a very important element which is Strategic Vision. A vision, gentlemen, is not a new management tool, like discounted cash flow or the experience curve of Boston Consultants or the directional policy matrix. Vision has always existed, every leader has a vision. Margaret Thatcher and Tony Benn have a vision. The problem with vision is twofold. In a large company several managers can have several vision, and you can have frictions. And the second point, which is more important, because vision is such a powerful tool if your vision happens to be wrong it can be devastating. Ghandi also had a vision for India for example. I personally believe that it has done enormous damage to

India. So I have a few things to say on how can you institutionalise vision. How can you make that the vision is shared, you know, that it is a common vision. And then, instead of becoming an element of friction, it becomes an element of dynamic. And secondly, how can you be sure that your vision is sound. And I would like thirdly to discuss it as part of the institutionalising process. I think that you can come to a vision not only by a lightening strike of genius but by merely asking the right questions. Now a number of elements of strategic vision have started in Japan. Like I choose Shell Oil for Option Planning I would like to choose Japan for strategic vision. In general I would like to make an observation. It is very regrettable that Shell does not make more use of its roots in Japan to learn what we could get from Japan. It is a pity; there are many interesting elements which could be highly stimulating for us. First Japan has really the richest material for observing remarkable planning. It is amazing. Let me just quote two elements that we now take for granted, the steel industry and the car industry. The steel industry. I was in Japan when steel development was discussed.

The Bank of Japan was strongly against it. For a very good reason, Japan has nothing to justify the steel industry. It has poor domestic coal, much more expensive than imported coal, no iron ore and very poor technology. And on top of this, as you well know, steel is an industry that is highly capital-intensive compared to the other options. And Japan in the early 50's was a dramatically capital-poor country. So it was not obvious at all. But you had a few people who had the vision maritime-located steel plants benefiting from declining maritime transport cost could make a difference. Steel is the case where the success was achieved by symbiosis between the steel industry and MITI. The car industry is an example of where the success was achieved against MITI. MITI was happy with Nissan and Toyota but was strongly against Honda and Mitsubishi, they wanted the two only. Now in the car industry, do you know for instance that Toyota was bankrupt in 1951, bankrupt. My first trip to Japan was in 53 and the second one was 58. During both trips you would never have guessed what Japan has become, such as a big car manufacturer. And to become a car manufacturer it is much more difficult than to become a steel manufacturer. Because in the car industry not only do you have to put your own house in order to be a good company, you have to have good component manufacturers, you have to build a whole system of component supply, which has to be good also. The second reason why Japan is very interesting to watch: In most cases in Japan their strategic vision is really the product of a group, it is not the product of an individual which makes it very interesting. And, thirdly, I have not discussed it but I consider the increasing complexity as important to deal with as uncertainty. Look, each of us already suffer from the enormous overload of information. And the great difficulty to distinguish what is really significant to watch, compared with the enormous noise. I would like to suggest that this present suffering will increase very strongly in the next 20 years, unless you do something about it. Now, the Japanese, as you will see, have a great gift for complexity reduction. And finally the Majol effect. For those of you who don't speak French I am going to translate it. In many cases knowledge comes from wonder, from amazement. And in Japan one's capacity for wondering is constantly aroused. So there are very few things you can transplant, but this wondering is an enormous advantage. If you speak to a Japanese company a well¬managed Japanese company, on planning you will hear two things. First you in the West are over-planned. We don't believe in planning like you do in the West. We just have a clear vision of what company we want to be. And this is usually said with a little smile. The next thing you would hear is the following. To put it black and white, Japanese see corporate life as a Darwinian struggle. Like you have an animal in a given habitat and this animal has to rely on some strong parts. Some animals rely on their speed, some other animals rely on their bite, some on their claws. Each animal will prosper in a given habitat, but you must have some strong points. The same thing for a company. For a company to prosper it must have a few strong points. Take Sony. Sony has chosen for its habitat the world market for consumer electronics. Contrary to Philips they do not go into professional electronics, only consumer electronics. And for prospering they have decided to become an innovative company, to produce products that no other company can produce. For two or three years, and to make money out of this. Let me stress that one of the biggest competitors of Sony, Matshushita who sells under the brand names of National and Panasonic is exactly in the same habitat but Matshushita is not an innovative company. Matshushita relies on other strong points. They don't pretend to invent and to innovate, they want to produce cheaper and better those products that have been innovated by others. But one of their strong points: they cover the whole range of electronic products. So they can go to the market place and say to a shop: Look, we give you enormous progressively increasing rebates if you sell Matshushita the whole lot. And Sony cannot match that. Sony has decided in order to prosper in its habitat by being an innovative company to become excellent. They have a word that means to become the number one in 7 capabilities at the same time. Let me stress a very striking constant in all Japanese strategies I have seen. The two most important inputs are input by the R&D vice—president and by the personnel vice-president. Always you have key inputs on these sides. How many times could we say so in Western strategy. And it is fundamentally realistic. Now Sony has decided to be excellent in 3 technologies at the same time. They recognise that some other company will be as good as Sony or better in one of the technologies but they say none will be as good as we are in all three at the same time. They are colour, solid state and magnetic tape recording. Then, Sony will have a very strong marketing policy. This was not the case at the beginning. You must know that Sony was founded by two friends, two engineers. One was in the army and the other one was supplying the army. They started a small company and the first thing they needed was to produce 100 rice cookers. Now rice cookers seemed a good idea in Japan but this did not succeed at all, they sold 5 of the 100. So they really learned the hard way what marketing is. Also when they got the first cassette player they marketed it themselves to the ... (?). They got this vision only 7 years after the founding, when they changed the name. Before they thought Sony was a crazy name but 7 years after they got the whole idea, what they wanted to be, they changed the name and created a strong image of a company of high quality and reliability. And they assured me that they can prove that they can sell and exactly similar product in the US market 15% higher in price than a similar local product. Nearly 10% more in Europe but only 5% in Japan. Sony in Japan has a far less exalted image than in the west. Then they have a finance policy that is very different from other Japanese companies. I mention this because it is very important to realise that in a strategic vision everything must hang together, it must be congruent. Normally in a Japanese company are financed by banks for 80% of their assets. This is normal. Sometimes it goes to 90. Now in the research of an innovative company you can be sure that sometimes you will make errors. If your break-even point is so high your high debt is dangerous, and you could not survive. So they have a very specific finance policy, based on much lower borrowing, and not involving the keiretsu Zaibatsu big banks. They were the first Japanese company quoted on the NY stock exchange. Like many Japanese companies they have a clear view of the type of people they want to hire. Now I would need 10 minutes to tell you what this really means: they hire people with a strong will to live. Now let me stress, Matshushita, their competitor, is very different, Matshushita hires people rather average Japanese. Matshushita is like Michelin, they don't hire the top of the universities like Sony, they hire average people but expose them to a very intensive in-house training, and then bring them to a much higher level than they would otherwise be, and so develop incredible loyalty. Sony takes five (?) people. But Sony takes—you know, the helmeted students which you see fighting the police. Well, if they are bright they can join Sony. Sony also hires from other Japanese companies which is something that is not done in Japan. And they have a people-centered management. It would require even more than 10 minutes to put flesh on this. Let me say in one word: they strongly believe in what Peter Drucker calls the knowledge worker. To get the best of the knowledge worker you need an exciting atmosphere and Sony is really de facto a company which is made for the knowledge worker. An exciting atmosphere. Now they think that being excellent in these 7 critical variables will achieve what they need. Forget about Sony, and forget about Japan. This is what I would like to tell you about strategic vision.

Some companies who are not Japanese have a strategic vision. Dow Chemical have a strategic vision. Siemens has a strategic vision. Michelin. So it is not only Japanese companies. It is a system for dominance. Every word is important. It is a system. It is not one decision, it is the combination of decisions. One decision never makes a strategy, it is a coup and it goes away. This is a lasting strategy in a system. For dominance. You really want to dominate one part of your habitat, one segment of the market. If you don't want that then you don't need a strategic vision. It is cumbersome. Be careful: you probably have read this remarkable article Marketing Myopia by Levitt. You remember when he said that if only the American railway companies—the biggest companies in the early stages of American industrialisation—if only they had said: we are in the transport business, instead of the railway business, then everything would have been different. This is not a strategic vision. Unless you have explicitly said how you are going to be successful in the transport business it is not a strategic vision. I would like to stress very strongly that strategic vision is not merely the product of a quick brainstorming at the end of an afternoon. It is really rooted in serious analysis, on both sides, the business environment and competitive relationships. And you have a clear view of what are the critical factors for success. It is not merely brainstorming. It is expressed as a commitment to excellence in a few key capabilities, more than 2 but less than 10. Sony has 7, I have seen cases of 4,5 and 8. None of these capabilities are given, but each is achievable with effort. And it is combined, coalesced into a unity and it is existentially experienced as a clear vision of what company you want to be. Now, I am not happy with the word vision. Especially in French vision is not a good word. There would be a German word which is much better. You know in German you can invent a word that nobody knows, that does not exist in the dictionary, but everyone understands you. Now "Ieitbild" would much better convey what we had in mind. Like leitmotiv, what leitmotiv is for music leitbild, a guiding image, is for strategy. But we suspect that maybe a German word would not take root, so if you find something better than vision we would be glad. Insight would be better but a vision is not only one insight. It is the coincidence of several insights.

Let me show you a few consequences of such a vision. Gentlemen, strategic vision is the ideal counterpart of scenarios. What scenarios are for dealing with uncertainty in the business environment, strategic vision is for dealing with uncertainty on the strategy side. We all realise that in a world of discontinuity you cannot have rigid plans, obviously. But, you know, we also realise that we cannot change every 6 months. We need an element of permanence. Because the way it is constructed a strategic vision is such an element of permanence in a turbulent world. It is only in the most extreme circumstances that you have to change one or two elements of a strategic vision. But normally it stays.

It is a marvellous complexity reducer. It changes your daily life. Suddenly you know what is really very important to watch. This is one of the greatest practical advantages of strategic vision. Those of you who know Japan know how much Japanese companies use their personnel as a tool for gathering information. Now if you would do this without a framework of what is essential you would only increase your overload of information. You can only do so if people are trained to see what is relevant and then it becomes meaningful. If it is really based on what does success mean for our time horizon, let's say 7 years ahead, and then, instead of looking directly you look indirectly for what you need for this success it is not so . . . I am very doubtful on strategic vision, I told you the case of Ghandi, what I try to show you is the difference between a healthy one which is based on critical factors of success and a wish. If it is merely a strategic vision without under-pinning it can be dangerous. But if it is well-constructed . . . Remember this first chart, the danger is making a slogan. You can only start this if you have done your analysis well, both on the business environment and on the competition.

This is also an important feature of a strategic vision. Most of our infor-mation systems is focused on the operational profit, which are very impor-tant. But next to the operational focus you have something very important, the profit potential. I know the case of a large European operating company who 15 years ago had a marvellous profit potential and this potential has been eroded without any red lights flashing. And now that it is clear every-body knows it but too late. We have very little information which is focused on this. Let me make a little detour, because I would like to show you some-thing. In Japan I had the opportunity to have discussions with Chimamura. Shimamura is really the inspirer of Japanese economic strategy between the end of American occupation and the Tanaka plan in 1972. It was based on Japan becoming excellent in 5 capabilities. Let me just say one thing, in 1953 Japan was a very unlikely case for fast economic growth. Dodge who was responsible for economic affairs under McArthur left a testament before leaving which was very gloomy for the future of Japan. And in 1954 the principle workshop in Japan for all the specialists was also very gloomy. They decided to become the country with the highest rate of investment per unit of gross national product. It made Japan the most underdeveloped country, more underdeveloped than India and Egypt. They decided to have the highest level of investments. And you know Japan has 37%-38% invest-ment on GNP. Now some people say this is because Japanese people are thrifty. Gentlemen, this is dangerous substitute for thinking. Because the Japanese had a lower rate of saving than Germany or France. This was really achieved by policy. Let me give you an example. You must have a balance between investments and savings, otherwise your economy is out of balance. And there are three types of savings. Private savings, company savings and government savings. Japan decided to increase all these three categories of savings. Let me give you a few examples. Traditionally you had bonuses in Japan twice a year, once at new year and once in the sum-mer. Now when Japanese companies became prosperous in the 50's and 60's these bonuses are now 40% per month. Now they get paid in two lump sums. At new year they get 300% of their normal wage, which is quite something. It is very clear that labour unions exercise an enormous pres-sure to integrate this in the monthly payment. No way, on this point they were absolutely inflexible. It was part of their vision, they wanted to have the highest possible savings. Let me give you another example which nearly touches on inhumanity. Traditionally also Japanese retire at 55. And tradi-tionally they did not have a pension system as we have now, they started however, the large companies start to have a pension since the early 70's. But before they got a certain multiplier of the last year of wages, never less than 3 years, but seldom more than 7 or 8. A good scheme is 5 or 6 times your last annual wages. Now at 55 the average life expectancy is 23 years. And you cannot hope to live for 23 years just on your 5 times last wages. So what you do, you increase enormously what economists pompously call the propensity to save. Savings after 40 enormously increased in Japan. And they invest this lump sum. Again, there was a lot of pressure to have a western style system, but people were inflexible. The reason that I show you this is the following. Shimamura said: this has made Japan the most underdeveloped country, more underdeveloped than India, more underdeveloped than Egypt. And he said this in the early 70's when Japan was already on its way. What he meant is the following: Development is a relative concept. You are developed compared to your development potential. If you increase your development potential at the same speed, or faster, than your development you stay underdeveloped. While Egypt presently is practically at its development potential, can do no more. Because its policy was really geared to increase its development potential in Japan, despite the high rate of growth Japan stayed underdeveloped. The same thing: a strategic vision has as it objective to focus on the development potential. And I have really not described anything from the concerns with the operational profit which is of course very important, but which should get an equal attention to the development of the profit potential. And this is the great advantage of the strategic vision.

And there is a last feature of a strategic vision that I would like to stress, All companies that have a strategic vision, Dow as well as Sony impress the external observer, who sees that the concern for the future is really brought into daily decisions. And this is an enormous advantage. Why? For a very clear reason. A normal plan, if it is expressed in financial terms, or even a policy statement I bet you, nobody has the memory of the policy statement in a normal daily discussion. It is impossible to compete with the fascination of operational problems. Only a strategic vision, because it is qualitatively different, can keep a share of the attention. And this is a way in which you bring the long term into daily decisions. And it is a great advantage.

### Summary

Gentlemen, you'll remember where we were at the end of my introduction. We saw that traditional planning, which is normally based either on forecasts or on enlightened intuition, which is based on passed experience and which is basically the same is now in a kind of evolutionary cul-de-sac, like hard skin. You must get out of this cul-de-sac and we really think that scenario planning is a way out. And if we didn't have scenarios we would really push for having it. But by scenario planning we mean more than just scenarios. We mean a whole nervous system. We mean the global scenarios, yes, which really focus on understanding the forces that drive the system. Which really analyses all the elements which are pre-determined. And puts the uncertainty right on the table. Which also sensitises you to novel information. Then from this you go to specific scenarios, which really is the fruit-bearing part of scenario planning. Where you get the most of the scenario approach and you focus them either around a large project or a strategic issue. And you develop of course the feedback.

Competitive Positioning, the world of relativity, where the difficulty is not uncertainty, the difficulty is to go to the scale of observation where you can really see black rocks and white rocks and you don't get stuck at the level of the grey powder. From these two things you get insights which are really helping you to develop a strategic Vision, what type of company you want to be. What is success for Shell Australia seven years ahead and what does it mean in terms of capability. You have your system which is a kind of magnified footprint for treating the option both at strategic business unit level and at corporate level in a neutral non-advocative mode. And the whole purpose of this is option finishing. I would like to start from an observation of one of our managing directors, who said that forecasting is not anymore a good way to think about the future, and the key word was "to think." Finding the right thing to do, finding the good strategy, in a reasonably stable environment is completely different from finding the right strategy in an uncertain environment. In the first case you have to calculate, to pick up THE best solution among a given set of solutions. In the second case the major difficulty: there is no. given set of solutions. The major difficulty is to create new solutions. And this nervous system is in fact a much better conceptual framework to think about the future, and to introduce creative foresight in our planning process. Let me make 5 points.

First a manager really has to assume responsibility for this part of the business environment, which is outside his control, which is outside the refinery gate, and which is now increasing in importance. You cannot say: I rely on the premises for the price of crude, given by the Centre. You must really internalize what are the consequences if these things change. This is the key piece, not optional. The second element: it is a process for creativity. Now I would like to demystify the word creativity. Sometimes when you use creativity you expect lighting of genius and then conversation stops. There are two types of creativity, output creativity and input creativity. I don't know better words but the phenomena behind them are very clear. Picasso is a very good example of output creativity. If you have seen the exhibition showing the life work of Picasso you'll remember that he changed his style completely every 5 years. Some people may imitate a picture he made in the past but nobody has made a picture that Picasso would have made 5 years later. This is really output creativity. But you have a completely different type of creativity in input creativity. Look, in natural science, in technology, in many cases you have fundamental breakthroughs, fundamental innovation, being made in different parts of the world by different people who have no contact with one another. Why? For a very clear reason. At a certain time the progress of knowledge is such that the basic building blocks are available and what you really need is a combining element. This is really input creativity. I would like to strongly suggest that this system is an approach which gives you much better building blocks on which to exercise your creativity. Not output creativity, input creativity. And if we are the first company to . . . You remember from the scenarios, one conclusion, a very strong conclusion that you can draw from the scenarios: no single large international oil company is well-adjusted for the type of habitat that we are going to face. Small companies, yes, they have quick-adjustment capabilities. But not a single large company. There is really an invention necessary and the company who can do the first and can come to the right solution has an enormous advantage. I would like to bet that with this approach you have much more creative plans. Not because lightening of genius but because of these very normal principles. It gives you much better building blocks on which to exercise your creativity. The third element. It does not suppress uncertainty, on the contrary, it sees uncertainty as an advantage, to be used by feedback loop, by the option planning, by the competitive positioning to understand the risks and to take only those risks that are really worth it. It is a marvellous complexity reducer, and very important, it is fun, it is great fun. Contrary to the form-filling mechanical exercise this is great fun. It is the most interesting part of the future-oriented management. It carries certain costs, but its cost is peanuts if you compare it to the penalty you incur with a wrong investment in a kind of . . . where the penalty is enormous. So the cost is really very small. It takes some time, I agree, but in all cases where I have seen it work I find that a good planning system generates much more energy than it consumes. It has this kind of breeder effect. Gentlemen, when you drive a car in winter we all hate snow, we all hate ice, or fog. But you all know the Rally de Monte Carlo which is just at the end of the winter, between winter and the beginning of spring. And the good drivers love when there is still winter because a good driver knows that they can bring all their capacities to bear in difficult circumstances. I can anticipate with certainty that you will have in the next 10 years your quite serious share of fog, ice or snow. And provided that you do well, I hope that you will take advantage of good driving, like the driver in the Rally De Monte Carlo.

## Work B—Wack's Original Manuscript, "The Gentle Art of Re-Perceiving"

The original manuscript "The Gentle Art of Re-Perceiving" is reprinted here with permission from the Harvard Business School Press, Eve Wack, and Jean-Pierre Wack. The manuscript was preserved by Napier Collyns and was issued as required reading in the Global Business Network's scenario training courses in the 1990s and 2000s. It remains the most comprehensive description of how scenarios evolved in Shell in the early 1970s and is a resource that teaches again and again each time it is read. The work pulls largely from transcripts of Wack's live presentations and was brought to completion with the help of Bruce Scott, Norman Duncan and Peggy Evans.

*Scenarios: The Gentle Art of Re-Perceiving*

One Thing or Two Learned While Developing Planning Scenarios for Royal Dutch/Shell

By Pierre Wack
9-785-042
Pierre Wack
Senior Lecturer
Harvard Business School
December 1984

*Scenarios: The Gentle Art of Re-Perceiving*

(One thing or two learned while developing planning scenarios for Royal Dutch/Shell)

Scenarios are clearly far more popular in the world of "futurists and commentators than in the world of decision makers. Futurists have learned to create "interesting" scenarios but rarely ones which attract more than passing interest from decision makers. There are important differences between scenarios which tell a story and scenarios which are of real help for decision makers—"decision scenarios." Scenarios that merely quantify alternative outcomes of obvious uncertainties (e.g., the price of oil may be $20 or $40 per barrel) are not helpful to decision makers. What makes the difference between such first generation scenarios and decision scenarios is the subject of this paper. It is illustrated by describing the evolution of the planning process in Royal Dutch/Shell, where there is not a considerable body of experience stretching over a decade in dealing with scenarios.

*Scenarios: The Gentle Art of Re-Perceiving*

*Introduction*

Very few companies today would say they are satisfied with the way they deal with an increasingly fluid and turbulent business environment. Traditional planning used to be based on forecasts, which worked reasonably well in the relatively stable 1950s and 1960s. But since the early 1970s forecasting errors have become more frequent and occasionally of dramatic and unprecedented magnitude. It is not that forecasts are always wrong, more often than not, they can be reasonably accurate. This is what makes them so dangerous. Forecasts are usually constructed on this assumption that tomorrow's world will be much like today's. True, the world does not always change, and forecasts work for a while. But sooner or later they fail—and just when they are needed most: they fail to anticipate major shifts in the business environment which can make whole strategies obsolete (see box: Two "a fortiori" examples).

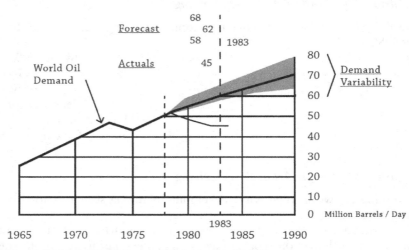

*Figure BM 1.1* World Energy Outlook, April 1978

Few areas have seen such a concentration of the best techniques, and many of the best brains in the profession, as short-term macroeconomic forecasting in the US Stephen MacNees, of the Federal Reserve Bank of Boston, has been analyzing the track record of the best known economic forecasters since 1970 (New England Economic Review November 1983). During more than half this period, forecasts were quite successful. But, on four occasions, the magnitude of error was sizeable. MacNees observes that:

- "Forecasts made from 1973 through early 1974 initially did not foresee the recession, and later misinterpreted the severe recession as an Energy spasm."
- "Forecasts made from mid-1977 through early 1978 did not capture the acceleration of the inflation rate in1978 and1979."
- "Forecasts made in 1981 and early 1982 underestimated the severity of the 1982 recession, and the deceleration of inflation that accompanied it." In the summer of 1981, according to MacNees, the median forecast had predicted 3.2 percent growth in US GNP for 1982. Instead, the economy plunged into a deep recession, with a GNP decline of 1.8%. As the journalist Warren Brookes commented, "This is like forecasting partly cloudy, and getting a 10-inch snow storm instead. After all, in economics as in meteorology, it's the ability to predict stormy change that makes forecasting useful."

Many business cases illustrate a similar phenomenon in longer-term forecasting. The oil industry which, prior to 1973, enjoyed the steadiest growth of all major industries—is still living with its failure to anticipate the turbulent changes that have occurred since then. Here is one major oil company's, (not Shell) forecast of oil demand, made in late as 1978. The example is chosen because this company allocates more resources to analyzing the future environment than most companies do and is well respected for its professionalism. Yet note how far outside the forecast demand range reality (the red line) proved to be.

The only solution, I believe, is to accept uncertainty, try to understand it and make it part of your reasoning. Uncertainty today is not just an occasional, temporary deviation from a reasonable predictability; it is a basic structure feature of the business environment. Therefore, the method used to think about and plan for the future must be made appropriate to the new nature of the business environment. The Royal Dutch/Shell Group of companies* has learned that decision scenarios are such a method. According to former Group Managing Director Andre Benard: "Experience has taught us that the scenario technique is much more conducive to forcing people to *think* about the future than the forecasting techniques we formerly used" ("World oil and Cold Reality," *Harvard Business Review, November 1980*).

Some planners say they know all about scenarios, that they have tried them, but their companies did not like them. I would answer that with two points (which will be developed at length below):

- Most scenarios merely quantify alternative outcomes of obvious uncertainties (e.g., the price of oil may be $20 or $40 per barrel). Such scenarios are *not* helpful to decision makers. We call them "first generation" scenarios. As will be seen, decision scenarios are quite different. (This explains why scenarios are usually more popular with futurists and planners than with the managers who are intended to use them).
- Good scenarios are not enough. To be effective, they must involve management, top and middle, in understanding and anticipating the unfolding business environment much more intimately than would be the case in the traditional planning process. Scenarios can be successful in structuring uncertainty only when (1) they are based on a sound analysis of reality, *and* (2) they change the decision makers' assumptions about how the world works and compel him to change his image of reality. This is different—and more—that simply designing good scenarios. A willingness to face uncertainty and to understand the forces driving it requires an almost revolutionary transformation in a large organization. And this transformation process is as important as the development of the scenarios themselves.

What makes the difference between first generation scenarios and decision scenarios, and how to achieve an intimate involvement of management in the process, is the subject of this paper. It is illustrated by describing the evolution of the planning process in Shell, where there is now a considerable body of experience in dealing with scenarios. As you will see, the concept and the technique we arrived at after some 10 years is very different from that with which we began—mainly because there were some highly instructive surprises along the way for all concerned.

### Predetermined Versus Uncertain

Let me begin by appearing to contradict myself. In Shell we did not reject forecasts altogether. We did use forecasting techniques—*not* to predict, but in order to understand the forces driving the system, and we used them within the conceptual framework of "predetermined" elements.

Strictly speaking, it is only possible to forecast the future when all its elements are predetermined. By predetermined elements, we mean those events that have already occurred (or which almost certainly will occur) but whose consequences haven't yet unfolded. For example, if there are extraordinarily heavy monsoon rains at the upper part of the Ganges River basin, once can anticipate with certainty that something extraordinary will happen within two days at Rishikesh, which is at the foothills of the Himalayas; in Allahbad three to four days later, and at Benares, two days after that. This is not fortune telling or crystal-ball gazing. It is simply recognizing the future implications of the rainfall that has already occurred.

This careful sorting out of the predetermined elements, this identification of what has already happened, is basic to serious planning. But great care is needed with the predetermined. Paul Valery, the twentieth-century French philosopher said, "Un fait mal observe est plus pernicieux qu'un mauvais raiseonnement." (A poorly observed fact is more treacherous that a faulty train of reasoning.) That, too is our experience: most of the errors of judgment in future-oriented studies come not so much from faulty reasoning but from poorly, insufficiently observed facts.

There are always some predetermined elements. But seldom are there enough of them that a single-line forecast will suffice to hand the residual uncertainty. And a single-line forecast for a situation that is not fully predetermined is an intellectual swindle: decision makers facing uncertain situations have the right to know how uncertain they are. Many decisions will always remain some kind of gamble, but it is dishonest to lead a manager to believe that he or she faces a safe, "business-as-usual" decision.

Accordingly, it is essential to try to put as much light on the uncertain elements as on the predetermined elements. They should not be swept under the carpet.

### How Scenarios First Came to Be Tried

#### Mechanical Planning Once Sufficed

The evolution of Shell's planning processes from 1945 to 1980 is outline in Chart I. For the first ten years, in the aftermath of the destruction of World War II, the planning needed to be physical only: the company obviously had to build new production capacity, tankers, depots, pipelines, and refineries. The main challenge was to coordinate properly and schedule new facilities. A PERT approach to planning could be, and was, used. Almost no economic planning was needed during this decade.

In the next decade, 1955–1965, financial considerations steadily became more important, but primarily on a project basis: the economics and the prospective rate of return on any given project were researched and evaluated. At the same time, Shell was introducing selectivity in its downstream sales objectives, choosing to develop those products and marketing channels that were most financially attractive. But no real integration of these projects was being made back to the crude oil production activities.

In 1965, Shell introduced a new system called, rather pompously, "Unified Planning Machinery" (UPM) to provide planning details for the whole chain of activity—from the oil in the ground, to the tanker, to the refinery, all the way to the gas station on the corner. UPM was a sophisticated, worldwide system that looked ahead six year: the first year in detail, the next five in broader lines. The system was designed, unconsciously, to develop Shell's businesses in a familiar, predictable work of "more of the same."

But six years was clearly a close horizon for an oil company, given the long lead times for new projects. Soon after the introduction of UPM, therefore, a study to explore the business environment of the year 2000—and Shell's corporation position in it—was initiated. The Year-2000 Study revealed that the familiar, surprise-free business environment of continued expansion simply could not continue, not even until 1985. The oil world would have to switch from a buyers' to a sellers' market, with major discontinuities in

| Steps in the Planning Approach in Shell 1945–80 | Chart I |
|---|---|
| 1945–55 | Mainly "Physical" Planning |
| 1955–65 | Project Planning + Selectivity |
| 1965–72 | Unified Planning Machinery |
| 1967 | Year-2000 Study initiated |
| 1969–70 | Horizon Year Planning Exercise |
| 1971 | Experimental Use of Scenarios in central offices, London |
| 1972–73 | Introduction of Scenario-Planning |
| 1975 | Introduction of Medium-Term Cyclical Scenarios |
| 1976–77 | Deepening "Societal Analysis" in Planning |
| 1978–79 | Deepening Geopolitical and Political Risk Analysis |
| 1979–80 | A Fresh Look at the Very Long Term + Development of Planning Capabilities Inside the Group |

*Chart BM 1.1* Steps in the Planning Approach in Shell, 1945–80

the price of oil and great changes to the interfuel competition. The huge size of the world oil and gas business projected in this study also signaled that major oil companies like Shell would become extremely large, heavily committed and much less flexible—almost dinosaur-like. And dinosaurs, as we all know, didn't adjust rapidly to sudden changes in their environment.

The discontinuity discerned in the Year-2000 Study generated a one-time exercise called Horizon Year Planning (1969–1970). A dozen of the largest Shell companies throughout the worlds, along with the main service company "sectors" in London and The Hague (such as Exploration and Production, and Marketing) were asked to look ahead fifteen years, to 1985.

One of the participating companies in the Horizon Planning exercise was Shell Francaise, for which the author worked at the time. We were familiar with the scenario approach of the Hudson Institute and were interested in experimenting with it. France was a perfect testing ground, for there were two major uncertainties: the availability of natural gas (recently developed in France and the Netherlands), which was the only fuel that could compete with oil; and the political uncertainty concerning how France would manage its energy business.

France, at that time, operated under an oil regime that favored French national companies and severely limited Shell's market share there. France, however, had just joined the Common Market and might have to change its oil regime to conform to EEC policy. There were therefore two options: France's oil regime would remain largely unchanged; or it would liberalize, after the transition period provided by the Treaty of Rome. Combining these two alternatives (Chart II) with the major uncertainty on gas availability gave us four scenarios.

|  | Liberalized | Same |
|---|---|---|
| **Large** |  |  |
| Natural Gas Availability |  |  |
| **Small** |  |  |

*Chart BM 1.2* French Oil Regime

Here is where we began to make some discoveries. First the amount of work required would be almost quadrupled if we provided the same sort of detail for each scenario that we gave to a normal UPM plan.

Accordingly, it quickly became clear that the same level of quantification and detail was not possible when planning with multiple scenarios. Just as the logistics of supply for an army have to be adapted to the type of war being fought, the logistics for scenario planning required a capacity to deal easily and quickly with alternatives. Without it, the whole process can be paralyzed by this bottleneck. In practice, this meant either developing flexible simulation models or having a number of specialists in key areas capable of rapidly assessing the consequences of different alternatives in a given field. We later found that both capabilities were needed.

Another realization was that simply combining obvious uncertainties did not help much with decision making. It was known beforehand that natural gas supply to France could be high or low and that French government control could stay as it was or be liberalized. Merely quantifying four Quadrants of Uncertainty didn't make for any gain in insight. The simply array of obvious uncertainties was a kind of trap: the way out would appear to be those already obvious solutions (in terms of strategies) which were often simplistic and unreconcilable—hardly a recommendation for such a time-consuming planning process!

But we intuited—we hadn't yet learned it—that we had discovered a useful search tool. By carefully studying certain of the elements suggested by this matrix design, the deeper understanding gained of the interplay of factors can lead, paradoxically, to the finding of some certainties, some inevitabilities amid the complexities of the situation. We began to appreciate the importance of additional sorting out of "PREDETERMINED elements" and "UNCERTAINTIES." In emphasizing only uncertainties, and only obvious ones at that, the scenarios we had developed were merely "first generation scenarios." They were useful in gaining more understanding of the situation so as to ask better questions and develop better "second generation scenarios" later—that is "decision scenarios." This dawning intuition—confirmed by all later experience—was an awareness of the critical importance of design. Scenarios will either help the decision maker, *or be of little use to him*, depending on how they are constructed and presented, not just on the information they contain. It is like architects who can create a well—or poorly designed building, even though both use all the same materials of construction

Although the initial attempts at scenario planning was not a success, it whetted our appetites. We believed the technique had promise and wanted to continue using it to experiment with second–generation scenarios.

HORIZON SEES DISCONTINUITY AHEAD

Meanwhile the Horizon Year exercise fully confirmed the conclusions of the Year-2000 Study. The most important ones were:

- The oil market—which had long been characterized by oversupply—was due to switch to a sellers' market.
- Soon there would be virtually no spare crude oil supply capacity in the secure, stable areas such as North America.
- Inevitably the Middle East, and in particular the Arabian Gulf, would be the balancing source of oil supply. In order to satisfy estimated world demand for crude oil, some 53MM B/D would be required from this region by 1985, compared to only 14MM B/D in 1970. (And this forecast allowed for discovery rates outside the Middle East some 40 percent higher than those achieved during the 1960s.)
- The very high demand on Middle East production would bring a sharp reduction in the Middle East reserve-to-production ratio.
- It seemed likely that this very sharp peaking in Middle East production would not in fact be allowed to occur and that many other factors would intervene, including:

  (a) A desire by Arab countries to extend the lifetime of their one valuable resource.
  (b) A cornering of the world energy market by Gulf producers for perhaps ten to fifteen years by limiting production.

- Something approaching a sustained worldwide depression would be necessary to reduce the growth of demand for Middle East Oil to levels where the anticipated sellers' market would be too weak to command substantially higher oil prices.

All of these developments would clearly have a major impact on the oil industry; yet in the Shell world, it was business as usual. (For example, some long-term contracts to supply products continued to be made at fixed prices—as if the fundamental changes projected by the Horizon Study would apply only on some other planet.)

After the Horizon Study was presented, serious doubts were raised about the UPM system's ability to provide realistic assumptions for the planning process: "How could it provide the 'right' answer if the forecasts on which it is based were likely to be wrong?" In 1971, therefore, it was decided to try scenario planning as potentially a better framework for thinking about the future than forecasts—which were now perceived as a dangerous substitute for real thinking in times of uncertainty and potential discontinuity. But Shell, like many very large organizations, is a cautious company. During the first year, when scenario analysis was done on an experimental basis, the UPM system continued in operation throughout the company. In 1972, scenario planning was extended to Central Offices and certain large Shell national operating companies. In the following year, it was finally recommended throughout the group and UPM was then phased out.

*Learning Scenarios*

Our next task at Shell was to find out how to go from a first-generation type of scenario to one that could become the basis for action. Somewhat to our surprise, we have found it is always a useful starting point to construct what we term, a "surprise-free" scenario or a "consensus-forecast." The surprise-free scenario is built on the implicit views of the future shared by most managers. While it is often the least likely outcome, its inclusion enables them to recognize their outlook in the scenario package. It is their entry—their bridge—into the future: without the surprise-free scenario, all possibilities may appear alien to the managers and they may reject the process out-of-hand.

*The 1971 First Generation Scenarios*

The Horizon Planning exercise indicated that the existing rate of growth for oil demand couldn't continue indefinitely; some break would have to come before 1985. Accordingly, 1985 was chosen as the horizon for the 1971 scenarios. Another significant date would be 1976, because the Teheran Agreement of 1971 (which established the level of oil producer-government taxes for OPEC) was to be renegotiated at the end of 1975.

Four scenarios were then constructed (Chart III).

| 1971 Scenarios | | | *Chart III* |
|---|---|---|---|
| I<br>Surprise-free<br>Scenario | II<br>High<br>Goverment<br>Take<br>Lower Demand | III<br>Very Low<br>Demand<br><br>Lower<br>Government<br>Take | IV<br>Other Energy<br>Intensive<br>Scenario |

*Chart BM 1.3* 1971 Scenarios

| Mm B/c Oil-equivalents | | | | |
|---|---|---|---|---|
| Scenario | I | II | III | IV |
| Total 1985 | 154 | 154 | 141 | 120 |
| Energy Demand<br>Supplied By: | | | | |
| Oil | 87 | 75 | 63 | 56 |
| Coal / Nuclear | 36 | 47 | 47 | 35 |
| Hydro / Natural Gas | 31 | 32 | 31 | 29 |

*Figure BM 1.2* MM B/C Oil-Equivalents

*Scenario 1:* A surprise-free, consensus scenario virtually lifted from the concurrent UPM work. It assumed median economic growth and led to an estimate of free world energy demand in 1985 of 154MM B/D oil-equivalent. While this was slightly higher than the 1971 UPM estimate of 150MM B/D, it fitted well with managers' expectations at the time, because the UPM had been consistently underestimating energy demand. (For orientation, 1971 free world energy demand was 78MM B/D).

*Scenario II:* Postulated a great increase—a tripling—of host-government tax take on the occasion of the renegotiation of the Teheran Agreement at the end of 1975, and further increases later. These assumptions of much higher oil prices would result in lower economic growth and energy and oil demand levels than those seen in the surprise-free scenario.

*Scenario III:* Treated the other obvious uncertainty: very low growth. Based on the recession years of 1970 and 1971, and a proliferation of already evident "me-first" and nonwork-oriented values, this slow-growth scenario premised an economic growth rate only half that under Scenario I. International trade would also slow down due to the lower growth and because the same attitudes would manifest themselves as nationalism and protective tariffs. Low oil demand would limit any oil price rises, and producer government take would increase less than in the surprise-free scenario.

*Scenario IV:* Postulated that demand for coal and nuclear energy would grow and much increased rates, mainly at the expense of oil. Other premises were kept similar to those in the surprise-free scenario.

All four of the scenarios assumed that the tax take of the producer governments would be increased at the Teheran renegotiation scheduled for the end of 1975. The assumptions are depicted in Chart IV.

The range of the free-world energy and oil demand in 1975 for the four scenarios was:

As is evident, the range of estimated energy demand was fairly wide, from 120 to 154MM B/D. The range of oil demand was even wider, at 56 to 87MM B/D.

This set of scenarios seemed reasonably well designed, and would fit most definitions of what scenarios should be. It covered a wide span of possible futures and each scenario was internally consistent.

When it was presented to Shell's top management, the problem was the same as with the French scenarios: no strategic thinking, or action could be taken from considering this material. True, we now had useful quantifications of the obvious uncertainties, and were sure that the range of uncertainties then considered relevant was reasonably well covered. But the scenarios were still useless for decision making.

It is this point which many companies reach in their efforts to use scenario planning, where the reaction of management must be similar: "So what!

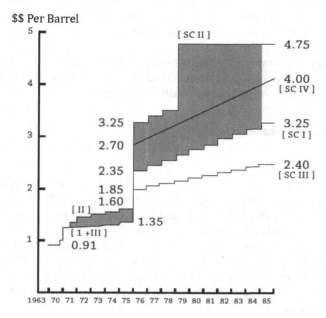

*Chart BM 1.4* Producer-Government Take, 1970–85

What do I do with these scenarios?" Many companies then abandon scenarios as useless—and indeed those are.

And yet this group of Shell managers was highly experienced in dealing with risk and uncertainty. For example, many of the decisions they take deal with exploratory drilling, a true uncertainty since you never know what is there until you drill. They are used to deciding whether to risk $5 million or over $50 million on exploration projects, and even to distinguish between these risks, say in Brazil or the North Sea. What was so different about the uncertainties of the scenarios? Quite simply, they needed structuring. In oil exploration, there were theories to call on, concepts to use, an organized body of geological and geophysical analyses, comparisons with similar geological structures, ways to spread the risk that were very familiar to the decision maker. Here, we had just presented the raw uncertainties. Our managers had no basis on which to exercise their judgment. The task for use was to devise ways to help them understand the nature of *these* uncertainties and to structure ways they could come to grips with them.

What, in time, we can to learn was that these first-generation scenarios are always learning scenarios; their purpose is not action, but to gain understanding and insight. The first-generation scenarios map out the future context. With that done and some of the predetermined elements identified, you then push to find others not obviously predetermined. The aim is to perceive more clearly the connections between various forces and events driving the system, and this understanding of the interrelatedness of the system shows that some apparent "uncertainties" are really "predetermined." In this way, we learned of many outcomes that were simply not possible under any reasonable set of assumptions.

Thus, our exploratory scenarios became good search tools. They had yet to become effective planning devices, but without them we would have been unable to develop the next generation of scenarios.

### Expanding the Predetermineds

### The Triangle Study

Our next step at Shell was to look more closely at the principal actors in our business environment: the OIL PRODUCER COUNTRIES, the OIL CONSUMING CONTRIES, and the OIL COMPANIES (see chart V). The roles they would play would be determined largely by their overriding concerns as producers, consumers and commercial interests; but there would be very significant differences in behavior within each group. We undertook the Triangle Study to understand better the characters in the drama and the behavior they would unconsciously be compelled to display when the discontinuity we saw ahead began to unfold.

#### PRODUCER COUNTRIES

We analyzed the major oil-producing countries one by one—not just OPEC and non-OPEC producers as groups—to try to determine their interests. As we did so, we saw that Iran's interests would differ from those of Saudi Arabia or Nigeria, and we expected that their strategies would show corresponding differences.

Our analysis of Iran is shown in the two panels of Chart V.

In the lower panel, Iran's oil production, as its share of projected oil demand under in the four scenarios just described, is shown. We had expectations, too, about Iran's discovery rates and additions to reserves (the shaded areas in the lower panel indicate the range). For the first five years, we expected the industry to find more new oil than Iran would be producing under any of our four scenarios and, hence, reserves would grow. For the second five years, the reverse would be true and reserves would fall.

Reserve / Production rations would be dropping rapidly in all scenarios (upper panel). This, we felt, would be viewed with considerable alarm, since it could signal the virtual ending of Iran's oil export capability by the end of the century. Our conclusion was that Iran would strive to change its oil policy from one of expanding production to one of increasing prices and possibly curbing production. This change in policy would stem not from any anti-Western attitude, but simply from the logic of national interest inherent in the situation. If we were Iranian, we would behave the same.

Number of Years       Reserves 10⁹ bbl

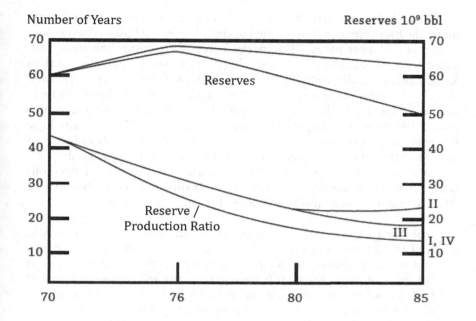

Production / Discoveries (Average)
$10^9$ bbl / a

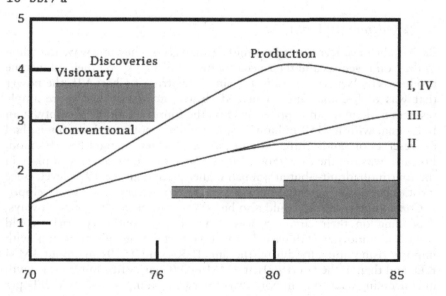

*Chart BM 1.5* Iran, Reserves / Discoveries / Production

The Saudi Arabian situation appeared to be very different. Its production under the four scenarios (lower panel of chart VI) would lead to the revenues shown in the upper panel. All scenarios except the gloomy, low-growth III, called for production levels that would generate much more revenue than Saudi Arabia could spend in purposeful ways (Absorptive Capacity). Even allowing for some of the surplus to be "manageable" doesn't change the basic outcome. Note especially that the surprise-free scenario had the Saudis producing 20MM B/D by 1985—what might be termed and oil-company logic but politically an outcome difficult to believe. Production levels sufficient to meet the national revenue needs are spotted on the lower panel in red.

Our conclusion was that Saudi-logic would have to prevail over oil-company logic. Accordingly, we were not too surprised when Sheik Zhaki Ahmed Yamani, Saudi Arabia's Minister for Oil Affairs, later said:

> Inability to spend our surplus income inside our own countries will lead us to reconsider the value of keeping our revenues in the banks and realizing interest on them as compared with the appreciation in the value of our crude oil if it were to be left in the ground. We should find that leaving our crude in the ground is by far more profitable than depositing our money in the banks, particularly if we take into account the periodic devaluation of many of the currencies. This reassessment would lead us to adopt a production program that ensures that we get revenues which are adequate for our real needs.

*Platt's Oilgram, 10 Feb. 1972*

Each of the producer countries could be analyzed in the same way, according to their oil revenues and their need for and ability to spend their oil income productively. When arrayed in the simply matrix of Chart VII, the power that was to become OPEC emerged clearly: no nation had more ample reserves and ample absorptive capacity; the fourth quadrant is empty. If an Indonesia, with its 150 million people and enormous need for funds, had the reserves of Saudi Arabia, the surprise-free scenario might have been on. But such was not the case. (Someday, the Soviet Union might find a place in the fourth quadrant—but at a much higher price than the 1971 level, since most of the Soviet potential oil was expected to be very costly to develop.)

*Consuming countries* could also be expected to behave in different ways, depending on their circumstances, when the discontinuity crisis would come. Oil import growth was already a well-established phenomenon, with imports rising annually during the late 1950s and 1960s by about 1MM B/D, and then in the late 1960s at 2MM B/D (Chart VIII). But now, growth in consuming countries' imports was forecast to jump to 3–4 MM B/D per annum, under the "surprise-free" scenario.

Different reasons for the jump could be ascribed to the US, Europe and Japan. In the US, domestic oil production had recently peaked, and now

## Maximum Absorptive Capacity
## Infrastructure Investment Possibilities
## Government Take (Oil Revenues)

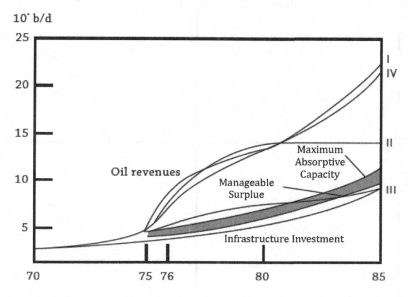

10° b/d

Oil revenues

Maximum
Absorptive
Capacity

Manageable
Surplus

Infrastructure Investment

I
IV
II
III

70    75  76    80    85

## Production Levels Following from Scenarios and
## Maximum Absorptive Capacity

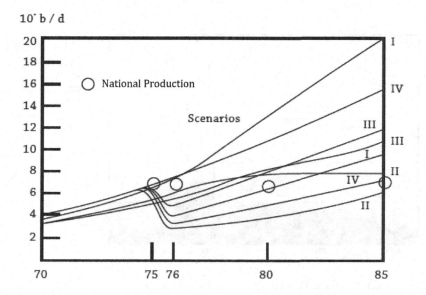

10° b / d

○ National Production

Scenarios

I
IV
III
III
I
II
IV
II

70    75  76    80    85

*Chart BM 1.6* Saudi Arabia

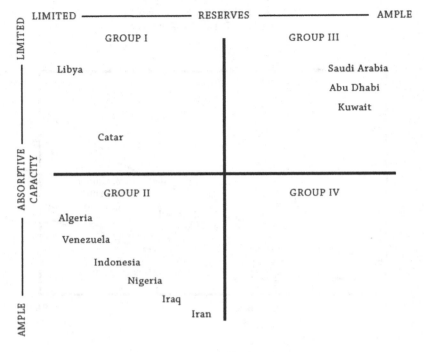

*Chart BM 1.7* Major Oil Exporters

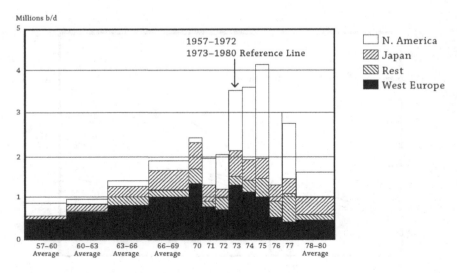

*Chart BM 1.8* Annual Growth in Import Requirements

imported oil not only had to match demand growth but falling domestic production as well. Natural gas was not able to take up the slack because regulated price had discouraged its supply and its production was also in decline. Coal production could have been readily increased, but its use was discouraged by environmental concerns, by ample availability of cheap imported fuel oil and by nuclear power's perceived future in electricity generation. Because of the large demand base in the US, when a 3%-4% increase in energy demand had to be met solely by imported oil, the US share of oil import growth along was more than 1MM B/D.

In Japan—which was then like a new continent emerging on the world economic map—the phenomenon was somewhat different. In 1953, at the end of US occupation, Japanese industrial production was 40% of the U.K.'s; in 1970, it was more than double. The country was growing at 11 to 12 percent a year, with oil demand growing at times by 20 percent a year. This large oil dependency, combined with Japan's rapidly growing economic size, created huge increases in the nation's oil imports.

Insight and "soft" information were as important to use as these quantifiable data. For example, the Japanese always become anxious when there is any risk of critical imports being denied them. Their psyche would be particularly tested about any tension over oil supply. Furthermore, they would project onto multinational oil companies the type of behavior their own companies would normally display in a crisis situation being loyal only to the home country and ignoring the rest of the world. This would add to the probably overreaction to tension over oil supplies.

Oil import growth projected for the US, Japan, and West Europe is shown in Chart IX.

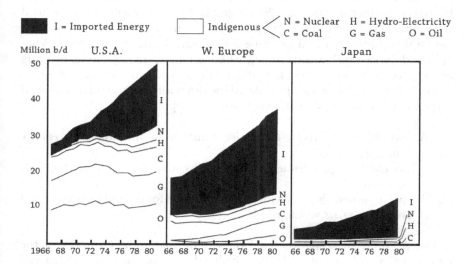

*Chart BM 1.9* Energy Demand by Sources

We also did a number of other analyses aimed at increasing our understanding, expanding the PREDETERMINDS and striving to get to the core of the UNCERTAINS. We looked at:

- Oil demand by Class of Market and How It Might Grow at Differing Rates.
- Implications of High Oil Price on Country Balances-of-Payments and Inflation.
- Inter-Fuel Competition and How This Might be Changed by Higher Oil Price.
- Changing "cut of the Barrel" (the yield of gasoline and light fuels versus heavy fuel) as Driven by Changing Inter-Fuel Pricing.
- Possible Reactions of Consumer Governments to Higher Oil Price (Free Markets vs. Dirigism).
- Construction, Already Committed to, in Refiner, Marine and Market Facilities.

With all of these "building blocks," we were beginning to understand the forces driving the system. Could we now tackle the 1971 scenarios again and devise a set of scenarios that would catch the decision maker's attention, and help him cope with the coming discontinuity and focus usefully on its uncertainties? We now felt we could design scenarios that might provide a proper framework for decision making, but we realized that we would have a formidable communications task.

### The 1972 Scenarios

In September 1972, we presented to Shell's top management an array of possible futures, gathered in two families, A and B. All of our analyses had pointed with great likelihood to the early surfacing of a major discontinuity, namely, the impeding scarcity of oil and an ensuing sharp increase in its price. What appeared "uncertain" was its timing (although it couldn't be too many years away) and, more particularly, how different actors would respond to it.

*The A-family of scenarios* postulated the discontinuity and then examined three ways in which circumstances might develop:

A1 would be a private-enterprise *solution* to the emerging energy shortage;
A2 would have governments intervene to solve the problem, the dirigiste *solution*;
A3 presupposed that solutions would not be found early enough, and an *energy crisis* would result.

The A-family of scenarios fixed the timing of the discontinuity at the end of 1975, coincident with the scheduled renegotiation of the Teheran price agreement. (In reality, the discontinuity came in the fall of 1973—not yet caused by demand outrunning supply, but when the oil embargo was imposed after the outbreak of the Israeli/Arab war in reaction to US assistance to Israel.)

Moderate economic growth was assumed through 1976, with growth thereafter threatened by a possible scarcity of energy. Most oil-producing countries would be reaching the technical limit of their capacities by 1976, while the others would be reluctant to increase output further due to their inability to absorb the additional revenues. Accordingly, producer countries oil prices would increase substantially at the end of 1975. Consuming countries, confronted with the possibility of physical shortages of energy supplies and with greatly increased oil import bills, would experience shock waves.

The essential point in the A-family of scenarios was discontinuity. Shell would have to prepare for a sudden change in the behavior of both producing and consuming countries that would result from their awareness of an impending imbalance between demand and supply of oil. The discontinuity might arise from a situation of tension, created by the producing countries' imposing a limit on the amount of oil they produced. It might also come about if these nations announced a gradual decrease in the rate of production growth, or if they gave advance notice of such a policy. In any case, the awareness of an impending energy gap constituted only the first stage of the process. The most important consideration, it was felt, was the timing and direction of the "active responses" to such awareness.

The A-family of scenarios emerged as the most likely outcomes from our analyses, but they were at sharp variance with the implicit "world view" then prevailing in Shell. That view was one of EXPLORE AND DRILL, BUILD REFINERIES, ORDER TANKERS, EXPAND MARKETS. But how could we be heard?

We therefore created a set of "challenge scenarios," the B-family. Here the basic premise was that somehow, sufficient energy supply would be available, and as discontinuity of energy supply would appear. These three scenarios would serve not only to challenge the assumptions underlying the A-family of scenarios, but could also destroy many of the comfortable business-as-usual aspects of the "world view" so many in Shell were still operating by.

The A-family and B-family scenarios could then be shown as either alternative responses to different outcomes (Chart X-A) or different paths pursued into the structure (Chart X-B).

———Chart X-A and X-B———(p. 51)

This might be a useful point to remark parenthetically about two aspects of the scenarios that we learned only later. Six scenarios are far too many. The ideal number is two, which highlight the principal uncertainty being focused on, plus the consensus or surprise-free scenario.

Another insight later gained was the importance of naming the scenarios. A well-chosen name conveys to the decision maker the essence of what drives the scenario; it also reduces the detail you must provide him and not only encourages him to fill in the detail (making the scenario alive for him) but leaves him room to do so.

THE B-FAMILY OF SCENARIOS

With hindsight, the critical assumption of discontinuity for the A-scenarios looks rather obvious. At the time, however, it was seen as quite the reverse. We believed in the A-scenarios, we put them forward very strongly as the most likely direction of events. But they did represent a major revolution in thinking for an oil company—and many Shell managers (like their counterparts in other companies) still wanted to believe in futures without discontinuity.

The B-family of scenarios therefore described how discontinuity might be avoided.

*B1*, was a protracted *low-economic-growth scenario*, requiring at least 10 years of low growth to force a demand fit to the oil supply presumed available. While low growth had seemed plausible in the downturn of 1971, by 1972 we could see signs of a coming economic boom. We did not know, of course, the extent of this period of above-average growth, or that growth in 1973 would be the most spectacular since the Korean War. But we could already see that our low-growth scenario, B1, was extremely unlikely: it would require an immediate and sharp drop in the growth rate of the world economy, which we had no reason to anticipate. Moreover, the negative cultural trends of the late 1960s in industrial countries were waning. Governments and the public perceived that rising unemployment was a problem and were consciously seeking growth. So, the B1 scenario, premising very low growth for a long period, had low credibility. However, it performed its function of highlighting the major discontinuity most effectively, simply because it was not a likely way to avoid the discontinuity.

*B3*, a more important alternative, postulated a very *high supply of oil*. We called it the "three miracle" scenario, because it required three extremely unlikely situations simultaneously. First, it required an exploration and production miracle. Our original surprise-free scenario had predicted a certain level of demand for oil. To meet that demand, rapid development of Middle Eastern reserves and extensive new discoveries were necessary. Our Exploration and Production staff believed that there was a 30 percent likelihood of finding the necessary reserves in each of the oil provinces individual, but that there was only a very small percent change of finding the necessary reserves in all the areas. Meeting the forecast 1985 demand would require not only 24MM B/D from Saudi Arabia, but also 13MM B/D from Africa and 6MM B/D from Alaska and Canada. Many new discoveries would be needed for these figures to become reality.

The second miracle demanded by the B3 scenario was a sociopolitical one: all major producing countries would be happy to deplete their resources at the will of the consumer. Countries with low absorptive capacities would agree to produce huge amounts of oil and put their money in the bank, exposed to erosion by inflation, rather than keep their oil in the ground for future generation. This scenario projected onto the oil-producing countries the values of consuming countries—a kind of Western cultural imperialism that was extremely unconvincing once examined rationally.

The final miracle of B3 started with the recognition that there would be little, if any, spare capacity over projected demand under the high-supply scenario. Previously when minor crises developed in the Middle East, there had always been additional oil available to meet sudden, short-term needs. (For instance, in 1956 during the Suez crisis, Texas and Louisiana helped out with their spare capacity. Similarly, during the June 1967 Middle East conflict, Iran called on its spare capacity to meet consumers' needs.) Under Scenario B3 there would be no spare production capacity. The miracle, then, was that there would be no need for it—no wars in the region, no acts of God, no cyclical peaks of demand higher than anticipated. Again, nothing short of miraculous.

The B3 scenario also performed its function very well by demonstrating that the high-supply assumption was extremely unlikely. Its essential role was educational.

B2, a totally artificial construct, was a *middle-of-the-road* scenario premising that despite all the problems, a muddling-through approach could be more or less successful. A widespread sentiment, particularly among the Anglo-Saxon managers, is well expressed by William Ogburn: "There is much stability in society. . . social trends seldom change their directions quickly and sharply. . . revolutions are rare and evolution is the rule." We couldn't really justify this scenario, but we knew that the worst outcome is not always the one that develops, and we imagined a situation in which the most positive outcomes were the norm. Oil-producing countries would take a live-and-let-live approach in order to obtain military and other concessions. Consuming countries, with great foresight, would take immediate steps to curb the rapid growth of oil consumption by encouraging energy saving.

The great danger was that the B-2 scenario coincided with the best estimates for oil demand by the major operating companies. It was thus a surprise-free environment as long as we did not probe too deeply into current forces. As soon as we did any serious digging into what underlay this scenario, it became much less convincing.

Both the A—and B-family scenarios were fully quantified in terms of volumes, prices, and their impact on individual oil producing and consuming countries as well as on interfuel competition in different markets. Our presentation of them succeeded in gaining the attention of top management principally because the B-family of scenarios destroyed the ground any of them may have chosen to stand on.

Two decisions were then taken

- to use scenario planning in the central offices and the larger of the operating companies, and
- to advise informally governments of oil-consuming countries about what we saw coming.

To implement the first decision, Shell asked its major, downstream operating companies to evaluate their current strategies against two A-type scenarios, using the B-2 scenario as a sensitivity check. A series of oral presentations was also made to the governments of the major consuming countries, starting in October 1972, followed by the distribution in May 1973 of a brochure, "The Impact on the World Economy on the Market for Oil." The brochure was based on a single scenario which stressed discontinuity, and traced its effects on oil-consuming countries' balance of payments, rates of inflation, resource allocation and so on.

Within Shell, the next step was to present the A and B scenarios to the second echelon of management. For most of them, it was their first exposure to scenarios. The meeting was in stark contrast to the traditional UPM meetings which dealt with forecasts and trends and premises—all with an avalanche of numbers. Scenarios focused less on outcomes and more on understanding of the forces that would compel the outcome; less on figures, and more on insight. This meeting was positive and unusually lengthy, and the audience clearly appreciative. We thought we had won over a large share of them.

In reality, the following months would show that no more than a third of Shell's critical decision centers were really acting on the insights gained through the scenarios, and actively preparing for the A-family of outcomes. The scenario package had created an intellectual interest, but it failed to change behavior in much of the Shell organization. For us, this came as a shock and compelled us to rethink how to design scenarios geared for decision making.

Reality was painful: most studies dealing with the future business environment, and now including these first scenarios, have a very low existential effectiveness. (We would define "existential effectiveness" as single-mindedness; but the Japanese express it much better—"When there is no break, not even the thickness of a hair, between a man's vision and his action.") A vacuum cleaner, for example, has an effectiveness of 30 to 40 percent; the rest is heat and noise. Future studies, particularly when they point to discontinuity, have an effectiveness below that of a vacuum cleaner.

If your role is to be a corporate look-out, and you clearly see a discontinuity on the horizon, you have better learn what makes the difference between a more or less effective study. Here, we learned a lot just by watching.

One of the differences involves the basic psychology of decision making. Every decision maker has a mental model of the world in which he or she acts. The model is based on past experiences and on the information which have been internalized. When someone has a decision to make, he confronts alternative ways of behaving with his mental model. When it proved to be a good decision, others say he has good judgment. In fact, what he has is a mental map that largely matches the real world. We call this mental model or map the decision maker's "microcosm,"—the small model in the head— as opposed to the "macrocosm," which is the large, real world out there.

There is also a corporate view of the world, a corporate microcosm. During a sabbatical year in Japan, I became acutely aware, for example, that Nippon Steel was not "seeing" the steel market the same ways as Usinor, the French steel giant, and this led to marked differences in their behavior and priorities. Each had a view of the world and acted rationally, consistent with that view.

The perception a company has of its business environment is in fact as important as it infrastructure of investment, because the strategy the company adopts will be the product of this perception, of how it sees the world—*its* world.

I cannot overemphasize this point: unless the microcosm—individual or corporate—is changed, no change in behavior will occur; the internal compass must be recalibrated.

From this realization onward, we no longer saw our task as producing a documented view of the future business environment five or ten years ahead. Our real target was the microcosms of our decision makers: unless we influenced the mental image, the picture of reality of critical decision makers, our scenarios would be like water on a stone. This was different and much, much more than producing a relevant scenario package.

Our initial aim had been to produce scenarios that we would not be ashamed of when subsequently confronted with the reality. From this point on, we wanted to design scenarios that would lead our decision makers to question their inner model of reality and change it as necessary, in order to take action *they* would not be ashamed of later. This was a fundamental change in perspective, as fundamental as when on organization switches from selling to marketing.

## Impacting the Decision Maker

### The 1973 Scenarios—The Rapids

"It was ordained at the beginning of the world that certain signs should prefigure certain events," Cicero noted twenty centuries ago. All the signs at the end of 1972 and early 1973, as we set about preparing the next set of scenarios, still pointed to that major oil discontinuity.

We had done new analyses that again told use that a very tight supply-demand relationship would exist during the coming decade. Even in 1973, '74 and '75 (before the anticipated renegotiation of the Teheran agreement), demand could be expected to push right up to available production capability. And that supply would already be stretched, since it predicated that certain countries, such as Saudi Arabia and Kuwait, would produce contrary to their logic.*

Now we saw even discontinuity as totally PREDETERMINED. Prices, then, would rise rapidly, and oil production would be constrained, not because of a true shortage of oil, but for political reasons—talking advantage of the very tight supply-demand relationship. Discontinuity would thus be our surprise-free scenario. What was not known was *how soon* the discontinuity would occur, *how much* of a price increase there would be, and *what the reactions* of the various players would be. Our company was like the canoeist who hears the white water around the next bend, and now needs to prepare for "THE RAPIDS" he will soon have to negotiate.

To reframe the outlook of our managers, we portrayed the situation for the 1973 scenarios as in Chart XI. From the calm up-river of the TRADITIONAL ENVIRONMENT, we would be plunged into the turbulence of THE RAPIDS, and have to learn to live in a NEW HABITAT for oil producers, for oil consumers, and—especially our concern—for oil companies.

The alternate branch of the river (the B-challenge scenarios of 1972) had now been dammed off. The "No Growth-No-Problem" possibility (B-1) now seemed completely noncredible as economies, fully recovered from the recession of 1971, boomed. "Three miracles" (B-3) still seemed just that—three supply miracles. And from our discussions to warn governments about impending crisis, we concluded that any reaction from governments would be *after the event*. (Obviously, we hadn't yet learned how to impact the microcosms of governments either!)

Another technique we used in the 1973 scenarios to keep the B-branch of the river dammed was to allow for delay in the onset of the discontinuity. In Phantom Scenario I we assumed a delay of five years; in Phantom II, fifteen years. (These, respectively, were typical times for bringing a new oil facility into service and for its amortization.) What we sought with these phantom scenarios was to measure the "regret" we would experience if Shell planned for the discontinuity but it did not in fact occur during the phantom years.

In the booming economy of late 1972 and early '73—with growth exceeding any period since the Korean War, trade expanding at a record clip and oil consumption higher than ever our bullish reference line—it was particularly difficult to convince an oil company having an affair with expansion that now was the time to slow down, to hold off on expanding refineries to stop building tankers and so forth.

And the phantom scenarios *did* measure a considerable "regret" if expansion continued and we didn't go with it. But, again, only two developments could delay the discontinuity, enabling business-as-usual to continue for any period of time; and both seemed so implausible that discontinuity soon had

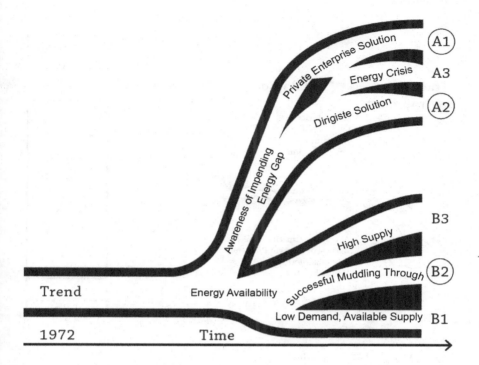

*Figure BM 1.3* 1972 Scenarios

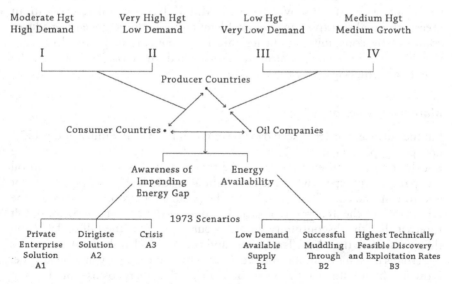

*Chart BM 1.10* 1973 Royal Dutch/Shell Scenarios

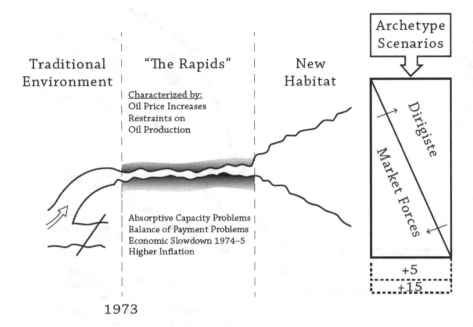

*Chart BM 1.11* 1973 Scenarios

to be regarded as a PREDETERMINED. (The two situations allowing for a continuation of the existing pace of oil demand increase and which were ruled out, were: the discovery of new Middle East-size oil reserves in an area with no absorptive capacity problem; and, the dominance of producer countries by consuming countries through some sort of political or military intervention.) The phantom scenarios acted, therefore, to reinforce the unpalatable message we were sending.

### More than Water on a Stone

On the surface, the 1973 scenarios were much like the A-family of the 1972 group (see page facing p. 28), but we saw them very differently. We were not driven by a sense of urgency. The time apparently available for an oil company to anticipate what the new habitat would be like, to prepare for it and to respond to it, had shrunk greatly. (Remember, too, we expected the crisis close to the Teheran renegotiation date at the end of 1975; we didn't forecast that the discontinuity would occur as early as the fall of 1973, on the occasion of that Arab/Israeli war and the Arab oil embargo.)

Perhaps even more important, we wanted to be more that water on a stone: How could we impact the view of reality—the microcosms—of decision makers? The easy part would be to destroy their existing view of the world (i.e., of orderly, predictable expansion of oil demand, a world of adding to oil fields and refineries and tankers and marketing outlets). We had been at this job of destruction for several years, and by 1973—the first year scenarios were used without the UPM—we were not even allowing for the conventional possibility.

But exposing and invalidating an obsolete world view was just the necessary first step. Reconstructing the new inner model of reality would be the task of decision makers themselves. The planner's job is to help by listening carefully to what he says he needs, and then to provide the highest quality materials for him to use. The planner will succeed, however, only if he can securely link the outside world, the business environment he scans, to the microcosm of the decision maker. Good scenarios provide this vital "bridge"; but it must be firmly anchored on both sides—it must deal with managers' real concerns, as well as external reality. Otherwise, there is a risk that no one will bother to cross the bridge.

If the "package" is well designed, a manager can then use the scenarios to construct a new model of reality by selecting those elements he believes are relevant to his business world, or, perhaps, what his "gut" tells him, or, perhaps, none of these things. After all, he is the decision maker and his track record has shown he is good at it.

What we later came to understand better is to make the scenarios relevant to the deepest concerns of the decision maker in the circumstances that he was facing. That requires knowing a lot more about the decision maker and his concerns than we knew then, or even suspected we needed to know. We did know that the scenarios would have to serve as a bridge to carry in the new elements and fashion the new microcosm. In later years, however, we built quite a few bridges that did not get used. The lack was always a failure to design the scenarios so they were relevant to the deepest concerns of the decision makers. I will come back to this very important aspect of scenarios in the CONCLUSION.

### Building Blocks for New Microcosms

At the time, we realized that if decision makers were to reframe their microcosms quickly, they would need to have a clear overview of that new model of reality. Chart XII was one such attempt to provide a global view of the 1973 scenarios. It summarizes the business environment foreseen and its key elements. On the left, in the rectangle, are the PREDETERMINDS— events which were already in the pipeline: the fact that oil reserves would soon be developed according to oil-producing countries' logic and that a scramble for oil would develop in this new sellers' market. In the centre of the chart were the major discontinuities: PRICE INCREASE AND INSECURE SUPPLY.

Attention was focused on some singularities of the industry's business environment:

> *Alternative Fuels* could be developed only very slowly; none could be available before the 1980s, even under a wartime crash development program. The cost, moreover, needed analysis, and this was considered in three thresholds. First, other fuels might replace oil as "underboiler" fuel, that is, for power generation and for steam generation in large industrial settings; coal and nuclear energy were the competitive alternatives. It was clear that oil-producing nations would not be impressed by alternatives that replaced their precious hydrocarbons in underboiler applications. On the contrary, they believed their oil was far too valuable for such uses and would welcome coal and nuclear power to displace oil in those low-value markets. The next threshold, oil used for heating, was the one that really counted. For such uses, burning coal as such would not be satisfactory: it would be necessary to gasify coal at great expense or to transform it into electricity, with the accompanying thermodynamics loss.

The price for this threshold, then, was very high, and we did not expect the oil price to exceed it in the near future. The third threshold, oil used in transport, was an even higher alternative fuel cost than the second, and therefore was not relevant to our analysis.

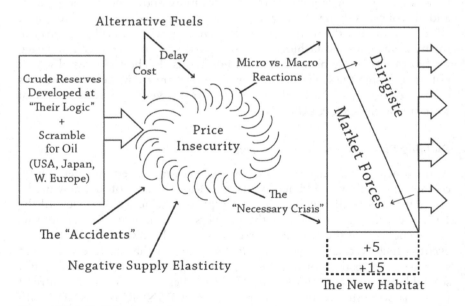

*Chart BM 1.12* Price Insecurity

"*Accidents*" constituted another major and inevitable factor. In our terminology, accidents included internal and external political incidents as well as physical ones. Anyone familiar with the oil world considers such events likely. It is like the Filipino who knows that his roof must be built carefully; even though the weather in the Philippines is usually balmy, typhoons are frequent enough that the only uncertainty is when the strength of one's roof will be tested. So it would be with accidents in the world of oil, when there was no spare capacity in the system.

*Negative Supply Elasticity* would be another key element. Unlike other commodities, the supply of oil would not increase when its price rose, at least for a number of years. On the contrary, for major exporting countries, the higher the price the lower the volume of oil it would be in their national interest to produce. This reaction from major exporters would more than compensate for any increases in production by smaller exporters.

As planners at the center of a group of companies, we also faced a special problem. The message of our scenarios had to be useful for our managing directors, but it would also have to be of use to the operating companies in Canada and Germany, in Japan and Australia. Yet the dramatic changes we anticipated would affect each and every nation differently. What basic message could be conveyed from the center that would be meaningful for managers in many diverse companies around the world?

We borrowed the concept of archetypes from human character analysis. Just as we are accustomed to viewing individuals as composites of archetypes (for example, introvert and extrovert, even though no individual is wholly one or the other), so we sought archetypes that would enable us to examine differing national responses to the coming upheavals.

In our view, nations would try to cope with this major discontinuity by either a market-force approach or by a government-intervention (dirigiste) approach. In their pure forms, these responses became our archetypes, and we explored each of them fully. We did not imagine that any country would follow either archetype absolutely, but we believe, for example, that West Germany's response would be heavily market-oriented, while that of its neighbor, France, would be more dirigiste. The actions anticipated under each archetypal response in terms of price increases, taxes, alternative fuels development, regulations, were analyzed by class of market.

## Taking the Decision Maker to Water

We didn't yet fully understand that really impacting the decision maker required a tailor-made fit between the scenarios and the decision makers' deepest concerns. Intuitively, however, we knew in 1973 that events were giving us just this type of fit in several ways, and for Shell they were very deep and important. The arrows on the far-right sides of Charts XI and XII symbolized four of the resultant implications we stressed to our decision makers.

We told our upstream people (those engaged in exploration and production), something nearly unthinkable for an oil company: "Be careful! You are about to lose the major part of your mining rents." This meant that the traditional base of profit in the upstream world would be lost—a revolutionary message for an oil company, and that new relationships had to be developed between the company and producing nations.

To the downstream world (the refineries, transporters, and marketers), we said something equally unthinkable, "You are about to become a low-growth industry." Again, this was revolutionary because oil demand had always grown more rapidly than GNP. Our management culture and its reflexes, were based on growth. In the past, the consequence of overinvestment was not too adverse; one or two years of normal market growth would cure any premature moves. Now we could expect that future consumption in industrial countries to increase less than GNP, which meant fewer refineries, no new service stations and so forth. New instincts and reflexes would have to be developed to function in a low-growth world.

A third major implication was the need to decentralize further. We believed that one basic strategy could no longer be valid for operating companies in most parts of the world. It had been the strategy of Shell companies generally, for example, to aim for a higher share of conversion in refineries, and it had been quite successful. (Shell, which was already decentralized compared to other oil majors, did in fact, decentralize further, which enabled it to adjust faster to the turbulence experienced later. For some time now, it has in fact been the most decentralized of all the major oil companies.)

Finally, we alerted decision makers to the possibility that, since we didn't know when the discontinuity would come, we should prepare for it in different phases of the business cycle. We developed three simulations: in each we anticipated both a cyclical downturn *and* the expected oil discontinuity, but in differing relationships. In the first simulation, the oil shock occurred before the downturn; in the second, the events were simultaneous; and in the third, the oil shock followed the downturn. These simulations led Shell to prepare for a far more serious decline in economic activity than might otherwise have been expected.

### And Most Drank

The 1973 scenarios were a happy coincidence of the right material and the deepest concerns of decision makers. And if any were not yet fully convinced, the events of the fall of 1973 soon made them believers. We had set out not to produce a scenario booklet summarizing views but to impact the microcosm of the decision makers, to help them restructure their world view. Only now, however, did we appreciate the unique power of scenarios—which really becomes apparent in turbulent times, and has immense value in a large, decentralized organization.

Strategies are the product of a world view. When the world view changes, there must be some common view of the new world throughout the group, or the decentralized strategic decisions that result could lead to anarchy. Scenarios provide a powerful way to express and communicate a common view of the new realities to all parts of the organization. Decentralized managements in operating companies worldwide thus have a shared understanding which they can adapt and use for strategic decisions appropriate to their varying local circumstances. Their initiative is not limited by planning instructions dictated from the center, but all "speak the same language" in adapting to the changing business environment. Still companies from Finland to New Zealand now knew what "The Rapids" connoted, were alert to the implications of "Producer Logic," etc., and of the consequent need to prepare for a totally New Habitat.

We learn, from studying evolution, how an animal suited to one environment must adapt, must become a new animal to survive when the environment undergoes severe change. It was that sort of change we foresaw, and we believed that Shell would have to become a new animal to function in the new world. Business-as-usual decisions would no longer suffice. This element of the message was really our most important.

## Scenarios: The Gentle Art of Re-Perceiving (Part II)

### Shooting the Rapids

#### Adrift in the Short-Term Economy

Most companies I have seen use scenarios for planning five to ten years ahead. For a variety of reasons, however, the application of the scenario technique to the short term is very interesting and can be particularly productive:

1    You must, in any case, explore the short term in order to get to the long term; changes in the business environment over the next two or three years can have a major effect on the alternatives possible five or ten years ahead.

2    Short-term scenarios can have a striking impact on the microcosm of the decision makers because they are "immediate." Unlike long-term scenarios, they deal with events and information that are already part of managers' day-to-day concerns.

3    They help to establish credibility—which is essential to the process—because their usefulness is quickly tested against reality; you don't have to wait five or ten years. In addition, managers tend to regard planners who deal only with the long term as mere theoreticians.

Up to 1974, planning in Shell had traditionally focused on the medium and long term, seeking to describe the environment in which today's investment decisions would come to fruition. In this context, the cyclical nature of growth in the short term was taken for granted.

But in the aftermath of the first oil shock, everyone's attention was focused on the short-term economy and its cyclical fluctuations. Such short-term fluctuations would pattern not only economic growth, but oil demand and inflation rates, currency and interest rates, and the sensitive OPEC supply-demand relationship and its politics. Could the scenario approach provide insight?

This second part of my paper describes the development in Shell of our first short-term scenarios, which were presented in May 1975. I include this example not only for what it teaches, but also because the long-term "Rapids" scenarios described in the first part of the paper were somewhat atypical: the major discontinuity was seen to be predetermined; the critical uncertainties were perceived only in the reactions to the discontinuity. The short-term scenarios also represent a different application of the technique.

As I have already indicated, we felt there was no point in doing single-line forecasts in turbulent times. It's perhaps unfair to cite other forecasts gone wrong, since we too have had our share; but here is an OECD forecast of growth for 1975 (made in December 1974) compared with actual growth:

|           | West Germany | France | Italy | U.K. | US   | Japan |
|-----------|--------------|--------|-------|------|------|-------|
| Forecast: | +2.5         | +3.0   | −0.3  | +1.8 | −2.0 | +2.0  |
| Actual:   | −3.2         | −1.2   | −3.7  | −1.8 | −1.8 | +2.1  |

We would strive instead to apply all we had learned in the previous scenario exercises"

- expand the predetermineds
- scenarios would then deal with the uncertainties
- link to those deepest concerns
- keep the scenario number small
- give them names

## Identify the Predetermineds

There is, in the minds of most managers, an extraordinary reluctance to entertain the concept of alternative futures; most managers crave certainty. Scenarios of the future will only be accepted when their common elements, the PREDETERMINEDS, have entered the mind of the decision makers, unfold in it, and are accepted. We call this process "rooting." It is like transplanting a tree. "Nemawashi" is the term the Japanese use for the technique of careful preparation of the tree roots by grafting the together to give them strength for the transplant ordeal. Similarly, scenarios, if they are to live and develop within a mind-set, have to be "nemawashi'd."

To be successful, this rooting process requires:

- A deep analysis of the predetermineds. You must go back in time far enough to provide for a common interpretation to events and data.
- Perceptions to be organized in a global framework (as in Chart XIII). This is material directed to the right part of the brain the one that thinks in terms of pattern and connectedness. Metaphors are frequently helpful to transpose a conceptual framework from the old domain of experience to what will be a new one.

Scenarios on their own,—i.e., the mere description of alternative courses of events—would be effective and alive just as long as a tree without roots. And many of the scenarios I have seen suffer this fate.

*THE PREDETERMINEDS IN THE 1975 SCENARIOS* ARE DEPICTED IN CHART XIII

It is immediately apparent that a great deal of analysis was given to the "roots" part of the scenarios. We will present these in some detail because in most scenarios sets, this part is absent or nonexplicit.

1973—THE FIRST WAVE: INFLATION

Like a large rock dropped in a lake, the oil price increase of 1973 generated a series of waves, the first of which was the impact of quadrupled crude oil prices on the general level of inflation. The dynamic effect turned out to be larger than simple cost-through-the-system arithmetic had indicated (on

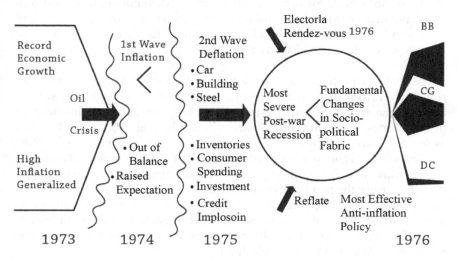

*Chart BM 1.13* Predetermined Part of the Present Evolution

average, 3–4 percent), because world economies in a simultaneous boom were already affected by high inflation prior to the oil shock, and were working close to capacity limitations. Further the immense publicity given to the oil price increase—coming as it did with production cuts and selective embargoes—created a climate in which major economic actors (trade unions, entrepreneurs, and consumers), overanticipated the actual inflationary impact. This and later overreaction added fuel to the fire and led to a substantial increase in the rate of inflation.

## 1974—THE SECOND WAVE: DEFLATION

A contradiction in demand to well below production capacity was increasingly apparent from mid-1974. The extra cash outflow to OPEC acted like an external excise tax on consumer demand of some $60 billion per annum—or, say, 2.5 percent of OECD economies. And this was compounded by government anti-inflation policies which pushed demand way below production potential. The economic dominos fell one by one:

- The automobile industry, always on the margin of discretionary spending and vulnerable to both the real increase in gasoline prices and the "oil link" in the consumer's mind, suffered an immediate decline, with extensive multiplier effects through the balance of the economy.
- Building and construction, also a major engine of economic activity, went some six months later as government anti-inflation policy caused a credit crunch.
- Some nine months after the oil shock, and while most sectors had slipped into recession, the world iron and steel industry was still an island of continuity high activity. Propped up by a backlog of orders (from shipyards, for instance) plus some stock-building, large and welcome orders from the communist world kept it buoyant longer than the oil sector, until eventually the domino effect of automobiles and construction worked its way through.

Two other aspects of behavior deepened the recession: *Inventories* were run down drastically. Credit controls when demand was already shrinking, and the expectation that prices would fall, guaranteed a drastic drop in inventories. When inventories are reduced by eight days, it's the same as foregoing six months of 5% economic growth; and inventories in many segments of the economy were reduced by more than eight days. *Consumer Expenditure*, long the stable engine of OECD economies, next took a nosedive. For really the first time since recovery started in the early 1950s, consumers stopped buying and started saving for a number of reasons—e.g., anxiety about high inflation, unemployment growth, world conditions, or future financial security. Basically, they began to worry for the first time in years about what the future might hold.

All this explains why the recession was the most severe since the war:

| | Decline in Industrial Production | | |
| --- | --- | --- | --- |
| | Measured from the Previous Cyclical Peak | | |
| | USA | Europe | Japan |
| This recession | 14% | 9% | 19% |
| (at last quarter 1975) | | | |
| Previous post-war recessions | 7% | 2% | 2% |

ELECTORAL RENDEZVOUS: ANOTHER PREDETERMINED

The governments of the three major OECD economies would face the electorate in 1976: Japan Germany, and the US It's an old truism that people vote their pocket-book, and presiding over a recession is an invitation to defeat at the polls. The incentives for these incumbent governments to go for growth would therefore be overwhelming.

REFLATION IN THE PIPELINE—A PREDETERMINED TOO

Not only were politicians' eyes on the 1976 elections, but there was also a keen awareness that much of the 1975 hardship was unnecessary and self-inflicted—the deflation was too harsh. With excess capacity now so widespread, reflation could be undertaken safely and expanding output could reduce unit prices and further curb inflation. Moreover, such reflation would be largely self-financing through taxation on increasing income, sales, profits and lowered costs for unemployment benefits.

Long-term unemployment was becoming evident as a social problem. Unemployment falls most heavily on the young, and few governments could afford to do nothing at the prospect of a third graduating class moving from the classroom to the welfare rolls.

All of these predetermined factors combined to make reflation attempts a virtual certainty.

1975 SCENARIOS FOR THE RAPIDS—THE UNCERTAIN PART

We had spent a lot of time developing the PREDETERMINEDS. The bridge we had built was now firmly anchored in our decision-maker's experience, since we had gone back far enough to include those events which had already unfolded and of which they were painfully aware. We also took care in this rooting process to develop those matters which, while not yet evident, would almost certainly occur. Reflation of economies would be the expression of the "Predetermineds." What was unknown was the timing of the recovery and the nature of it.

We designed two recovery scenarios:

> *Boom and Bust*—a vigorous recovery which had within it the seeds of its later destruction.
> *Constrained Growth*—A kind of muddling-through recovery but fundamentally different than earlier business cycle recoveries.

The two scenarios are depicted in Chart XIV. We allowed, too, for the possibility that reflations might not happen (for whatever reason), but including a *Depression Contingency*; it seemed so improbable, however, that it was not considered relevant for planning.

A. *Boom and Bust* described a world which develops in cycles of greater amplitude and shorter duration than those of the 1960s, more characteristic, in fact of the 1950s. It was clear that the longer the recover was deferred, the more likely this scenario would become as governments turned to panic measures to reflate their economies.

Boom and Bust was founded on apparent surprises.

### FIRST SURPRISE—RECOVERY COULD BE VERY RAPID

The first surprise would be the rapidity, strength, and forcefulness of economic recovery. It would not be abnormal, for instance, to see the US economy grow by 11 to 12 percent in eighteen months. (See Chart XV.) In GNP terms, this would be equivalent to the appearance on the world map of an

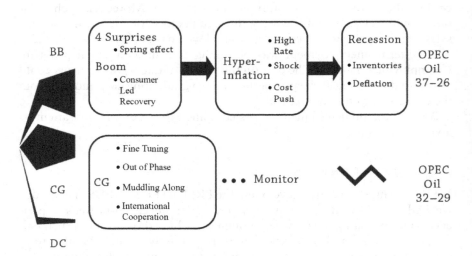

The world knows now how to reflate, but accidental shocks defer recovery.

*Chart BM 1.14* The Uncertain Part: Two Scenarios for the Rapids

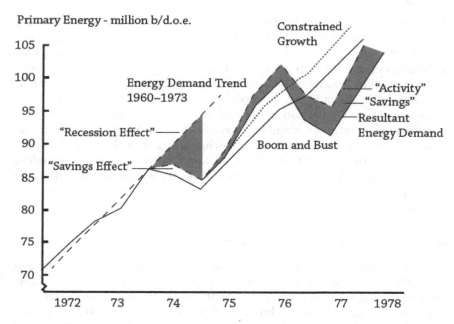

*Chart BM 1.15* WOCA: Energy Demand Recession and Savings

economy the size of the U.K. in this short time span. The potential for this lay in the depth of the then current recession and the amount of US production potential underemployed, which—like a coiled spring—would rebound and sustain very rapid growth for a short period. An annual growth rate of 8%, typical of past booms, would certainly not imply spectacular achievements but only reflect the depth of the 1973–1975 dent in the economy.

SECOND SURPRISE—THE RECOVERY COULD BE OIL-INTENSIVE

The energy intensity of the coming boom would constitute the second surprise. Newspaper reports of energy savings would persuade the intelligent layman that "Western" responsiveness would largely negate OPEC's initial negotiating strength. This, however, could not stand up to analysis. The largest single factor reducing oil consumption had not been any fundamental change in behavior, but rather the extent of the recession, which had cut both industrial and consumer demand. A boom in 1976 or 1977 would therefore find the majority of consumers reverting to their previous patterns of behavior and consumption. Energy savings could be very important in the 1980s, when it might be surprising how much GNP could rise without increasing energy use. Not, however, in 1976–77, when economic growth would be fueled by a major increase in demand for energy (Chart XV) and particularly for oil.

THIRD SURPRISE—US OIL IMPORTS COULD BOOM

The third surprise would be the rapidity and the magnitude of the increase in US oil imports. One could forget all about "Project Independence," President Ford's import reduction targets, and alternative energy projects. Our estimates indicated that in the first year of recovery, US imports would rise by 2.5MM B/D (i.e., more than Britain's total imports or Kuwait's current exports). In the second year, there could be a further increase of 2MM B/D, (in aggregate, more than Britain's total energy consumption). We had seen that the normal recovery in the USA. would be equivalent to the sudden creation of a new economic nation, somewhat larger than the U.K. We could now add that this new nation, like Japan would be almost totally dependent on oil from the Middle East. Consumer countries would once again realize they were in a trap, and that their recovery was entirely in the hands of a few Middle East governments.

FOURTH SURPRISE—ALTERNATIVE ENERGIES WOULD BE STAGNANT

The fourth surprise would be the discovery that alternative energy programs consisted largely of empty words and paper tigers. Most nuclear plants were operating well below design capacity and many had been deferred or cancelled. In the coal sector, little had been done, and the OECD nations were slipping progressively further behind their target forecasts. The world was far removed from the "crash programs" of which one had heard so much in the dark days of the oil embargo, and alternative energies would provide little relief to consumer countries' growing dependence on Middle East oil.

THE BUST, OR SECOND RECESSION

The next threat in the Boom and Bust scenario was high levels of inflation—approaching hyperinflation in many of the weaker OECD nations. In broad terms, the inflation rate would exceed the highest levels of 1973–75 plus, a further 5 percent. These levels would become intolerable in sociopolitical terms, and would be the signal to governments in the industrialized world that the boom was getting out of control. They would then have little choice but to reapply the deflationary measures so recently removed. Credit restrictions would be imposed and interest rates would climb; import controls might appear here and there and measures to reduce the consumption of oil imposed. Just as reinflation was likely to have been surprisingly rapid, so the downturn could be very sharp. Inventories would play an important role: stock building, starting from depths of the current recession would contribute to the growth of production during the upswing. But as liquidity disappeared in the face of strong deflationary measures, stocks would be run down rapidly, making the downturn that much sharper.

PROBABILITY ASSESSMENT FOR BOOM AND BUST

We felt that this scenario's dramatic implications for all sectors of the world economy made it difficult to be objective and give equal attention to the other scenarios. Nevertheless, we considered it to be less probably than the alternative scenario, Constrained Growth. We would make no forecasts about when a boom could start, although we believed it could take off any time from third quarter 1975 onwards. But the longer recovery took to get underway, the more likely that it would be of the "Boom and Bust" variety (see following table).

*Probability of Scenarios Starting:*

|  | Mid-1975 | Mid-1976 |
|---|---|---|
| Constrained Growth | .60 | .30 |
| Boom and Bust | .30 | .65 |
| Depression Contingency | .10 | .05 |

B. *CONSTRAINED GROWTH*

Everything in Boom and Bust was normal; the "surprises" were typical of business cycles that had happened previously. Constrained Growth on the contrary had a genuine surprise: recovery would be different, slower and more halting, than that experiences in post-World War II cycles.

The central idea was that the underlying high-growth trend of the past twenty-five years had come to an end. This would not result simply from the oil shock or the eclipse of the Bretton Woods monetary order. It would be because the very success of the post-war economies induced certain limits to continued vigorous growth. Along with unprecedented economic growth had come unprecedented expectations in standards of living and social welfare programs. These, in turn, led to a new kind of rigidity as governments became locked in to ever-increasing taxes needed to pay for these social programs. Industrialized countries were now slower to change and adjust to new factors—whether it be a response to an oil crisis or to new competitors like Japan and the newly-industrializing countries of Southeast Asia.

*Constrained Growth* would characterize the first years of this new economic world (which, in a long-term scenario introduces in the previous year, we called the "World of Internal Contradictions"). We concluded that all the motors of economic growth—consumption, international trade, government expenditure and investment—would work with less power in the next fifteen years due in particular to the trend for governments to become top-heavy with the impact of growing social welfare commitments.

Investment was especially emphasized as a change which we called the "technological recession," and would be dramatic and quickly felt. From the end of World War II until the early 1970s, the best new technology in basic industries could replace existing technology *on its own merit*. A new steel plant, for example, was more economic than an existing one, per ton of capacity; so too were new cement and paper plants, new refineries, tankers or new power generation plants per kilowatt of capacity. But from the late 1960s or early 1970s, technological progress became incapable of beating inflation. The cheapest method now to get new capacity was not to buy new plants, but to acquire existing capacity. Thus, there was both a slowdown in technical progress and an increase in inflation.

We felt that a situation had been reached—at least temporarily, for perhaps ten to fifteen years—wherein both the unit capital and operating costs of almost all new plants in basic industries would exceed those of existing equipment. This was a major discouragement to new investment in most industries that had been the engine of economic growth since the war, and would result in a structural change in the global economy. It could further accentuate inflation in any future upturns. Similar analyses were done for the other motors of growth: government spending (budget deficits and more rigidity); consumer spending (increased maturing in the life cycle of a large range of consumer durables), and international trade (accumulating imbalances and frictions).

The overall conclusion that economic growth prospects were perceived to be well below past achievements and the trends of the sixties and early seventies. We could enter—by means of the Constrained Growth period—this completely new "World of Internal Contradictions": a world of lower economic growth in stark contrast to the booming economies of the previous twenty-five years.

*Focused Scenarios*

Let me give one final example of how global scenarios were then used to focus on specific issues or projects. From one viewpoint, scenarios are like cherry trees: cherries grow neither on the trunk nor on the large boughs; they grow on the small branches of the tree. Nonetheless, a tree needs a trunk and main branches in order to grow small branches.

The global, macro-scenarios just described are the trunk; the large branches are country scenarios developed by Shell operating companies, in which factors individual to their own countries—predetermined and uncertain—are taken into account and added. But the real fruits of the scenarios are picked at the small branches, the focused scenarios which are custom tailored around a strategic issue or a specific market or investment project. One example of focused scenarios follows.

As OPEC oil is the balancing factor in the world energy system, its fluctuations reflect cyclical economic fluctuations but several times amplified. A given percentage decline in economic activity translates into a larger decline in world oil consumption, and into a much larger decline in OPEC oil demand, because: energy-intensive industries (like cement and steel) are more that proportionally affected in a recession; non-oil energies are usually cheaper than oil; and finally because OPEC oil has to be paid in foreign exchange as opposed to domestic oil. Conversely, in a recovery, a small increase in world energy demand. In the Boom and Bust scenario, a 13 percent increase in world energy demand in the first two years of a recover would be translated into a 23 percent increase in world oil demand and into a 34 percent increase in OPEC oil demand. How would this demand match available supply?

The fluctuations of OPEC oil production develop in a narrow band between two danger zones (see Chart XVI): the upper one, dangerous for oil-consuming countries, is set by technical production capabilities and is called "OPEC willingness to produce"; the lower one, dangerous for oil-producing countries, is the threshold of "OPEC dissatisfaction" where the solidarity and discipline of OPEC comes under severe stress and when prices might erode.

We made two simulations (Charts XVI and XVII). The demand changes implicit in a normal boom starting in late 1975 would become clear in winter 1976–77, when supply would be dangerously tight and prices under severe pressure. A boom starting only in late 1976 would be less dangerous.

### The 1975 Scenarios in Hindsight

As events turned out, economics develop mainly along the lines of Constrained Growth in the recovery of 1976, 1977 and 1978, *and* we were introduced to the World of Internal Contradictions. What had been the floor for long-term economic growth expectations before 1973 now became the ceiling. What turned out to be particularly fortuitous for Shell was that many managers took full cognizance of this new slower growth era they were now entering and hedged their business plans accordingly. The leanness and restructurings that the 1980s would demand were thus helped by beginning the diet regime early. That Shell saw this new world earlier than most could be seen by comparing the various energy forecasts made at the time. Shell consistently projected one of the lowest energy growth paths for the 1980s.

There are two main purposes of scenarios: one is to avoid regret; the other is positive and creative—to see new strategic options that you were not previously aware of. This positive aspect is in the long run the more important, and will be developed more fully in the conclusion to this paper. But let me add here that, despite the fact that the "Boom and Bust"—the most dramatic and (for Shell companies) dangerous of the two scenarios—did not occur, the exercise proved useful enough for our managers that short-term scenarios were prepared every year thereafter. As K. MacMahon of the Bank of England has so successfully observed:

"No time is as usefully wasted as that spent guarding against disasters that do not in the event occur."

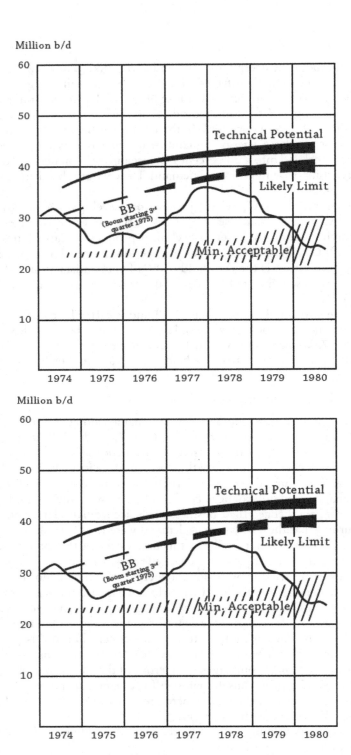

*Chart BM 1.16 and 1.17* OPEC Production Boundaries and Seasonal Requirements

# Conclusion

Scenarios are clearly much more popular in the world of "futurists" and commentators than in the world of decision makers. Futurists have learned to create "interesting" scenarios, but rarely ones which attract more than a passing interest from decision makers. There are important differences between scenarios which "tell a story" and scenarios which are of real help for decision makers, "decision-scenarios."

Scenarios that merely quantify alternative outcomes of obvious uncertainties—first generation scenarios—never raise a management team to enthusiasm. Most managers do not like to face such alternatives. They yearn for definiteness when dealing with the business environment, even after they have had their fingers burned for relying on past forecasts. The same managers who are superb at deciding on alternative courses of action where they are in control often come unstick when confronted with alternative futures they don't control and don't really understand. This is partly cultural. Many such managers developed their reflexes and skills in the 1950s and '60s, a management era shaped by unusually high predictability. To be competent then was to know the right answer; it was incompetent, unprofessional, to say, "Things could go this way, or they could go that way."

There is still deeper reason that cases many decision makers to reject scenarios. The quality that most lifts managers to the top of large organizations is their good judgment. They identify with it and trust it, their faith in it is a key motivation. Most scenarios confront them with uncertainty where they cannot easily use good judgment. The use of this best quality is denied them, and the tendency then is to say "Why bother with all that scenario stuff? We'll go on as before." The desire for a framework, within which they can exercise their judgment, is so strong that many managers continue to rely on forecasts, even though they know that forecasts often miss major turning points in their environments.

What distinguishes "decision-scenarios" from their sterile namesakes is subtle. All too often this critical factor falls outside the field of vision of scenario designers: they don't even realize that it has been missed!

Almost by definition, scanning the business environment and crystalizing the findings in a set of scenarios deals with the world *outside* the corporation, e.g., evolution of demand, supply, prices, technology, competition, business cycle changes, etc. This is only a half-truth, and is dangerous because there is another half. Because the raw materials of scenarios are made from this stuff of "outer-space," it's not realized that something more is needed: scenarios have to be made alive for "inner-space," the microcosm of the decision maker—this stage of the mind were alternatives are played out and where judgment is exercised. Scenarios deal with two worlds: the world of facts and the world of perceptions.

Decision-scenarios explore for facts out there, but they aim at perceptions *inside* the head of critical decision makers. Their purpose is to gather and transform information of potential strategic significance into fresh perceptions which then lead to strategic insights that were previously beyond the mind's reach—those that would not even have been considered. This transformation process is not trivial; it is genuinely creative. It is an "aha!" experience. Scenario planning is a discipline for *rediscovering* the original entrepreneurial power of creative foresight in contexts of accelerated change, greater complexity and genuine uncertainty.

In this concluding section of the paper, we look first at some "do's" and "don'ts" of the discipline: they all derive from facilitating the transformative process, in particular when they appear at variance with common practice. Then we examine a key aspect which makes the discipline creative.

### A Discipline

Decision-scenarios are *not* a mere range of possibilities . . . or a sensitivity analysis around one critical variable . . . or an optimistic case and a pessimistic case . . . or a different mix of premises . . . or interesting stories of what could happen in the future.

Scenario analysis is a disciplines way to *think* about the future. It demands above all an understanding of the forces that drive the system, rather than reliance on forecasts (that is someone else's understanding and judgment crystallized in a figure, which then becomes a substitute for thinking for the person who uses it). It is as different from relying on forecasts as judo is from boxing: you want to use the outside forces to your competitive advantage and make them work for you, in order that $2 + 2 = 5$ or much more. There is little or no power in merely accepting information about an outcome (such as the future price of oil, or the future level of demand); the power lies in understanding the forces behind the outcome. For this it is fundamental that decision makers develop their own feeling of the nature of the system, the forces at work within it, the uncertainties that underlie the alternative scenarios, and the concepts used to interpret key data.

Scenarios structure the future context into predetermined elements and genuine uncertain elements. The foundation of decision scenarios is exploring and expanding the predetermined: (1) events "already in the pipeline," but whose consequences have yet to unfold; (2) interdependence within the system (surprise outcomes often arise from interconnectedness), (3) trend breaks i.e., unfoldings that cannot continue, and (4) the "impossible." One of the most useful structuring of decision scenarios is to focus on and rule out the impossible events; decision-scenarios usually deny much more than they affirm.

Contrast the 1971 scenarios (p. 11) with the 1973 scenarios (p. 37): a major difference is the work done on the predetermined. The first set covered the range of possibilities and included everything believed plausible. The second set ruled out ever-increasing demand and low-priced oil; it said that muddling through was not on, that alternative fuels could not come to the rescue; and so forth. The difference in these two scenario sets was primarily the amount of work done of exploring and expanding the predetermineds. A set of scenarios which stresses uncertainty only, that is alternative developments, I like a tree without roots; a vital part is that which is common to all of the scenarios, the predetermined.

Scenarios acknowledge uncertainty and aim at structuring and understanding it, *not* merely by crisscrossing variables and producing dozens or hundreds of outcomes, but by creating a few alternative and internally consistent pathways into the future. Neither are decision scenarios a group of quasi-forecasts, one of which is like to be the right one. Instead, decision scenarios describe different "worlds," not just a different outcome of the same world. Never more than four (or it becomes unmanageable for most decision makers); the ideal number is "1 + 2"—i.e., the surprise free implicit view (showing explicitly why and where it is fragile), and then two other "worlds" or different ways of seeing the world, whose "logic" or main theme focuses on the critical uncertainties.

The point, to repeat, is not so much to have one scenario which "gets it right" as to have a set of scenarios which illuminate the major forces driving the system, their interrelationships and the critical uncertainties. The purpose, in short, is to help decision makers sharpen their focus on key questions about the environment, and to aid them via additional concepts and a richer language system through which to exchange ideas and new data.

The most dangerous scenario design is three scenarios that describe alternative outcomes along one dimension only, because many managers cannot resist the temptation to identify with the middle one as a "base line" and treat it essentially as a forecast. A scheme based on two scenarios raises a similar risk if the two are easily seen as "optimistic" and "pessimistic." Reality must be somewhere between and could easily be seen as "splitting the difference"— an outcome not very different from starting with a single line forecast.

What is characteristic of decision scenarios is that they focus at the end on critical uncertainties possibly very different from those which seems "obvious" at the beginning. It is characteristic also that, despite this focus on uncertainty, they do not paralyze decision makers. Rather, the deeper understanding of the risks that is gained often makes the decision maker capable of confronting apparently greater risk.

Scenarios are also an effective device for organizing a variety of much seemingly unrelated information, economic, technological, competitive, political, societal—some quantitative, some qualitative and translating it into a framework for judgment (in a way that n model, for instance, could do).

### Important:

A planner who tries to develop a set of decision scenarios without knowledge of his decision maker's microcosm and deepest concerns is attempting an impossible job. When the scenarios described in this paper were done, we did not fully appreciate this. We were lucky, however; our managers' concerns turned out to be precisely those we were dealing with because of their magnitude and obviousness when they were developed. Later we learned techniques of interview to find out the deep concerns of managers, and to illuminate the existing decision-framework. Now, the interview discipline is one of the first steps taken when starting a scenario exercise.

The decision-scenarios described in this paper were global or macro-scenarios. To do specific analyses of parts of the business, one develops "focused scenarios" custom-tailored around a strategic issue, or a specific market or investment project. But you cannot start with such focused scenarios because you will almost certainly miss key things, or cast the focused scenarios in the wrong way. You must wide-angle first to get the big picture, and then zoom in on your business specifics.

Finally, scenarios are most effective when used with two other tools.

### Strategic Vision

A clear, structured view of what kind of company you want to *be*, which precedes what you want to do (investing, divesting, penetrating a new market, etc.).

### Option Planning

In most planning approaches, strategies are put forward on a single line (which is more dangerous even that single line forecasting), and options—if there are any—are merely straw men, not real options. Option planning is a discipline to be practiced both at the level of business unites and at the corporate level, in which all options are put forward on a neutral, nonadvocative mode.

The purpose of this combined approach is "option generation." If the scenario process does not bring about the emergence of strategic options which were previously not even considered, the process has been sterile.

### Scenarios and the Gentle Art of Re-perceiving

"Genius, in truth, means little more than the faculty of perceiving in a non-habitual way" (William James).

It is well known that companies differ greatly in the effective-ness and speed with which they can transform the potentialities of scientific progress into innovation (that is, new products or new processes). Similarly, in times of rapid change, the effectiveness and speed with which companies identify and transform information of strategic significance into strategic initiatives can differ just as much. Today, this capacity is obviously critical.

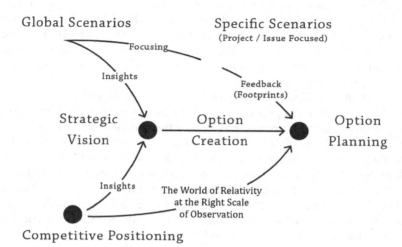

Global Scenarios    Specific Scenarios
                    (Project / Issue Focused)

Focusing

Insights

Feedback
(Footprints)

Strategic        Option        Option
Vision           Creation      Planning

Insights    The World of Relativity
            at the Right Scale
            of Observation

Competitive Positioning

*Chart BM 1.18* Option Generation

Unless particular care is taken over this process, really "new" (novel) information that is outside the span of expectations may not penetrate the core of the mind of a decision maker—that intimate stage of the mind where possible futures are rehearsed and where judgment is exercised.

There are many well-documented historic examples: Stalin, after concluding the non-aggression pact with Hitler in 1939, was so persuaded that the Germans would not attack as early as 1941, and certainly not without a prior ultimatum, that he ignored 84 warnings that "Operation Barbarossa" was about to be launched. According to Barton Whaley in *Codeword Barbossa* (M.I.T. Press, 1973), these included warning such as personal communications from Churchill, from Soviet spy Richard Sore in the German embassy in Tokyo, withdrawal of German merchant shipping from Soviet ports, and evacuation of German dependents from Moscow. Pearl Harbor, as documented by R. Wohlstetter, is another such case. The fundamental problem throughout this intelligence failure was "noise," the massive volume of signals. "To discriminate significant sounds against this background of noise, one has to be listening for something or for one of several things . . . on needs not only an ear, but a *variety of hypotheses* that guide observation." (R. Wohlstetter: *Pearl Harbor Warning and Decision*, (Stanford University Press, 1962), emphasis added). It is revealing that the Japanese commander of the Pearl Harbor attack, Mitsuo Fuchida, in his different microcosm was surprised at achieving surprise and asked "Had these Americans never hear of Port Arthur?" (an episode famous in Japan where the Japanese navy destroyed in a surprise attack the whole Russian Pacific fleet at anchor in Port Arthur).

Cases in the business world are, for obvious reasons less well documented. The author could personally observe the French steel industry with the "FOS project," the tanker market before and after the first oil shock, petrochemical investments in Europe in the seventies and a large American car manufacturer's misinterpretation and dismissal of Japanese competition during a good part of the seventies.

In all of these cases, a number of manager were involved (not just one individual), the inappropriate behavior extended over several months or even years (not just a one-time error), and the stakes were very high. They were all *crises of perception*—inability to see—and not cases of wrong strategic reasoning. Within the context of the view of the world these decision makers persisted in their strategy made sense; sometimes it was brilliant.

In our times of rapid change and discontinuity, these crises of perception—the inability to see a novel reality emerging by being locked inside obsolete assumptions—have become the main cause of strategic failures particularly for large and internally well-managed companies.

When failures are clearly visible, opportunities missed by not seeing them in time are probably more important. "The greatest danger in times of turbulence is not the turbulence; it is to act with yesterday's logic" (Peter Drucker).

The following graphic example illustrates, at the most elementary level, the process of persisting in seeing only what we are prepared to see. If one sees a face, to start with (below), one can go a long way and still see a face. The important point is: it is almost impossible to break out of an inappropriate mental frame while perceiving and experiencing within it. As the Chinese proverb says "The fish is the last to know it swims in water."

*Chart BM 1.19* Faces

Central to decision-scenarios, where they succeed or fail, is the micro-cosm of the decision maker: his inner model of reality, his organized set of assumptions which structure his understanding of how and why his business environment is going to unfold, and what are the critical factors which make and will make for success. This inner model *never* mirrors reality: it is always a construct: microcosms are basically superior "simplifications"; they deal with complexity by focusing on what really matters.

In stable times (business-as-usual, more-of-the-same), there will be a reasonably good match between the mental model of a successful decision maker and unfolding reality. A little adjustment and fine tuning will do. Decision-scenarios would have little or no leverage here.

But it times of rapid change and increased complexity the mental model becomes a dangerously mixed bag: enormously rich detail and deep understanding can coexist with dubious assumptions, selective inattention to alternative ways of interpretive evidence, and projections that are a mere pretense—blind spots and dead angles. It is here that the scenario approach has leverage and can make the difference.

In such circumstances, a microcosm based on past experience and prolonged by the usual type of forecasts is inherently suspect and most likely inadequate; yet it is almost impossible to break out of one's world view while operating within it. When one is committed to a certain way of framing an issue, it is extremely difficult to see solutions which lie outside this framework.

Decision-scenarios, by being alternative "ways of seeing the world," are a systematic method for breaking out of this one-eyed view. In a proper sense, such scenarios confer a gift of second sight and can achieve something very precious: the ability to re–perceive reality. In times of change there is definitely more to see than we normally perceive—more information potentially relevant to us lying around unnoticed because, being locked into our way of looking, we fail to see its significance.

It has been my repeated experience that the perceptions which emerge when the disciplined approach of scenario analysis is practiced are not only richer and substantially different in critical aspect from the previous implicit view. They are also qualitatively different. The process of converting information into fresh perceptions has something of a "breeder effect": it clearly generates energy, much more energy that has been consumed during the process of scenario analysis in terms of time and effort. . .

A mere "high" and "low" around a base-line would never achieve this conceptual reframing. The re-perception and discovery of strategic openings which follows this breaking out of one's own assumptions—many of which are so taken for granted that one is no longer aware of the—is, after all, the essence of entrepreneurship. Scenario planning, to repeat, is a discipline aimed at rediscovering the original entrepreneurial power of foresight in contexts of accelerated change, greater complexity and genuine uncertainty.

It is precisely in these contexts—*not* in stable times—that the real opportunities lie to gain competitive advantage through strategy.

"Uncertainty, my friend . . .
. . . discontinuity, mon amour!"

## Acknowledgement

The charts in this paper are reproduced with the kind permission of Shell International Petroleum Company. The author would like to acknowledge the many original contributions to the development of scenarios by his former Shell colleagues—both managers and planners, and by members of that unusual unit called Group Planning. The conceptualization of scenario analysis has benefitted greatly from discussion with Harvard Business School colleagues, in particular Bruce Scott and David Bell. This paper would never have been written had it not been for the encouragement and editing help of Norman Duncan and Peggy Evans. This paper expresses what the author has learned in the process; it should not be inferred that this represents Shell's current planning views or practices.

## Notes

* In this paper I use the words "Royal Dutch/Shell" or "Shell" to describe the Royal Dutch/Shell Group of companies, or sometimes as convenient shorthand to describe the management and planning functions within the central service companies of that Group in London and The Hague. Usually I should be taken as excluding the Shell Oil Company, U.S.A, which—as a majority-owned public company in its own right—has undertaken its own planning for its own operations. I also use words like "company" as shorthand when what is really described is a complex group of companies of varying degrees of self-sufficiency and independence of operation, most of which are obliged to plan for a future in their own national economic and political environments as well as to be an integral part of the Group of which they are members. I would not like to mislead anyone into thinking that any one person, manager or planner is able to have a clear view of it all.

1 The details of these new supply/demand studies needn't again be told here but are described in Pierre A. Wack, "Learning to Design Planning Scenarios." Harvard Business School Working Paper 1–785–006, pp. 26–30.

# Photographs

*Photo 1* Les parents de Pierre Wack (the parents of Pierre Wack): Jean-Jaques and Elisabeth, 1921

*Photo 2* Wack canoeing in France circa 1938

*Photo 3* Advertisement in Paris for *L'Occident*, a fashion magazine started by Wack and his friends after World War II, 1947

*Photo 4* Wack in Fontainebleu, France, 1961

*Photo 5* Wack and Indra, location unknown, circa 1966

*Photo* 6 Wack's formal photograph for Shell Francais, circa 1968

*Photo* 7 Wack and either Newland or van der Heijden in Wack's office at the Shell
Centre in London, circa 1981

*Photo 8* Wack, Newland and de Geus at Wack and Newland's retirement party, 1982, Shell Centre, London

*Photo 9* Wack and Newland (with Ged Davis in the background) at the Shell Centre in London, circa 1981

*Photo 10* Wack and Baudoin's marriage, May 1993

*Photo 11* La Johannie—Wack's home in the Dordogne Valley, Curemonte, France (Photo by Jean-Pierre Wack via Drone, September, 2016)

Photo 12 The style of Pierre Wack, a cockfighting cage purchased in Asia used as a lampshade at La Johannie in Curemonte, France

Photo 13 Wack's cat, Tao

*Photo 14* Wack on a visit to Avebury in England with Eve and Napier and Pat Collyns in 1993

*Photo 15* Wack and Jean-Pierre Wack in Wisley Garden driving Jean-Pierre to college in England, 1994

*Photo 16* The bamboo garden at La Johannie

*Photo 17* The garden terrace at La Johannie: Wack used to sit under the tree for hours, looking out over the garden below

*Photo 18* Wack and Davidson with Davidson's two dogs (Frodo and Bilbo) on Vancouver Island, Canada, 1994

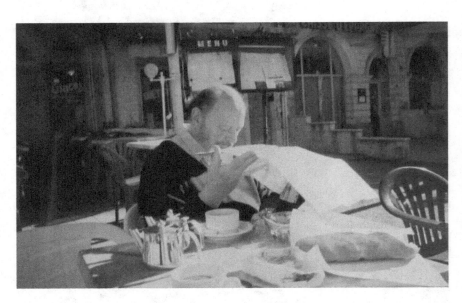

*Photo 19* Wack looking at a map on the way to Lurs with Eve, 1994

*Photo 20* One of Wack's favorite scrolls—the monk and the sleeping tiger

*Photo 21* Wack at La Johannie in Curemonte, France, 1996

*Photo 22* The start of the spiral stone staircase at La Johannie in Curemonte, France

# Index

Printed in the United States
by Baker & Taylor Publisher Services

Printed in the United States
by Baker & Taylor Publisher Services